THE
FOLLY OF
REALISM

THE FOLLY OF REALISM

HOW THE WEST DECEIVED ITSELF ABOUT RUSSIA AND BETRAYED UKRAINE

ALEXANDER VINDMAN

PUBLICAFFAIRS

New York

PublicAffairs
Hachette Book Group
1290 Avenue of the Americas, New York, NY 10104
www.publicaffairsbooks.com
@Public_Affairs

Printed in Canada

First Edition: June 2025

Published by PublicAffairs, an imprint of Hachette Book Group, Inc.
The PublicAffairs name and logo is a registered trademark of
the Hachette Book Group.

The Hachette Speakers Bureau provides a wide range of authors for speaking events.
To find out more, go to www.hachettespeakersbureau.com
or email HachetteSpeakers@hbgusa.com.

PublicAffairs books may be purchased in bulk for business, educational,
or promotional use. For more information, please contact your local bookseller
or the Hachette Book Group Special Markets Department
at special.markets@hbgusa.com.

The publisher is not responsible for websites (or their content) that are
not owned by the publisher.

Print book interior design by Bart Dawson

Library of Congress Cataloging-in-Publication Data has been applied for.

ISBNs: 9781541705043 (hardcover), 9781541705067 (ebook)

MRQ-T

1 2025

To those killed in the Russia-Ukraine War . . .
May we learn to avoid such tragedies

CONTENTS

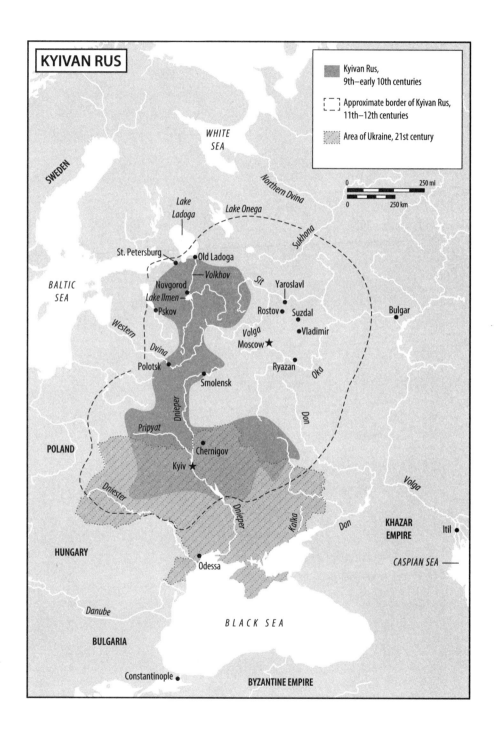

KYIVAN RUS

Kyivan Rus,
9th–early 10th centuries

Approximate border of Kyivan Rus,
11th–12th centuries

Area of Ukraine, 21st century

0   250 mi

0   250 km

SWEDEN

WHITE
SEA

Northern Dvina

BALTIC
SEA

Lake
Ladoga

Lake Onega

Sukhona

St. Petersburg

Old Ladoga

Volkhov

Sit

Yaroslavl

Bulgar

Novgorod
Lake Ilmen
Pskov

Rostov

Suzdal

Vladimir

Western

Dvina

Volga
Moscow ★

Polotsk

Smolensk

Ryazan

Oka

Dnieper

Don

POLAND

Pripyat

Chernigov

Kyiv ★

Dniester

Dnieper

Kalka

Don

Volga

KHAZAR
EMPIRE

Itil

CASPIAN SEA

HUNGARY

Odessa

Danube

BLACK SEA

BULGARIA

Constantinople

BYZANTINE EMPIRE

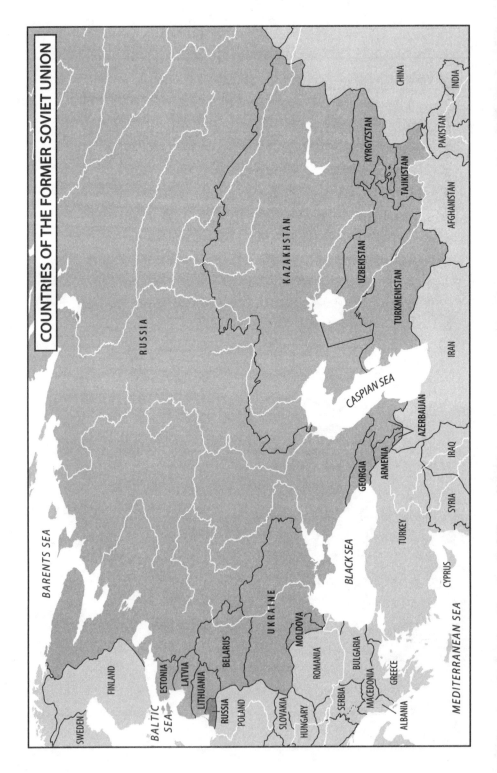

COUNTRIES OF THE FORMER SOVIET UNION

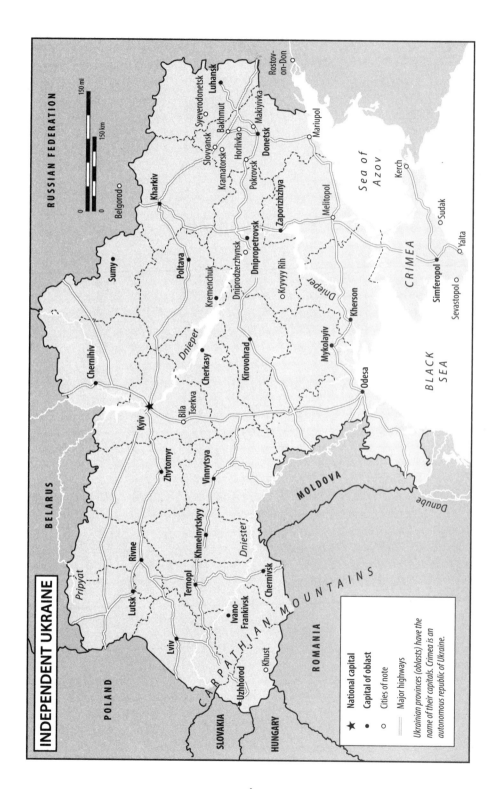

INDEPENDENT UKRAINE

150 mi
150 km

RUSSIAN FEDERATION

Rostov-on-Don
Luhansk
Syeverodonetsk
Bakhmut
Slovyansk
Kramatorsk
Horlivka
Makiyivka
Donetsk
Pokrovsk
Mariupol
Belgorod
Kharkiv
Zaporizhzhya
Melitopol
Sea of Azov
Kerch
Sudak
Simferopol
Yalta
Sevastopol
CRIMEA
Sumy
Poltava
Dnieprodzerzhynsk
Dnipropetrovsk
Kremenchuk
Kryvyy Rih
Dnieper
Kherson
Mykolayiv
BLACK SEA
Chernihiv
Dnieper
Cherkasy
Kirovohrad
Kyiv
Bila Tserkva
Odesa
Zhytomyr
Vinnytsya
MOLDOVA
Danube
Rivne
Khmelnytskyy
Dniester
Ternopl
Chernivsk
Pripyat
Lutsk
Ivano-Frankivsk
ROMANIA
Lviv
Khust
Uzhhorod
C A R P A T H I A N   M O U N T A I N S
POLAND
SLOVAKIA
HUNGARY
BELARUS

★ National capital
● Capital of oblast
○ Cities of note
═ Major highways

Ukrainian provinces (oblasts) have the name of their capitals. Crimea is an autonomous republic of Ukraine.

INTRODUCTION

A NEW WAY

It cannot be stressed enough that without Ukraine,
Russia ceases to be an empire, but with Ukraine
suborned and then subordinated, Russia automatically
becomes an empire.

—ZBIGNIEW BRZEZINSKI[1]

At dawn on February 24, 2022, nearly 200,000 Russian troops, having massed on the Ukrainian border intermittently for almost a year amid denials by the Kremlin of any intention to invade, crossed the border from three bordering compass quadrants—north, east, and south—while Russian forces bombarded Ukrainian targets throughout the country. The invasion was underway.

The ensuing Russian war to conquer Ukraine, to reverse the national independence established in 1991, and to subjugate the country to Russian control—supposedly in three days—has now gone on for three years and, as of this writing, appears likely to continue through most of 2025. Ukraine will take almost two years to train and prepare for another major operation following the 2023 counteroffensive. Ukraine's new offensive will likely take place on the heels of a mobilization of both personnel and the military-industrial base, with significantly more Western support in both materiel and training. On the geopolitical tailwinds of a Democratic victory in the 2024 US election, and with a successful 2025 offensive, Ukraine would be in the best position to begin a negotiation process and wind down Europe's largest war since World War II.

But any such success requires the West to cast off the presumptions underlying the repeated missteps of the last thirty years of relations with Russia. As the history presented here will show, Russia's rationalizations for mounting the attack on Ukraine—rationalizations expressed publicly, for years, by Russia's president Vladimir Putin, even as he denied a desire to conquer Ukraine—involve long-standing Russian delusions and falsehoods regarding the two countries' historic relationship. Putin once famously described the collapse of the Soviet Union as the greatest tragedy of the twentieth century; in fact the greatest tragedy for Russia was the loss of its empire. Taras Kuzio described the independence of Ukraine from Russia this way: "Millions of Russians are convinced that, without Ukraine, it is impossible to speak not only of a great Russia but any kind of Russia at all."[2]

US ambassador to the Soviet Union Robert Strauss, writing from Moscow in November 1991, just weeks before Ukraine's independence referendum, put the meaning of Ukraine shedding Russian domination even more directly: "The most revolutionary event of 1991 for Russia may not be the collapse of Communism, but the loss of something Russians of all political stripes think of as part of their own body politic, and near to the heart at that: Ukraine."

Ukraine, and particularly the centrality of Ukraine to the myth of Kyiv as the progenitor of the Russian state, is essential to Russia's exceptional sense of its status as a great power.[3]

That toxic Russian delusion underlies the series of fatal missteps, taken by the United States and the West generally, that played a decisive role in bringing about the Russian war of aggression that rages today.

For it is the US and its allies, I argue, that have enabled the ongoing tragedy in Ukraine. The West's failings to constrain Russian aggression and harden Ukraine against it have nourished the Russian sense of impunity, and the West's missteps threaten to foster even larger crises and encourage even greater danger from other resurgent authoritarian regimes.

The fundamental problem arises from a combination of delusion, faulty priorities, and misplaced hopes and fears. Starting with the fall of the Soviet Union at the end of 1991, extending throughout six US presidential administrations, and ranging in mood from fear to skepticism, from hope to anxiety, US policymakers have bought fully into Russia's vision of itself as the exceptionally and naturally dominant player in the post-Soviet space. At nearly every turn, for nearly two generations, US foreign policy for the region has been driven by very slight variations on a fundamentally Russia-centric philosophy that persistently relegates the US relationship with Ukraine to a secondary and derivative status. In moments of crisis, the US routinely took up an active hyper-focus on a Russia-centric approach. In 1991 and through the mid-1990s, the basis for that approach was fear of the fracturing of the Soviet Union, nuclear proliferation, and loose nuclear weapons. In the post-9/11 period, the basis was a mirage of cooperation with Russia. After the start of the 2014 Russia-Ukraine war, the basis was fear of a confrontation: the West deterred itself from supporting Ukraine and challenging Russian aggression. The West has thus repeatedly reinforced a Russian belief that it can act with impunity on historical fantasies of regional dominance. In the process, the entire post–World War II and post–Cold War liberal world order has been thrown into perilous chaos.

As I will show, this faulty Russia-centric policy has a background in the Cold War. Given the peril of that period, and the optimism over partnership and peace that arrived at the Cold War's end, a policy focus on integrating Russia with the West was at least somewhat understandable in the 1990s. Nevertheless, overinflating the importance of Russia after the fall of the Soviet Union, and giving primary attention to the global war on terror after 9/11, contributed to obscuring both a clear US understanding of Russia's ambitions and the value of a close partnership with Ukraine and the newly independent states of the region.

Long before the invasion of February 2022, it should have become glaringly obvious to all responsible parties that such a policy had already proven catastrophic, throughout the region, for the persistence and growth of the fundamental Western values of self-determination and liberal democracy. The stubborn continuation of Western policy made Russia's invasion of Ukraine and the resulting crisis in the world order seem nearly inevitable.

They weren't. Missed opportunities for drastic course correction arose again and again. They were simply passed up.

But the US government, and the West generally, has clung to a doomed and delusional policy, across party lines, through political upheavals, and in the face of more and more open aggression by Russia. How did we get to this point? How might things have gone differently? And what can we do to bring about the fundamental changes of approach to all our foreign relations that, even if

terribly late, would still offer a chance for establishing a more genuinely stable world?

Those are the questions I address in this book—and the stories
this book tells.

THE FOLLY OF REALISM. This book's title, a deliberate seeming
contradiction in terms, serves as shorthand for one part of the
answer. The long-standing overreliance on the "realist" philosophy
of US foreign policy has been largely, though not solely, to blame
for the persistence of Western delusion regarding Russia. The realism school, associated with diplomats and scholars such as Henry
Kissinger, John Mearsheimer, Stephen Walt, and Kenneth Waltz,
came to prominence during the superpower nuclear standoff of the
Cold War and emerged from a pushback against an earlier approach
famously associated with the internationalist president Woodrow
Wilson, who framed the historic purpose of US entry into World
War I in a desire that "the world be made safe for democracy." In the
classic Wilsonian view, American values of democracy and freedom,
as well as the institutions that ensure them, represent a universal
good, morally obligating the US to engage internationally: what we
might call an idealist approach.

The realists, responding to perceived setbacks for US power,
took a posture seemingly harder-headed than Wilson's: the lofty
ideal of advancing US values around the world is not always feasible. Instead, advancing vital US interests—defined as an aggressive
national defense, immediate commercial prosperity in trade, and
short-term crisis aversion in pursuit of greater stability—should
serve as the main standard for American engagement abroad. In the
1970s, with the thawing of the Cold War and the improvement in

the US relationship to China, realism could be seen as having major successes.

As I will argue, however, the history of US policy toward Russia and the current plight of Ukraine show just the opposite: that the benefits of a policy ranking pure national interest above all other considerations and ignoring national values—in that sense, a purely transactional policy—must always be short-term. In the George H. W. Bush administration, and to a degree in the Clinton administration, realism dictated a hyper-focus on denuclearization, which demanded that Ukraine and other states hand the Kremlin control of all Soviet nuclear weapons, with no concomitant demands made on Russia. The effects of that process reveal that, absent a commitment to the advancement of Western liberal values, even the somewhat cynically limited goal of securing US interests can't in the end be met. Realism's impulse to avert crisis at virtually any cost doesn't even avert crisis.

The post-Soviet history of US relationships with Russia and with Ukraine—presented in this book as a test case for the prevailing US approach to international relations in general—makes overwhelmingly clear that realism isn't, in its own too-simplistic terms, realistic. In the process of selling out our values, we have failed to deter an aggressive yet deterrable opponent, Russia, and lost a chance to form a strong relationship with a strategically critical, more likely Western-aligned partner, Ukraine.

The alternative approach, fundamentally different, is "neo-idealism." Far more likely to achieve better outcomes and, as we will see, so far embattled in US policymaking, neo-idealism has been discussed in depth by international relations theorist and scholar Benjamin Tallis—an originator of the term and conceptual author of and ardent advocate for the theory—in his paper "Neo-idealism: Grand Strategy for the Future of the Transatlantic Community" and elsewhere. In "The Rise of the New Idealists," Tallis calls neo-idealism

> a morally-based approach to geopolitics, grounded in the power of values conceived as ideals to strive for: human rights and fundamental freedoms, social and cultural liberalism, democratic governance; self-determination for democratic societies; and perhaps most importantly, the right of citizens in those societies to a hopeful future.
>
> Crucially, its proponents see the struggle for these ideals, and making progress toward them, not as luxuries to be set aside when hard-nosed interests are at stake. For the Neo-Idealists, our values are our interests.[4]

More consonant with American values than realism, and more literally realistic about achieving long-term stability and securing vital American interests, neo-idealism is emerging as a new way of thinking about foreign relations. In part, this approach requires of nations that seek engagement with the United States and the West a credible effort to adhere to agreed-upon, liberal, orderly standards of conduct among nations, as well as a credible willingness, at the very least, to pursue domestically the stability-enhancing institutions that secure liberty, equality, and democracy.

Neo-idealism thus departs sharply from recent approaches to foreign policy that seemingly reject the short-term, transactionalist basis of realism but have proven, in the end, merely fantastical— often with disastrous results. One such approach was that of the neoconservative school, known as the neocons—Dick Cheney, Paul Wolfowitz, Condoleezza Rice, Donald Rumsfeld, and others— who came to power with the election of George W. Bush in 2000 and led the US response to the terrorist attacks of September 11,

2001. The prosecution of a global war on terror meant that, when it came to Russia, the neocons became at least as transactionalist and short-term in their thinking as the realists. It was the neocons who doubled down on a Russia-first policy for Eurasia, trading cooperation with Ukraine for Russian support in the global war on terror.

Their failures triggered the emergence of a kind of idealism—but a faux and naive kind. The Obama administration made a rhetorical commitment to an idealistic mood while quickly reverting—especially, as we will see, with regard to the increasingly naked aggressions of Vladimir Putin—to short-term crisis management and prioritizing of Russian exceptionalism. Obama's classical-liberal style of idealism—focused on cooperation through international institutions, lead-from-behind multilateralism, and soft power, pursued in the face of Putin's repeated aggression and the growing malign influence of authoritarianism globally, and backed up by less-than-credible assessments of opponents' and partners' interests and objectives—proved utterly unsuitable for a world filled with realists, let alone with dictators and tyrants.

The realist, the neocon, and the latter-day liberal-idealist foreign-policy schools, not so different in their effects, have governed the past thirty years of US geopolitics; none has been able to focus on long-term interests in a tough-minded and clear-eyed way. The neo-idealism now emerging insists that serving Western liberal values transcends the transactionalism inherent in faux idealism, neoconservatism, and realism alike.

The ramifications go far beyond Ukraine and Russia. The current situation there should be seen as a devastating test, proving the need for a wholesale change in the US approach to foreign relations. Neo-idealism demands using a more nuanced and coherent understanding of interest, viewed through our values, along with other important inputs, to determine a compass heading for a US foreign-policy approach: understanding the relative importance of an interest, determining the resources that can be applied, and assessing the risks of action and inaction.

BENJAMIN TALLIS, WHO has produced much of the scholarship on the concept of neo-idealism, is doing admirable spadework developing the tenets and applicability of the neo-idealist approach. What I offer in this book is a historical and current vision—informed by my scholarship, shaped by my hands-on, up-close involvement in two presidential administrations, and supported by my one-on-one interviews with key officials with agency in both US and Ukrainian policy and politics—of the failure of US policy for Russia, Ukraine, and the entire former Soviet space, with an urgent call to action. And I share my prescriptions, in terms accessible to general readers, for why we must—and how we can—change course, even at this late and crucial date, for the betterment and greater security of our country and the world.

The origins of the story told here stretch back as far as the earliest days of the Russia-Ukraine relationship. The ramifications play out as immediately as Russia's ongoing war on Ukraine and the recent foreign policy of President Joe Biden. The story includes a behind-the-scenes look at how, in the waning days of the Obama administration, the foreign-policy community did in fact begin a major course correction, developing, before the term was current, a comprehensive neo-idealist policy for Russia, only to have the rug pulled out from under that policy by the chaotic irresponsibility of members of President Donald Trump's administration, including the president himself.

I'm not expecting everyone to readily embrace the vision I present in this book. Thirty years of policy repetition with worsening and now dire results implicate big-name diplomatic players across conservative and liberal parties in both the US and the wider Western policy environment, many of whom I admire personally and professionally. It's a tough critique.

Neo-idealism does not, however, call for an overnight replacement of everything. We need to begin with a new set of guidelines—to be created, it's true, under the urgent pressure of this moment—for developing and executing a truly durable policy. Neo-idealism is not unworkably purist or rigid; like any other set of precepts, it will at times have to yield to unforeseen contingencies. The currently prevailing mode, however—the veering between fear and hope, too often causing paralysis—has not, as we will see, enabled US policymakers to establish a practical playbook that enables tough-minded assessments and decisive, effective action. The absence of principle-based idealism has led to the dangerous trend, now exploding, of instability and insecurity.

The proof of the pudding is in the eating. The sequence of events recounted in the ensuing narrative, focusing on the thirty-five years since the collapse of the USSR, demonstrates the manifest failures of both realist and faux-idealist approaches. Ukraine is currently a proving ground for Russian aggression, but that ground can shift—to Moldova, to Latvia, to Finland, and beyond, into the Pacific, to China and Taiwan.

If it does, we will need a tough-minded, clear-sighted way to respond. And to that end, we need a shared vision: a basis for thinking through our responses, well in advance of the moment when decisive action is required.

CHAPTER ONE

FROM THE COSSACKS TO CHERNOBYL

A TALE OF TWO NATIONAL IDENTITIES

On April 26, 1986, a design test was underway for a safety system of the Unit Four reactor of the Chernobyl Nuclear Power Plant, located on the Dnieper River near the Belorussian border in the northern part of the Ukrainian Soviet Socialist Republic, a strategically critical heartland republic of the Soviet Union. The reactor was to be shut down, after the test, for scheduled maintenance. At about 1:23 a.m., therefore, when the test began, it was conducted in a reduced-power mode that increases loss of coolant throughout the reactor, bringing coolants to the boiling point. Given the reduction in power, the impact is typically minor, usually negligible.

About forty seconds after the Chernobyl test began, however, a rapid increase in power unexpectedly sent explosive steam pressure from damaged fuel channels into the reactor's exterior cooling structure and caused an explosion, instantaneously destroying the reactor casing, bursting through and blasting off the upper reactor's upper plate, and blowing off the roof of the whole reactor building. That was the first explosion.[1]

The second explosion, more powerful than the first, occurred about two or three seconds later, damaging the core, ending the nuclear chain reaction, and compromising the reactor containment vessel. It shot out hot lumps of nuclear graphite, which caught fire on exposure to air and spread beyond the immediate area with stunning speed, full of radioactive fallout. A survivor running outside and looking up saw a laser-like blue light, caused by glowing ionized air, "flooding up into infinity."[2]

The Chernobyl plant was operated jointly from Moscow, the Soviet capital, about 500 miles away, and Kyiv, the Ukrainian capital, less than 80 miles away. And yet in the first few hours, the government of Ukraine received little information about the disastrous accident that had occurred within the republic's borders. As huge volumes of radioactive material entered the atmosphere, the nearby city of Pripyat was not evacuated. Within a few hours, people there were experiencing severe headaches, metallic tastes, coughing, and vomiting.

Not until the following day would buses begin evacuating Pripyat. Fifty-three thousand people, able to bring just a little hand luggage with them, were taken to villages near Kyiv, in the expectation that the situation would be resolved in two or three days. However, officials quickly realized they had to evacuate a ten-kilometer radius; ten days later, the evacuation zone was reset to thirty kilometers.

As evacuations went on, health problems continued to spread far beyond the expanded zone. The Dnieper reservoir system, one of the largest in Europe, supplied water to the 2.4 million people living in Kyiv. Aquatic systems became contaminated with radioactivity for months after the accident. The zone itself was even further expanded.

When I visited Chernobyl and Pripyat in 2009, it was clear that those evacuees who thought they were leaving their homes for two to three days never did return. The zone remains deserted today, and the whole city looks like a postapocalyptic landscape out of a fantasy movie: giant catfish the size of Volkswagen Beetles swim in the pond outside the nuclear plant. Desolate apartment blocks, carnivals, and classrooms dot the landscape—one moment they'd been vibrant with humanity, the next completely abandoned.

The Chernobyl nuclear disaster represents an especially dramatic marker of a shift, beginning as early as the mid-1980s, in the Ukrainian people's long and difficult relationship with the Soviet Union. That relationship began in 1917, when the Russian Revolution brought Soviet Russia into existence. By the 1980s, much of the Soviet nuclear arsenal, then the world's largest, was stationed in Ukraine. The immediate risks to life and health, on a mass scale, presented by vast amounts of nuclear material, weaponized or not, were brought home to Ukraine by the Chernobyl disaster. The prospect of denuclearizing began to look attractive, even essential to some Ukrainians and their leaders.

Chernobyl was of course by no means the only issue driving this shifting Ukrainian perception. The 1980s saw other events, both related and unrelated to the denuclearization issue, that caused friction in Ukraine's role as a main republic of the Soviet Union and inspired more Ukrainians to hope for greater autonomy.

One factor was the release, in 1987 and 1988, of Ukrainian dissidents who had long been held prisoner in the Soviet Gulag. Some began to take leadership positions in the nascent Ukrainian opposition to Soviet domination.[3] The year 1989 also saw the end of the regime of Volodymyr Shcherbytsky, the head of the Ukrainian government and a member of the Soviet Politburo and a strong proponent of the Russification of Ukraine. Shcherbytsky's downfall arrived as part of the general purge of hard-liners by Mikhail Gorbachev's glasnost and perestroika campaigns in Moscow. By the end of the decade it was clear that at a fundamental level Ukraine was readying itself for a new relationship with Moscow, one that granted it much greater autonomy and self-determination.

That readiness would lead to a series of dramatic events involving Russia, Ukraine, and the US, which culminated in the Russian invasion of Ukraine in 2022 and a geopolitical earthquake in world affairs ensuing from that act of Russian aggression. I maintain that the West's and the United States' missteps throughout the collapse of the Soviet Union and the post-Soviet period enabled the current crisis. The ensuing chapters will show that a policy of short-term transactionalism, torn between the realist school of international relations, whose famous authors include Henry Kissinger, John Mearsheimer, Stephen Walt, and Kenneth Waltz, and a fickle form of liberal idealism—supposedly a values-based alternative to realism but, as we will see, not so in practice—has led to failure after failure in our relationships with both Ukraine and Russia, emboldening Russian aggression at almost every turn. I argue that we urgently need a new approach: we must reject the unrealistic cult of realism, embrace a true and tough-minded idealism by which the US confidently asserts its own values, make values-based demands in our relationships with other nations, eschew fear- and hope-driven short-term transactions, and prioritize long-term interest and stability.

The ramifications of the neo-idealist ethos I'm calling for go far beyond US policy for Russia, Ukraine, and Eurasia. The current disaster for Ukraine, caused by Russian aggression and unwittingly enabled by US policy, serves as the most urgent kind of test case. The principles it encapsulates are evident in a host of other flash points around the world, each made more dangerous by a cynical and highly nationalistic local power-monger. But none is so brazen at the moment as Vladimir Putin's Russia.

In coming to terms with the urgent requirement for real change, it's important to keep in mind that our relationship with an independent Ukraine is recent and that the US will be only 250 years old in 2026. By contrast, the interconnected histories of Russia and Ukraine, now coming to another historic climax, have been playing out for more than a thousand years. The West and its policymakers must better understand the depth of that history if better decisions are to be made regarding the future of this history-defining region.

In some ways, the two countries might seem to overlap. They are geographic neighbors. Their capitals are only about 500 miles apart. Both nations are majority Slavic peoples, speak Slavic languages, use Cyrillic alphabets, and practice Eastern Orthodox Christianity (though Ukraine is richly multiconfessional).[4] So before looking at how Russia and Ukraine extricated themselves from one another in the 1990s, before looking at the issues developing in the post-Soviet period, before looking at how those dynamics brought Russia, Ukraine, and the US and the West to the current crisis, it is critically important to have a sense of how Russia and Ukraine, beginning more than a millennium ago, came to see their own relationship in such conflicting terms and how in modern times Ukraine was brought into the Soviet sphere, from which it emerged only in 1991.

BY 1922, UKRAINIANS forced to become citizens of the Ukrainian Soviet Socialist Republic and subject to rule by the Communist Party of Ukraine—a subordinate of the Communist Party of the USSR—had long fostered a powerful sense of themselves as a distinct national people. And yet Ukrainians had never enjoyed the benefits of a modern, independent nation-state.

Russia, by contrast, long before establishing Communist rule in Ukraine, and indeed before its first emergence as a regional power, had a particular sense of the critical importance of Ukraine to Russian existence as a nation. The relationship between Russia and Ukraine thus turns on complex and delicate questions of identity: national, political, geographical, cultural, and, crucially, emotional. Discussions of these often focus on Russia as the subject, with Ukraine its object. *Without Ukraine, Russia is a country; with Ukraine, it's an empire*: this saying accurately describes the Russian elites' self-identity. Ukraine is the means by which Russia achieves imperial scale.

But that definition makes Ukraine a subject; Russia is either enhanced or diminished by the presence or absence, within Russia, of Ukraine. Missing is the Ukrainians' own long history: first acting as the regional hegemon; later diminished and subordinated to other regional powers, even before Russian hegemony began in the seventeenth century; and then, in times of Russian weakness or opportunity, asserting a political identity that exists independently of the ups and downs of Russian power.

Ukraine and Russia do share an origin story. Both countries see themselves as having sprung from the loins, politically speaking, of Prince Volodymyr, also known as Saint Volodymyr, the tenth-century ruler of an ancient, Slavic-dominated regional power that historians call Kyivan Rus. Centered on what is now the capital of Ukraine, Kyiv, Kyivan Rus long practiced pagan religious ways.

According to both Russian and Ukrainian histories, when Prince Volodymyr converted to Christianity, he became the originator of an Orthodox Church and the founding father of the ancestral state common to Russia and Ukraine.[5]

The prince's religious conversion involved important matters of trade, security, economics, and, crucially, self-determination. In the tenth century, Slavic-speaking people had long been subject to a vigorous slave trade, carried out both by the powerful Vikings of Scandinavia to their north and the Muslim caliphates to their south. By converting to Christianity, Volodymyr allied himself and his subjects with the strongest and most relevant state, the great Christian power to the Slavs' west: the Byzantine Empire.[6] From a Western Europe–centric point of view, the Byzantine world looks eastern, but from the point of view of Volodymyr and Kyivan Rus, the new association was western, and it was this westward lean that succeeded in opposing and deterring some Viking and Muslim depredations and kicked off the development of a nation out of an early tribal ancestry, making what would become a Western-connected Ukraine the main regional player.

In the eleventh century, Kyivan Rus grand princes were ruling much of what today is Ukraine and Belarus when certain principalities north and east of Kyiv began to claim autonomy. They would later become known as the Russian princes, as they declared their principalities independent of the Kyivan capital.[7]

Russia thus begins as an eastern effort to declare independence from the Western-looking region that was to become Ukraine, and for a time, Russia remained in that sense a sidebar in developments centering Ukraine. In the thirteenth century, however, after both an internecine struggle within Rus and a series of destructive Mongol invasions, Russian princes were able to consolidate their power by forming the Grand Duchy of Muscovy, centered on what was to become Moscow. By the fifteenth century, self-defined Russians had established themselves as a distinct power center, free both from the yoke of the Turkic tribes known as Tatars and from Mongol vassalage.[8]

From that point onward, Russian rule began to expand in all directions. This expansionism would lead to the creation of a state well-known for both its sheer size and its enthusiasm for absorbing regions strikingly remote geographically from its point of origin.

Yet as early as the sixteenth century, the royalty and aristocracy of the tsardom, having amassed sufficient strength to make Russia the most formidable descendent of Kyivan Rus, inaugurated what would become a persistent claim on all of the ancient lands of their claimed ancestry—Ukraine, that is—based on the notion that Russia was now the inheritor state of the Kyivan Rus principalities, Kyiv-centered Rus having all but disappeared from the maps by the early thirteenth century. In that claim—historically fantastical, yet deeply worked into Russian public consciousness—lies the origin of Russia's baseless, ahistorical claim on Ukraine. Russian elites would go on making that claim throughout the Russian imperial, Soviet, and post-Soviet periods. Searching for a Russian identity that solidified regional hegemony, Vladimir Putin enflamed a doctrine of regional exceptionalism that first emerged in the sixteenth century and remained a deeply rooted nationalist and imperialist dream throughout Russia's history. It is this vision of Russia to which the West has given far too much credence.

THE MODERN HISTORY of Russia-Ukraine relations begins in the seventeenth century and involves the famous Cossacks. The term "Cossacks" was originally used to define representatives of nomadic people out of the steppes of eastern Ukraine and southern Russia, who provided military service to the region's emerging and often competing empires. On January 8, 1654, a Cossack council, assembled in the town of Pereiaslav in what is now central Ukraine by the "hetman" (military commander) Bohdan Khmelnytsky, pledged Cossack loyalty to the authority of the Russian tsar in exchange for protection from the Polish-Lithuanian Commonwealth, the Ottoman Empire, and the Crimean Khanate.

To the Cossacks, this agreement was conditional. They intended only to preserve their nascent Cossack autonomy, a need that had arisen out of their struggle to carve out a Cossack state between the Polish and Ottoman empires. But the tsars viewed the Pereiaslav Treaty as permanent, progressively subordinating Cossack lands to the Russian Empire, and the agreement in fact created and set conditions for Russian imperial rule in the region, especially with regard to Ukraine. It also accelerated Russia's continuous expansion beyond the limits of the young Russian kingdom, recently converted from the small regional kingdom of Muscovy.[9]

The Cossacks on the one hand enforced Russian rule. On the other, they continued to try to play the various empires against each other and formed clans, fighting among themselves and undercutting efforts to achieve autonomy. In eighteenth-century military campaigns against Poland, Sweden, and the Ottoman Empire, Russia wrested lands from both the competing powers and the Cossacks' own leadership; by 1764, the Russian Empire, having subdued the Tatar Khanates, ruled territories from the north and east of modern-day Ukraine through Ekaterinburg in the Ural Mountains to Khabarovsk in the Far East, with Cossack forts extending throughout the sparsely populated territories of Siberia. The remarkable multidirectional expansion of Russia that had begun in the 1500s would ultimately swell the state across eleven time zones.

That push continued through every phase of Russian political and economic history. Its first reversal would happen only after the Soviet collapse in 1991: Putin's aggressions outside of the Russian Federation, beginning in 2004 in the non-military sphere and in 2008 in the military sphere, represent attempts to revive Russia's sense of its expansionist destiny. Formerly, the Russian Empire's inexorable growth had incorporated sparsely populated northern territories; individual city-states in Central Asia; and parts of the declining Ottoman, Persian, and Chinese Empires, with significant populations of non-Slavic peoples. Russia thus established a state stretching from the Baltic and Black Seas to the Pacific Ocean and the North Sea, incorporating the Caucasus and Central Asia—territories conquered, in significant part, thanks to the military service of the Cossacks, themselves a people more and more subordinated and occupying north, central, and southeast Ukraine.

This expansion, so far-ranging from Russia's origins as the kingdom of Muscovy, and enabled by the help of the Cossacks, also helped create Ukraine as an entity both emotionally and politically central to Russia's identity. With the partition and absorption of the Kingdom of Poland in the eighteenth century, imperial Russia accrued western lands and control over the preponderance of what today is the western part of Ukraine. In 1783, when it absorbed the territory of the Crimean Khanate, Russia annexed what became southern Ukraine and Crimea. By the beginning of the nineteenth century, Russian tsars believed they had justly reestablished control over the Kyivan Rus lands, divided, in their belief, some six centuries earlier and now reunited under their imperium.

Ukraine's modern borders thus represent an inheritance of acquisitions made first by Russian and then by Soviet rulers, part and parcel of Russia's relentless efforts to expand its empire.

For most of modern history, Russia has considered Kyiv and the surrounding lands to be Russia's interior periphery: in Russian, the word for "Ukraine," *Krayna*, translates literally into English as "border." This legacy of territorial "right" and claim, developed over the centuries, resembles the legacies and vestiges of other empires.[10]

For this reason modern Ukrainians take offense when people say "*the* Ukraine." The term suggests that the country serves as the western border of Russia. "Ukraine" in fact refers to a separate, independent country, whose origins many Ukrainians rightly see as both preceding Russia's and looking more westward than eastward.

UKRAINE HAS ALWAYS embraced a history of unique identity and independence that shapes both its domestic politics and its international relations with Russia. From early times, however, outside of the Cossack lands, Ukraine lacked a coherent historical political class and therefore was never fully a *nation*: a modern construct, originating in the seventeenth century and rooted in a sense of shared tradition with an imperial center, yet not fully developed until the industrial age. In the nineteenth century, rapid urbanization led to new feelings of national solidarity, connected to rapidly developing modernity. In that sense, a nation is fundamentally a political act, directed toward the future. Ukraine did ultimately experience aspects of those patterns: rapid consolidation of people in cities throughout the center and east of the country. Yet its achieving an actual national government was obstructed by the strength of the Russian Empire in the early and middle nineteenth century and the active repression of Ukrainian nationalism. Taras Shevchenko, for example, Ukraine's most famous poet, whose statue stands near Dupont Circle in Washington, DC, was exiled from Ukraine for promoting the Ukrainian language and nurturing Ukraine's national identity.[11]

By the mid-nineteenth century an urban populist movement in Ukraine was asserting that the country had long possessed a language, a culture, and a historical narrative markedly different from Russia's: a cultural identity, never properly represented politically and governmentally. From 1917 to 1920, in the wake of the Russian Revolution, Ukraine enjoyed a brief period of independence with a socialist government; it was not until 1920 that Russian Communist forces secured control over eastern Ukraine, and not until 1921 that those forces came to control large portions of western Ukraine, issuing in the Soviet period. Despite the brevity of that first independence period, Ukraine had managed, over centuries, to develop a sense of identity similar to those formulations of national identity emerging in so many places during the industrial age. That sense carried Ukraine into the Soviet era and presaged its emergence as an independent state in 1991.

In 1922, however, after Communist forces defeated the remaining Ukraine Republic forces, Ukraine signed the Constitution of the Union of Soviet Socialist Republics (USSR), officially joining the Soviet Union and establishing the Ukrainian Soviet Socialist Republic. Even that Moscow-backed Communist victory involved concessions to Ukrainian nationalism. The compromise between Vladimir Lenin, the founding head of the government of Soviet Russia, and Ukraine's, Georgia's, and other countries' own Communist nationalists compelled the creation of national Soviet republics, rather than absorption into a large Communist Russian superstate. An effect of that compromise with nationalism sounded the death knell of Russian empire: seventy years later, it would permit the breakup of the Soviet Union into independent states. Because the

Soviet Union's policies of the 1920s and the early 1930s initially offered the republics' nationalists some latitude in sustaining identity, Soviet Ukraine retained important elements of its own national feeling through the later decades of the Soviet Union.[12]

Yet despite the persistence of nationalism, Soviet Ukraine was now subjected to a slow process of Russification. That process degraded cultural unity.

The Russification of Ukraine involved a number of factors, related both to Soviet efforts at utter dominance and to the Soviet period of industrialization. For Ukraine that meant breaking the link between landowning peasants and their holdings and consolidating populations into industrial manufacturing centers in cities. By the 1930s, Russian efforts were underway to reduce the threat of rising nationalism within all of the Soviet republics. Joseph Stalin, Lenin's successor, directed widespread terror campaigns against nationalists of all stripes, including even pro-Communist nationalists. Notoriously, Moscow also used the Holodomor—organized mass starvation of Ukraine's landed peasantry—to break the power of landowning peasants known as kulaks and subordinate agriculture to the industrial-planning forces of the state. To force the collectivization of farms, more than 3 million and by many accounts up to 10 million Ukrainians were starved to death.[13]

Meanwhile, eastern Ukraine and the Donbas region had become industrialized as part of Stalin's attempt to rapidly develop the entire Soviet Union, an effort powered by coal, making coal-rich parts of Ukraine crucial to Moscow and Russia's other important industrial cities.[14] The brutal agricultural collectivization dovetailed with making eastern Ukraine and the Donbas the Soviet Union's economic engine. In that process, major cities of the Donbas drew much of their industrial labor force from all across the Soviet empire.

Upon absorption into the USSR, Ukraine became the second-largest state, and Kyiv the Soviet Union's third-largest city, thus indispensable to the Soviet Union's economic, military, and national power. And through both industrialization and collectivization, eastern and southern Ukraine and Crimea were populated with ethnic Russians to a higher degree than central and western Ukraine.[15] Thus, the east and south were seen as even more central to Russian power and national identity and as indivisible elements of Moscow's industrial base and military-industrial complex. Crimea also housed the Black Sea fleet and enjoyed the status of the premier Soviet vacation destination: Russian military retirees and senior party apparatchiks maintained dachas—vacation homes—there and retired to the region after government service, fostering a higher percentage of ethnic Russians in Sevastopol, the headquarters of the Black Sea Fleet, and in Simferopol, the capital of Crimea, than in any other territory in Ukraine, or indeed anywhere else in the Soviet Union outside of the Russian Federation.

In the later referendum for Ukraine independence, only in Crimea did the electorate come anywhere near voting to remain with the Soviet Union: some 40 percent voted to remain; 90 percent of the rest of the country voted to leave.[16] This degree of Russification engendered an identity, peculiar to the Donbas and related regions, that would pose a challenge to Ukrainian unity after independence in 1991. And while this peculiar identity would moderate toward Ukrainian national unity over the next thirty years, Russian aggression, in 2004, 2014, and 2022, would become the galvanizing force that led the Ukrainian population to reject Russia in the face of an existential threat and rally around a hard-won national Ukrainian identity.

In the late 1930s and the 1940s, the preservation and even extension of Ukrainian nationalism developed. With the signing of the Molotov-Ribbentrop Pact with Nazi Germany in 1939 and the start of World War II, the Soviet Union invaded Poland and thereby acquired eastern Galicia and Volhynia, former Hapsburg and Romanov provinces granted to Poland after World War I and inhabited by many ethnically Ukrainian people.[17] Ukraine thereby gained its current western boundaries and assimilated a host of western, culturally Ukrainian influences. The assimilation of Galicia in particular became key to helping Ukraine advance its national identity—and started giving the Soviets various headaches. Because these new lands included territories that had never been part of either imperial Russia or the Soviet Union, after the war both the Kremlin and the Ukraine SSR had to contend with the arrival of a western Ukrainian population with a coherent national identity, a prevalent Ukrainian language, and no Russification. Where the more homogenized and Russified eastern and central Ukrainian state had become, as a consequence of generations of Kremlin dominance, somewhat reconciled to Russian and Soviet power, the incorporation of western Ukraine counterbalanced the Russification of the east.

The Communist Party now had to deal not only with an ethnically coherent western Ukrainian identity, progressively strengthening the national identity of the whole of Ukraine, but also with a nationalist insurgency based in Galicia from the end of World War II through the 1950s. This was a far-right movement, often referred to as the Banderites or, in Ukrainian, "Banderivets," after its most notable leader, Stepan Bandera, a Galician-born Ukrainian with ties to Nazi Germany. Among some Ukrainian nationalists, Bandera would always symbolize the Ukrainians who fought tenaciously for Ukraine's independence against the overwhelming might of the Soviet Union. But his collaboration with Nazi forces and association with the murder of Jews and Poles understandably made him in the eyes of many simply a fascist and a murderer. The Bandera movement has long given Russia an excuse to brand any democratic-nationalist movement in Ukraine as fascist and Nazi by definition. Bandera himself, after multiple assassination attempts throughout the 1940s and 1950s, was murdered in 1959, in Munich, poisoned with cyanide by the Soviet security agency KGB on the orders of Premier Nikita Khrushchev.[18]

In 1954, in a last major change to Soviet Ukraine's borders, Ukraine attained the borders it would enjoy throughout the latter part of the Soviet period. Into the early 1950s, the Kremlin had retained direct control of Crimea; then on the 300th anniversary of the signing of the treaty of Pereiaslav that, according to Russia, granted the Russian state control over Ukraine, Crimea was transferred to Ukraine. The transfer occurred during anti-Stalinist reforms advanced by Stalin's successor, Nikita Khrushchev, mainly so that the Ukraine SSR would foot the bill for developing and maintaining the Crimean Peninsula.[19] Throughout the rest of the Soviet period, Ukraine's control over Crimea remained undisputed by Russia.

BY 1960, THEN—OR slightly past the approximate midpoint, as it would turn out, of Ukraine's Soviet period—a constant tension had come into play in Ukraine between Russification and nationalism. The conflict involved regional divisions within the country: Russia chauvinists especially influential in the south and east; nationalism on the rise in the west; Kyiv, the capital, the center of both anti-Soviet dissidence and of an increasingly pro-Russian, anti-nationalist government.

The ensuing decade saw upsurges in dissident action by nationalists and crackdowns by prominent Communist Party leaders who originated from the Black Sea port Odesa, Crimea, and the Donbas.[20] Wielding a sense of Ukrainian history and culture defined by what they called "Little Russia," those Russified elites ascended to power on a program of suppressing Ukrainian identity.

The conservative nature of the "Little Russia" Kyiv elites was rewarded when the Communist Party began a policy throughout all of the Soviet republics of selecting Eurasianists—Moscow-centric, imperial-minded leaders—rather than republic-centric nationalists, as party leaders. In 1972, the Ukraine SSR's first secretary, Petro Shelest, a pro-nationalist, was removed from power and replaced with Volodymyr Shcherbytsky, a Eurasianist utterly servile to Moscow, close to the Soviet leader, Leonid Brezhnev, and eager to hew to the Communist Party line.[21] Mass arrests and incarcerations of dissident intellectuals, including incarceration in psychiatric institutions, followed Shcherbytsky's ascent. The Ukrainian-language press was repressed. Ukrainian citizens were overrepresented among Soviet Gulag prisoners. The language itself was officially sidelined as much as possible; Shcherbytsky himself spoke Russian at official events.

Shcherbytsky's actions were driven in part by an ambition to succeed his mentor Leonid Brezhnev, Khrushchev's more hard-line successor, as head of the USSR. To that end, he felt he had to prove his Soviet orthodoxy and demonstrate the mettle required to lead the Soviet Union. A critical effect of that effort was seen in the summer of 1979, when the Ukrainian SSR began canceling Jewish refugees' flights out of Kyiv in response to deteriorating US-Soviet relations following the USSR's invasion of Afghanistan and the US boycott of the 1980 Moscow Olympics.[22] Where other Soviet cities continued such flights, Shcherbytsky, hoping to anticipate the Soviet line on the matter, wanted to show himself, if anything, ahead of it.

This reactionary policy had a direct impact on my family. My cousin Mila, deep into a pregnancy, was supposed to have her first child born in the West. Instead, her departure was canceled two weeks before she was to emigrate as a refugee: her child, Jane, spent the first ten years of her life in the Soviet Union.

But the political leadership in Moscow was changing rapidly, and Shcherbytsky's ambitions were thwarted. He was passed over for leadership of the USSR upon Brezhnev's death in 1982, when Yuri Andropov was given that role. In 1985, with the accession of Mikhail Gorbachev, who championed the liberalizing political philosophy of perestroika (reform and rebuilding) and glasnost (truth and transparency), Shcherbytsky's days in power were numbered. At the same time, the appeal of denuclearization was amplified by the Chernobyl disaster. An increasingly assertive Ukrainian nationalist movement, inspired and led by political prisoners newly released from the Gulag, began to gain traction.[23]

In 1989, amid Gorbachev's purge of conservatives, Shcherbytsky's membership in the Politburo of the Soviet Communist Party was rescinded. Gorbachev himself came to Kyiv and presided over the session of the Communist Party of Ukraine that removed Shcherbytsky from office.

Events beyond the immediate Soviet space inspired further assertions of Ukrainian autonomy. Later that year, in Germany, the Berlin Wall came down, the Sovietized East German government fell, and the difficult process of German reunification began, based largely on the free-market principles of what had been West Germany. Nationalist aspirations within Ukraine for greater self-determination coincided with and, in their bumpy way, were inspired by perestroika in the Soviet Union and an end to Communist rule in Germany and elsewhere.

With Shcherbytsky's exit, a group of moderately national-ist reformers turned the Verkhovna Rada—Ukraine's legislative body, formerly a creature of the Communist Party and the Soviet government—into a new parliamentary body subject to partially free elections. This body would shepherd Ukraine toward estab-lishing sovereignty over the territory defined by the uncontested borders arrived at in full in 1954, with Soviet transfer of Crimea to Ukraine.

The creation of a largely freely elected Rada was a historic accomplishment for Ukrainian self-determination and national identity. Yet, even as the Soviet grip loosened, ultimately to the point of true independence for Ukraine, the country as a whole remained both poorly equipped and reluctant to undertake major societal and economic reforms.[24] Democracy, as Western democracies know it, remained a difficult goal to fully realize for Ukraine, thanks to the history of elites' Russification and deference to Moscow, along with real physical and structural tethers. When the world-changing events of 1989 to 1991 began accelerating toward what nobody could yet see coming—the implosion of the USSR itself—Ukraine's struggle over its national identity would connect with the turmoil in Russia, and the rapidly developing policies of the United States and the West, to create new conditions for fostering familiar desires for empire, independence, and stability. That interplay would lead, ultimately though avoidably, to Russia's invasion of Ukraine.

CHAPTER TWO

UNGROUP

THE VIEW FROM WASHINGTON

Foreign-policy leaders in the United States, startled by the waning of Soviet power, were of course watching and responding to the history-changing events of the late 1980s, both within the USSR and in its Soviet Bloc allies, with intense interest. The US missteps that would contribute, ultimately, to the 2014 and 2022 crisis of a Russian war on Ukraine germinated in actions taken by the US beginning in the late 1980s.

The US assessment of the situation in Ukraine at that time conflated what would soon become the new Russian Federation with that singular great rival, the Soviet Union, involving a historical conception of the power of the Russian Empire. This acceptance of Russia's own account of its history and nature made Russia, instantly and immediately, the exceptional priority in regional relations. Washington, after forty years of Cold War antagonism, was all too willing to believe that Russia was at once more fearsome, due to upheaval and instability, and also more likely to form a productive partnership with the West than it ever really was.

That mentality has persisted throughout many twists and turns of events and ins and outs of politics in the US, in Ukraine, and in Russia. It began in the George H. W. Bush administration and continued, across otherwise deep partisan divides, throughout the administrations of Clinton, George W. Bush, Obama, and Biden, with Trump a possible exception: his personal approach was chaotic and, in opposition to his entire national security establishment, he was obsessed with manifesting a friendly relationship with Vladimir Putin, already proven a despot. The prevailing approach across administrations has been crisis management, a transactional mode of at once containing and courting Russia, which allowed little room for the long-term values-based approach that would have deterred Russian aggression and revealed opportunities to form productive, enduring strategic alliances with others—most crucially, Ukraine.

But in the late 1980s the US position seemed reasonable, in part because it operated within a larger Western context of nurturing a Soviet transformation away from hostility and toward peaceful coexistence. That context was by no means lockstep. Where Germany and France prioritized normalizing relations with the Soviet Union and avoiding major disruptions in normalizing relations, the UK prioritized limiting aggression, as did the former Eastern Bloc states that would eventually join NATO and the EU.

Both modes, however, were influenced by an acceptance of Russian chauvinist, imperialist, expansionist exceptionalism by the US. That attitude had deep roots in the Cold War period, influenced by the existential threat of nuclear Armageddon, a threat then coming to an end, with a future unknown to all participants. Beginning as early as 1949, when the Soviet Union detonated its first nuclear bomb, even as it launched a program of aggressive expansion that would change the face of the region and establish the Warsaw Pact, the Russia-US relationship came to be defined as both a contest over ideas about government and an arms race. It thus became the one relationship critical to the security of the entire planet. While other nuclear powers quickly came into existence, and while the US came to be at stark odds with Communist China as well, the bilateral nuclear superpower standoff with the USSR, with the fate of the globe seemingly always held precariously in the balance, was the gravitational force that shaped American thinking about international relations during the decades-long Cold War.

In the mid-1980s, much of that tense situation seemed to begin to drastically improve for the first time since the end of World War II. When Gorbachev came to power in 1985, and as he and President Reagan developed a notably positive relationship, US foreign-policy officials saw new potential for a more positive bilateral relationship between their countries.

Processing that shift, however, was not as simple for policy-makers as it might have looked to the public. In 1987, Reagan visited West Berlin and made a memorable speech containing the famous line "Mr. Gorbachev, tear down this wall!" That was a blunt, even confrontational demand, based on US values around self-determination—a demand made in one of the hottest Cold War spots of Europe itself, a Germany still starkly divided between NATO and Warsaw Pact protections. The president had been advised by his deputy national security advisor, Colin Powell, as well as by his chief of staff, Howard Baker—who were concerned about the possibility of worsening relations with Gorbachev and that the US president would sound extreme—to cut the line from the draft. Reagan ignored them.

As early as 1987, then, elements in US foreign-policy circles were more concerned, perhaps still reasonably, given nuclear and other stakes, with managing the Soviets on the basis of short-term and immediately urgent issues. They reflexively defaulted to a kind of negotiation with the USSR that became bargaining sessions akin to Yalta during World War II, with the Soviet Union charged with reforming Eurasia. The US approach assumed the USSR to be a solid, durable political fact, as well as a potential threat, when in fact it was hollowed out and about to collapse from within. The negotiations focused effectively on reducing nuclear weapons stockpiles, but they were scarce on values-based demands, relying on Gorbachev, a life-long Communist apparatchik, to drive reform within the Soviet Union. The US was reluctant even to support resistance to Soviet authority within East Germany, fearing the possibility of upsetting the applecart of warming relations. As a result, the autonomy of a Ukraine indistinguishable, to many, from Russia came to seem of tertiary importance at best, or simply a problem to be kicked down the road.

When events in Europe, Eurasia, and Russia began unfolding at a mind-blowing pace, amid a transition in the US presidency from Reagan to his vice-president, George H. W. Bush, US attention naturally remained fixed on immediate ways of avoiding danger and ameliorating the chaos that might arise from deterioration of centralized power within the Soviet Union. In 1989, with the fall of the Wall, the US focused on the complicated process of German reunification. Restlessness in the Baltic states, too, which would lead to the independence of Lithuania in 1990, strongly suggested to US policymakers that the Soviet Union's existence as a coherent and seemingly stable imperial power was also threatened. To Washington and Western capitals, this prospect was alarming. It elicited a hyper-focus on danger and thoughts of worst-case scenarios rather than a cool appraisal of opportunities for advancing the cause of Western values.

IN THE SPRING of 1989, Deputy National Security Advisor Robert Gates went to President Bush and advised him that, given the fall of the Berlin Wall and other events, the administration should start contingency planning for the USSR's collapse. Such a collapse was still seen as unlikely, but it was not out of the question. The president agreed.

Bush and Gates were committed to keeping this planning project very small, agile, and secret. Many of the other stakeholders who typically participate in policy planning, and much of the military and diplomatic enterprise, were left in the dark. They were driven by a concern that as long as the administration remained focused on supporting Gorbachev it could not be seen underwriting a project that speculated about scenarios that envisaged a regime without him, since to do so would undermine US-Russia relations. That July, the National Security Council (NSC) therefore established a group reporting to Gates, facetiously named the Ungroup both because it consisted of undersecretaries and to emphasize its official nonexistence.[1]

Participants in the Ungroup included Condoleezza Rice, Stephen Hadley, and Robert Blackwill from the NSC; Paul Wolfowitz and Eric Edelman from the Department of Defense; and Robert Zoellick and Dennis Ross from the Department of State. Its mandate was to analyze the waning power of the Soviet Union, investigate the still-counterfactual situation of imminent Soviet collapse, and establish US policy toward the region in the unlikely scenario of outright downfall.

Because the "counterfactual" soon became not only likely but a fait accompli, the Ungroup's findings and recommendations would chart US policy for Russia and the newly independent former Soviet republics throughout the George H. W. Bush and early Clinton administrations; even after its direct influence ceased, the Ungroup's legacy endured. Understanding its view and preconceptions is therefore critical to understanding the all too transactional nature prevailing in the US-Russia relationship and US attitudes toward the autonomy of Ukraine and the other republics.

The Ungroup's hyper-focus was on the Kremlin preserving control of the Soviet empire throughout any imperial collapse and national and regional restructuring. As Gates recalls, "The primary conclusion [the Ungroup] came to us with was the risk to nuclear weapons if the Soviet Union collapsed—a dispersal of the nuclear weapons. And actually," Gates goes on,

> their conclusions were the strongest argument against Cheney's position that we ought to try and make Russia as weak as possible. Their central conclusion, which became US policy under the president, was to do everything we could to maintain a strong central government in Moscow, because that was essential to maintaining control of the nuclear weapons. And therefore, it was important to do everything we could, once the collapse took place, to have Russia itself retain its territorial integrity, but further to be as strong a government as possible in Moscow in order to have command and control over the nuclear weapons.[2]

The Ungroup was fixated on risks emerging from the world's largest nuclear arsenal falling into the hands of potentially failed states, the proliferation of nuclear states, and the possibility of loose nuclear weapons, a calculation that fed a desire to prevent balkanization by preserving regional coherence through centralized Kremlin power.[3] In keeping with the hope for centralization and control, another of the Ungroup's key policies was to preserve a special relationship between President Bush and his key counterpart, Gorbachev.

But Gates also reports that the need to centralize control over nuclear weapons did not conflict with a desire to advance the independence of the Soviet republics and satellites as democracies ready to join the brotherhood of nations. The real issue was never, he says, to preserve the *territorial* integrity of the Soviet Union:

> This was all about Russia. And we were perfectly comfortable with the constituent republics becoming independent, and I don't recall any opposition to that at all. . . . Because there was consensus that there was enough going on in all of those republics. . . . It was clear where things were going. . . . We had no problem with those republics becoming independent and in fact sought, in our interest, for those republics to become independent, particularly if there was a way to get control of their nuclear weapons.[4]

Through the ensuing crises, this attitude of general support for the republics' independence, while retaining Russian control over nuclear weapons, would direct the US position.

The attitude reflects a hierarchy of interests that ranks national self-determination secondary to, even contingent on, nuclear security. Above all, the nukes had to be secured; in practical terms, that made self-determination for the republics contingent on the Kremlin's retaining significant control. While the idea would come up, as we will see, there was never any serious consideration of Ukraine retaining nuclear weapons as a hedge against Russian revanchism and aggression. This policy of ensuring Russian control over Soviet weapons—based on the institutional knowledge of the Ungroup, which to most members of the US government did not even exist—was in place well before the actual collapse of the USSR, and it showed a strong bias in favor of the USSR and Gorbachev over the republics: it prioritized the center, the Kremlin, over the periphery.

That bias was borne out on May 31, 1989, when President Bush spoke to German citizens and political leaders, including the West German chancellor Helmut Kohl, at the Rheingold-halle, in Mainz, West Germany. As suggested by its title, "Europe Whole and Free," the speech focused on the future of Europe, not Eurasia—and certainly not Ukraine, whose European elements US policy continued to subordinate to the historically misinformed, Russian-exceptionalist view of the country's nature and identity.[5] "For forty years," the president said,

> the seeds of democracy in Eastern Europe lay dormant, buried under the frozen tundra of the Cold War. And for forty years, the world has waited for the Cold War to end. And decade after decade, time after time, the flowering human spirit withered from the chill of conflict and oppression; and again, the world waited. But the passion for freedom cannot be denied forever.[6]

In the context of the passion for freedom, the president mentioned Poland and Hungary. He also mentioned "positive steps by the Soviets" that "would be met by steps of our own," proposing to liberalize old anti-Soviet trade restrictions and technology sanctions. He made no mention at all of the ongoing struggle for self-determination in any of the Soviet republics.

In Ukraine, as the 1990s began, the pace of change continued to boggle the mind, as did overall events regionally. Given the historic place of Ukraine in Russia's imperial self-conception, the Ukrainian drive toward establishing a de-Russified political and cultural autonomy posed a special challenge to the Soviet hegemony that US policy had now become focused on shoring up—or at least managing through an orderly decline. As a result, Ukraine did now draw the concerned attention of the officials most influential on US policy.

Ukrainian politics at that moment involved some cultural and historical complexities. The moderately nationalist forces in Ukraine that had succeeded Shcherbytsky and established the new, more democratic Rada favored their own brand of conservatism, an anti-Soviet form of Communism, in which liberalized markets were not on the agenda. An anti-nationalist mood also prevailed in the Donbas and parts of Crimea, where Russified populations and leaders were resistant to any change. Meanwhile, Russia's Black Sea Fleet remained in place, though in decline. Tracing its lineage to the 1780s, centered on Sebastopol and other Crimean ports, the fleet of some 25,000 military personnel and scores of capital ships challenged NATO's posturing on the northern shore of Turkey and above the Bosphorus. Its officer class in particular was Russia-chauvinist and adamantly opposed to any transfer of the force to Ukraine.

This persistence of the cultural "Little Russia" servility to the greater Russia, common among ethnic Russians in Ukraine and among some Ukrainian Russian-speakers—especially in the long-governed and more assimilated eastern and southern regions—combined with the Ukrainians' own conservatism to impede reforms that would have weakened connections with Russia and helped Ukraine strengthen its sovereignty in a period of seething transition in both Europe and Eurasia.

Nevertheless, by the summer of 1990, a convergence of moderately nationalist forces was gathering enough momentum to push Ukraine toward increasing independence from the struggling USSR. One driver was the People's Movement for Ukraine national party, also known as "Rukh" (*movement* in Ukrainian), which formed a coalition with liberalizing Soviet leaders and thereby surmounted the historical dominance of the Eurasianist bloc within Ukraine's Rada. In October 1990, that achievement enabled a declaration of Ukrainian sovereignty—not outright independence—which passed the Rada by an overwhelming majority.[7]

In US policy circles, this blizzard of unanticipated changes in Russia, in Ukraine, and throughout the region triggered a conflict regarding the proper approach to take, centered largely on a difference between the Pentagon and the White House. At the Pentagon, Secretary of Defense Dick Cheney advocated a policy of keeping the Soviet Union as weak as possible—maybe even to the point of final collapse, a result many others were wary of. Cheney was especially sympathetic to a scenario that involved Russian regime change in favor of the popular Gorbachev critic Boris Yeltsin. Once a Gorbachev ally and subordinate, then fired by Gorbachev, Yeltsin had become by 1990 his most charismatic opponent; as president of the Russian Supreme Soviet, Yeltsin accused Gorbachev of holding back from true democratic reform. Cheney seemed to view Yeltsin as the more aggressive reformer and the best vehicle to unwind Soviet power, a judgment that would prove correct. Yeltsin would in fact advance the creation of a sovereign Russian state in the final days of the Soviet Union, undercutting the office of Gorbachev as the secretary general of the Communist Party of the Union of Soviet Socialist Republics. Yeltsin would also accept the end of the Soviet Union as a fait accompli after the withdrawal of Ukraine and Belarus in December 1991.

Conversely, Gorbachev, favored by George H. W. Bush's secretary of state, James Baker, took steps to brace Moscow's control over the republics and maintain the integrity of the Soviet Union.[8]

So Cheney was correct: the policy of the Bush administration to support Gorbachev proved futile. Yet Cheney's approach too was based largely on short-term interests, not on the development of Western values. Eric Edelman, in 1990 the special assistant covering Soviet and East European affairs for the deputy undersecretary of defense for policy, recalls that he was "convinced," early on, "that the Soviet Union was decomposing. . . . And from our point of view, Ukraine was sort of ground zero, if you will, for the Soviet Union breaking up in a way that would make it much less of a threat to Central Europe, for obvious geographic and demographic reasons." The Cheney school, though it supported both Yeltsin and Ukrainian independence and focused on US interests, rested that support and focus less on the spread of liberal democracy than on immediate hopes for containing whatever the Soviet Union was about to become.

At the White House, the strongest trend among officials was continuing to push hard the other way. Jack Matlock, ambassador to the Soviet Union, while seeing potential both in Yeltsin and in the autonomy of the republics, also advocated a policy of maintaining closeness to Gorbachev and merely hedging with Yeltsin and other leaders in the republics.[9] National Security Advisor Brent Scowcroft and his deputy, Robert Gates, expressed a strong desire to keep a liberalizing Soviet Union going and to give full support to Gorbachev. If his political demise was inevitable, and regime change had to happen, the White House favored at least slowing the pace of change.

Gates puts it this way:

My recollection is that . . . the President and [Secretary of State] James Baker in particular thought that the longer we could keep Gorbachev in power, the better our interests would be served, because he was sort of single-handedly dismantling the Soviet Union. And a big concern was, what would happen with all the nuclear weapons in Ukraine, if Ukraine declared its independence. I think we were also very concerned that Gorbachev would be compelled to act militarily, as he did, in early 91, against Lithuania. . . . It really was more about a managed dissolution of the Soviet Union rather than a chaotic one.[10]

Given the nuclear stakes referred to by Gates, and the many preceding decades of global tension around the potential for nuclear war, it was probably natural that avoiding a crisis dominated White House thinking during this period. While Secretary Baker did see potential in Yeltsin's agitation for true and total reform of the USSR, he also feared the thing that was keeping many other US policymakers up at night: the Cold War threat of the Soviet nuclear arsenal might be made newly and dangerously chaotic once the Soviets lost control of their arsenal to a balkanized patchwork of its former territories, republics, and satellites. Bush and Baker were heavily influenced by the recent and ongoing example of Yugoslavia, a non-nuclear state, which was fracturing into constituent republics that in turn were splitting apart in violent clashes that would lead, in the 1990s, to regional disaster. And within the Soviet Union, Armenia and Azerbaijan were also seeing spiraling ethnic violence. As James Goldgeier and Michael McFaul noted, "The White House . . . feared that the breakup of the Soviet Union might present the worst of all nightmares: a Yugoslavia with nuclear weapons."[11]

The Pentagon, by contrast, when it came to the nuclear weapons in Ukraine in particular, "was never very worried about that," Edelman recalls. "The Ukrainians never had positive control of those weapons." Powell and others at the White House strenuously disagreed, and as for the president himself, Goldgeier and McFaul describe his attitude about the larger changes afoot this way: "Bush was reluctant to get ahead of history." He wanted the US to avoid getting caught up in actively trying to bring about historical change and viewed emerging questions of nationalities in the former USSR as an internal matter. They also note Bush's overall reluctance to explicitly push US values when dealing with foreign affairs, especially regarding Russia: "The Bush administration did not pass judgment on the Soviet Union's internal matters. Nor did Bush ever label the USSR an empire. . . . Bush never . . . call[ed] for the freedom of the Armenian, Ukrainian, or Russian peoples. He was not a Wilsonian champion of self-determination."[12]

Described elsewhere as "the quintessential realist" on foreign policy, Bush operated in the Kissinger-influenced realpolitik mode that criticizes idealism about America's global moral leadership as a crusading sentimentalism, one that is likely to be self-defeating and tends to foster global instability. As we will see, the realist tendency was to become increasingly unrealistic regarding US relationships with Russia and Ukraine, leading to drastically diminishing returns for global stability.

Looking back, Steven Pifer, President Clinton's ambassador to Ukraine from January 1998 to October 2000, sums up the overall situation at the time. "Washington was slow to recognize the Soviet Union's demise," Pifer says. "Moreover, once they realized its likelihood, many senior officials, including in the White House, became apprehensive at the prospect. Some even seemed to look for ways to slow the processes underway inside the Soviet Union, which the United States could hardly affect."[13] US long-range policy would have been better served by recognizing the centrality of values to interest and the importance of nurturing democracy.

President Bush and other US policymakers nevertheless felt they had good reason, in this shifting period, for prioritizing Soviet over Ukraine relations. Regardless of oncoming breakups, Soviet Russia remained a nuclear superpower with the means to annihilate the United States. A positive relationship could be security-enhancing; an adversarial relationship would significantly increase security risks. Soviet liberalizing forces, meanwhile, looked encouraging. The White House, not the Pentagon, drove policy, and the guiding idea of the moment was to keep Gorbachev in power.

US RESPONSE TO the dramatic Ukrainian claim on sovereignty was thus influenced by the desire to maintain Gorbachev's power in the USSR, as informed by the Ungroup's narrowly scoped policy for regional stability and control of nuclear weapons systems. US officials saw Ukraine moving headlong toward greater and greater autonomy—even independence. To the dominant policy players who accepted the long-standing Russian-exceptionalist view, despite an all too vague and general sense of support for democracy and self-determination, these moves seemed potentially profoundly destabilizing.

On July 30, 1991, President Bush arrived in Moscow for a two-day informal summit with Gorbachev. Alignment between the two was already both implicit and explicit: in 1989, at the Council of Europe in Strasbourg, Gorbachev had given a speech entitled "Europe as a Common Home," parallel to Bush's "Europe Whole and Free."[14] In that speech, he called the Cold War "a thing of the past." He departed from old Soviet doctrines, according to which any threat to socialist rule in any Soviet Bloc country threatened them all, which had justified the Soviet Union's military interventions in Hungary in 1956 and Czechoslovakia in 1968. He tacitly endorsed self-determination in East Germany, thus endorsing German reunification. Those gestures toward sovereignty, independence, and self-determination referred only to Eastern European states. Regarding the former Soviet republics, Russian exceptionalism prevailed, and the Kremlin suggested it was entitled to its vassals and satellite states.

In 1990, Gorbachev had also begun pushing the New Union Treaty, in which the USSR would be reformed along more legitimately federalist lines, acknowledging the kind of sovereignty Ukraine had declared while keeping the republics within the Soviet Union.[15] Ukraine had abstained from signing it.

In their meeting on July 30, 1991, Bush informed his Soviet counterpart that the US saw it as in the US interest that the Soviet Union should survive. He promised to advise Ukraine against declaring independence. "Gorbachev also warned Bush," as Paul D'Anieri says, "that Ukraine's independence might lead to a conflict similar to that unfolding in Yugoslavia—but with thousands of nuclear weapons involved"—the exact scenario on which the Ungroup was laser-focused.[16]

On August 1, Bush traveled to Kyiv and was met with an intense public turnout, reflecting the divided climate of Ukrainian politics in this moment of profound change. Crowds represented a wide range of viewpoints: some waved Ukrainian and American flags, some were reformist Communists, some were protesting any US support for Russia at all. Bush declined to meet with leaders of Rukh, the pro-independence party. Addressing the reconstructed, representative Rada, he gave a speech extolling an improved version of Gorbachev's New Union Treaty and praising Gorbachev as a reformer.

And while in the speech Bush expressed support for "the struggle in this great country for democracy and economic reform," he warned his Ukrainian audience against "rampant nationalism," advising Ukraine that "freedom is not the same as independence. Americans will not support those who seek independence in order to replace a far-off tyranny with a local despotism. They will not aid those who promote a suicidal nationalism based upon ethnic hatred."[17]

He also announced a hands-off approach by the US: "We will not try to pick winners and losers in political competitions between republics or between republics and the center. That is your business. That's not the business of the United States of America." Clearly reflecting the US realist bias for the stability of the Soviet Union, as well as the president's own recoil from any crusading Wilsonian commitment to active support for self-determination abroad, the August 1 speech sparked intense controversy both at home and in Ukraine. In the US, veteran cold warriors condemned Bush for pandering to Russia and selling out those very values of self-determination and democracy that had stood at the heart of the decades-long standoff with the Soviets.

William Safire, the conservative columnist, lambasted the speech as sheer cowardice: "chicken Kiev." In Ukraine, meanwhile, Ivan Drach, the chairman of Rukh, accused Bush of serving as "a messenger for Gorbachev."[18] To this day, Ukrainian policymakers invoke the "chicken Kyiv" speech to describe the sclerotic and schizophrenic US relationship with Ukraine.

Still, the New Union Treaty remained on the table. Ukraine's abstention might be overcome. Gorbachev was scheduled to issue a new draft, expected to create a true confederation of fully sovereign states. It seemed to many in the White House far from impossible that Ukraine's newly representative government would endorse that draft. If it did, the most historically and emotionally critical of the non-Russian republics would take an active part in shoring up the Soviet Union and lowering the highly concerning potential for nuclear balkanization.

ALL SUCH CALCULATIONS were overwhelmed by events. Later that August, with President Bush back in Washington, US officials abruptly found themselves facing dizzying history-changing developments in Moscow.

On August 18, hard-line Soviet Communist Party leaders, dissenting from Gorbachev's reforms and hoping to prevent signings of the New Union Treaty, dispatched agents of the KGB to detain not only Gorbachev but also Yeltsin, who had been elected, over Gorbachev's objections, chairman of the Supreme Soviet of the Russian Soviet Federative Socialist Republic.[19] The KGB did detain Gorbachev, but it missed Yeltsin, who now became the de facto leader of a popular movement, both in officialdom and on the streets, to overcome the hard-liners' putsch.

In the course of only two days, the popular movement succeeded. Pushback against the putsch ended the long reign of the Communist Party of the Soviet Union and, in that context, not only the role of the hard-liners but also, very soon, the leadership role of Mikhail Gorbachev.

Both Ukraine and the US responded quickly to the shocking news both of the attempted coup and of its failure. For Ukrainians, the New Union Treaty was now completely off the table. On August 24, the Rada joined a slew of other former Soviet entities declaring independence.[20] A referendum was scheduled for December 1, in which the question of Ukraine's withdrawal from the Soviet Union was to be decided by direct popular vote.

The other republics' withdrawals would weaken the Soviet Union—but a Ukrainian withdrawal would be fatal. Should the December referendum vote be to withdraw, the USSR, as Goldgeier and McFaul say, "would lose a significant economic base, fifty million people from a republic crucial to the balance among Slavs and Muslims in the empire, and a geostrategic position in the heart of Central and Eastern Europe."[21] By the end of 1991, the fate of the Soviet system was effectively in the hands of the people of Ukraine. For nearly 350 years Moscow had imposed its will on much of Ukraine; now Ukraine had the opportunity to determine its own fate and the means to end Russian empire. Ukraine was thus the primary culprit in what Vladimir Putin would later say was the greatest disaster of the twentieth century, the collapse of the Soviet Union.

The US response to the putsch, meanwhile—a "devil you know" bias for preserving status quo—amounted more or less to hoping for the best, not for the USSR but for Russia, for the Kremlin, and for Gorbachev. Throughout the end of that summer and into the fall, Bush and the White House continued to see the rise of Yeltsin and the republics' independence as complications in a narrative where the primary agent for change in the Soviet space was Gorbachev. As Eugene Fishel says, "Despite the fact that Gorbachev emerged from the August 1991 hard-line coup attempt severely—and probably mortally—weakened, Bush remained convinced that Gorbachev and the center could still play a role and that the United States should remain supportive."[22]

The US therefore reacted to Ukraine's response to the putsch and the result of the December referendum in Ukraine with grave concern. In *The Great Transition*, Raymond Garthoff describes the policy of the Bush administration as supporting the status quo in reacting to sovereignty claims from other republics. The only exception was the bolder language reserved for calling on the Soviet government to recognize the independence of the Baltic states—Estonia, Latvia, and Lithuania—whose incorporation in the Soviet Union had never been recognized by the United States.[23] The White House remained very wary of any further disintegration of the USSR, and in particular of Ukrainian independence.

Throughout this period of utter turmoil and unpredictability for Russia, however, the division between the White House and the Pentagon persisted, with particular regard to Ukraine. Thomas Graham, then at the Arms Control and Disarmament Agency (ACDA), recalls:

> [The] White House clearly had an interest in the Soviet Union sort of holding together. So, they continue to work with Gorbachev. I think Cheney and his staff were . . . much more interested in, I think, reaching out to the Ukrainians at that point, getting a better understanding of what was happening, and certainly not opposed to sort of encouraging separatist ideas in Ukraine, and not terribly keen on pushing back against nationalist forces, or anything that seemed to be separating Ukraine from Russia [and] from the Soviet Union.[24]

As the December referendum approached, Cheney and his aides at the Pentagon favored being "as forward leaning as possible" toward Ukraine, according to Goldgeier and McFaul.[25]

But they were up against a more powerful coalition centered on the White House. The long-range focus remained on maintaining

Kremlin control of weapons systems, a policy borne out in October 1991, when Undersecretary of State Reginald Bartholomew met with representatives of the republics of Russia, Ukraine, Belorussia, and Kazakhstan. A Moscow embassy cable shows that Bartholomew expressed an overriding concern that waning Soviet power "not lead to the creation of new nuclear powers" and issued a warning to the republics that, as Fishel puts it, "efforts by Republics to exploit or take exclusive control of nuclear weapons on their territory would be politically costly."[26]

Some of the representatives at the meeting raised the idea that the republics ought to have a degree of input into arms-control negotiations, but Bartholomew shot them down. The US government, he said, continued to view the central Soviet authorities as the US negotiating partner. Yeltsin's representative at the meeting aligned with Bartholomew's rejection of the republics' having a role, stating Russia had a "strongly positive view of President Bush's nuclear initiative."

On November 26, George Bush and the State Department agreed on a policy of postponing any official US recognition of Ukraine and most other emerging states. Three days later, in a phone conversation with Yeltsin, Bush went out of his way to underscore that he did not want Ukraine issues to cause division between the United States and the newly emerging Russian government, though "I hope you understand," he explained to Yeltsin, "that as a democratic nation, we must support the will of the Ukrainian people."[27] As Fishel says, Bush almost sounded apologetic.

Regardless of all these US concerns and inner divisions, on December 1, 1991, the Ukrainian people took matters into their own hands. In the referendum, 93 percent voted for independence. Ukraine, the empire's last, best underpinning, withdrew from the Soviet Union.

By THEN, THE monopoly power of the Communist Party of Ukraine had been abolished, but it continued to hold a lot of sway and to seek power. Ukrainian independence therefore represented a compromise among Western-leaning liberal nationalists, communists, old elites, and others. Leonid Kravchuk, chairman of the Rada, formerly a highly placed Communist Party official, became the interim head of state. Elections were scheduled, and on December 5, Kravchuk, elected the first president of the independent nation, took office. For the first time in its long history, Ukraine, within its current borders, was a sovereign state with a fairly democratically elected government.

These developments went largely uncontested by Moscow, where the struggle for power between Yeltsin and Gorbachev, as Yeltsin tried to eliminate Gorbachev's power base as the head of the Soviet Union, dominated everyone's attention. Ukraine, having fatally undermined the structural integrity of the USSR by declaring independence, became the critical agent in a massive historic collapse.

On December 25, 1991, Gorbachev resigned as president of the Soviet Union and the Russian tricolor replaced the Soviet flag over the Kremlin, and the following day the USSR legally ceased to exist when the upper chamber of the Supreme Soviet voted to cancel itself and with it the concept of a Soviet Union. The Russia-Ukraine relationship, having existed in emotional and political tension for almost a thousand years, had entered a new and very challenging phase.

Despite offering no real support for Ukrainian independence, the US had little interest in supporting a failed Soviet Union. The focus had always been first and foremost on maintaining the

Kremlin's central control of nuclear weapons. Supporting the jurisdictional and territorial persistence of the USSR and/or aiding its orderly decline were purely transactional policies—driven almost entirely by the desire to avoid "a Yugoslavia with nuclear weapons." It was a policy based not on principle but on a desire to achieve immediate results: arms control and the pacification of any emerging ethnic or nationalistic tensions.

As soon as the USSR had vanished, US attention focused primarily on the newly independent Russia. For it was to Russia that the central management of the USSR's massive national security apparatus now defaulted.

The Ungroup's gamed-out scenario, in which existential threats emerged from the world's largest nuclear arsenal falling into the hands of failed states, resulting in a proliferation of loose nuclear weapons, now became an immediate concern. Prioritizing control over nuclear weapons caused US policy to address relations with whoever was to become the Russian counterpart to President Bush. Once Gorbachev had resigned it was almost inevitable, despite Bush administration hopes, that they would be dealing with Boris Yeltsin. As for Ukraine, there was no planned US policy beyond the goal of denuclearizing the region as a whole. Worse yet for Ukraine's future, the US had too little understanding of Ukraine as a separate entity, with a distinct national identity, to warrant much consideration of Ukraine policy.

For decades, the United States had been locked in a bipolar struggle with a peer adversary. As soon as the forty-year Cold War ended, the United States became the sole superpower in what some have called the "unipolar moment." A mix of old habits and new anxieties would determine foreign policy going forward.

CHAPTER THREE

DENUCLEARIZATION

Having possessed the largest nuclear arsenal in the world, with thousands of nuclear warheads in its silos, submarines, and bombers, the Soviet Union could have destroyed the world many times over. After the collapse of the USSR, Russia inherited that capability, but Ukraine, Belarus, and Kazakhstan—newly independent states, with unclear prospects for cohesion or internal stability—also inherited thousands of those weapons.

Starting in 1989 with the work of the Ungroup, the US had determined that the greatest existential threat to its interests emerging from a Soviet collapse would be nuclear proliferation—the emergence of three more nuclear-weapons-armed states—and the appearance of a nuclear rogue state or a loose-nuke scenario. Realism, at its most short-term and transactional, was therefore to prevail, according to Ungroup thinking, against any supposedly misguided idealism about supporting the self-determination of the new republics as a fundamental Western value. Well before the fall of the USSR, the goal of Bush's nuclear initiative had been, as

Fishel says, "to protect and, if possible, advance existing arms control agreements with the Soviets, even under conditions of increased activism by the union republics."[1]

Boris Yeltsin's representative had expressed a positive view of Bush's nuclear initiative in October 1991.[2] That encouraged US leadership to believe that the existing US-Soviet nuclear position would now become the US-Russia position, thus easing fears of both nuclear proliferation and loose nuclear weapons: ultimately, under this program, all of the region's nuclear weapons would be consolidated in Russia.

In the immediate aftermath of the collapse, there was in fact some talk in US policy circles of letting the republics retain limited nuclear capability, as a hedge against a resurgence of Russian aggression. But the dominant optimism about a reforming Russia and doubts about Russia's ever regaining enough power to pose a significant threat to the United States combined to confirm the priority of limiting nuclear proliferation.[3] And enabling the safety of the republics via nuclear deterrence or other defense was of little concern in the US. Any fear of the newly independent states having to defend themselves against a resurgent Russia looked remote.

By early 1992, this US priority for the reduction of nuclear threat was well-aligned with the priorities of Russia. Suddenly a newly independent state too, Russia had the strongest possible interest in controlling the weapons systems that had now defaulted to it. And it had a special concern for the Soviet-era nuclear weapons stationed nearby, outside its borders. Arguably the country most at risk from loose nukes in the former Soviet republics was Russia itself. So a bilateral focus on denuclearization intensified throughout the early 1990s between the US and Russia.

UKRAINE, WITH ITS massive new nuclear arsenal, size, and population, was the country where the US and Russia most naturally focused shared attention: Ukraine bordered Europe and Russia, whereas Belarus was small and thinly populated and Kazakhstan was considered a part of Asia, much farther from NATO's sphere of interest; Ukraine was home to about 20 percent of the Soviet Union's intercontinental ballistic missile (ICBM) warheads and about 40 percent of its heavy bomber weapons. More than 4,500 nuclear warheads were distributed among the ICBMs, cruise missiles, and tactical weapons in Ukraine.[4]

US priorities for handling these weapons during the first years of US policy in the post-Soviet period dovetailed with President George H. W. Bush's views expressed in his 1989 Mainz speech, in which Bush "tiered" the European continent "into European states—nations meriting incorporation and integration into Europe's economic, security, and political structure—and other states, former Soviet republics." By setting the eastward boundaries of Europe at the old Soviet border—which meant Poland, Romania, Slovakia, and Hungary were "in" Europe, but Ukraine was not—Bush had framed the end of communist regimes in Central Europe as making Europe "whole and free." Ukraine, and other nations on what Fishel calls "the wrong side of the artificial dividing line," would still be subject to Moscow's authority.[5] As the 1990s went on, that policy vision advanced US relations with the Kremlin ahead of relations with the fourteen other former Soviet republics; with Ukraine, the US further subordinated broader policy to a denuclearization imperative.

The high prioritization of Moscow was rationalized by the idea that Russia was at once the greater threat and the more significant site of potential progress. Gains made with Russia, it was presumed, would be converted to gains for Ukraine and the other republics. Thus at the outset of a critical period of political and economic transition, the largest country in Europe, with a population of 50 million, received too little attention from the US and the West as a whole regarding the broad range of challenges it had begun facing as an independent nation, including but not limited to unceasing Russian coercion, stoked by the Russian elites' faith in eternal empire and Ukraine as core province and indispensable organ: "Little Russia."

The fact was that, with the collapse of the USSR, Ukraine remained from the beginning highly vulnerable to Russian revanchism. Ostap Kryvdyk, later the senior policy advisor to the speaker of Ukraine's Rada, puts the early situation of independent Ukraine this way: "Ukraine was lucky to emerge as an independent state during Russia's period of weakness."[6] The remark emphasizes the contingent, by no means inevitable nature of Ukraine becoming a nation-state, given its complicated relationship to Russia's historic sense of the region—a sense that, as many Ukrainians saw then, was bound to revive, should Russia gain sufficient strength.

Oleksandr Turchynov, Ukraine's former prime minister, former secretary of the National Security and Defense Council, and one-time acting president, puts the issue another way, asserting that "from the very beginning, the Russian Federation laid out a task for itself: the return of the Soviet Union. . . . [Thus] all of their actions from the beginning have been aimed at weakening Ukraine."[7]

Ukrainians were not being paranoid. From very early in the transition, Russian leaders were anything but timid about playing up the importance of Ukraine to the cause of Russian exceptionalism. Wanting to keep Ukraine in its sphere, Russia was already using the political, societal, and economic links established during the imperial and Soviet eras to influence Ukraine's elites to arrest Western reforms. Yeltsin advisor Sergei Kortunov, echoing Yevgeny Primakov, one of Russia's most important geopolitically minded policymakers, then serving as minister of foreign affairs, argued that only Western interference was impeding what he presented as a natural tendency for Ukraine to reintegrate quickly with Russia.[8] Yet Ukrainians' clear-eyed perceptions of Russian revanchist aims—to be borne out in part in 2004, 2014, and fully in the 2020s—remained hard to envision for the most senior Western and US policymakers at the outset of the post-Soviet period.

Consideration of Moscow, not Kyiv, drove US policy for the region, a phenomenon that Fishel has called "the Moscow factor." The US did attempt to conduct a broader foreign policy and to engage bilaterally with Ukraine—but only in areas where US concerns about a fractured and unstable Russia, and about controlling the nuclear arsenal, were not impacted. Even when Moscow didn't directly color US policy, Russia consistently took precedence in US leadership's time, energy, engagement, and financial support. If not wholly derivative of relations with Russia, relations with Ukraine were persistently ranked subordinate to perceived US national security interests around arms control.

The long-term potential for a threat to Ukraine, hence to the West and to Western values and global stability, was barely considered.

FOR UKRAINE, MANY of the new problems arising from independence were not first and foremost Russian or American but Ukrainian. Critical to understanding the development of US missteps in the longer period, beginning with denuclearization in 1990s, and leading to the crises of the 2010s and 2020s, is understanding the specific nature of the challenges facing Ukraine itself in its early independence.

All of the republics realizing independence at the dawn of the 1990s found themselves lacking the structures and processes necessary for governing. In Ukraine, the end of Shcherbytsky's conservative regime in 1989 had enabled a moderately nationalist, moderately reform coalition to establish the Rada that shepherded the country through independence. The driving force for that great change was the establishment of the Rukh national party, which, though aligned with sovereign Soviet leaders, surmounted the historical dominance of the Eurasianist bloc within the Rada and gained the declaration of sovereignty in 1990 and then, with the backing of the power-seeking Communist Party, saw true independence emerge from the 1991 referendum on withdrawal from the USSR.[9]

Independence by no means equated, however, with true or complete reform of government. The legacy of Russian imperial and Soviet rule left not only an absence of strong state-governing institutions but also a population whose demographics—Ukrainian and Russian, ethnically mixed, national-identity-muddled—inhibited appeasing Russia's wishes for a pliable neighbor and, at the same time, prevented pivoting fully toward Europe as a reformed, resilient, and prosperous state capable of defending itself against the Russian revanchism that many Ukrainians could already predict. The Ukrainian state began with no defense or security or foreign-policy structures. And the only functioning political parties were the old Communist Party and the nationalist Rukh movement established only two years before independence.

In the late Soviet period, the Communist Party boss elites had initiated a process to secure state property in the hands of a *nomenklatura*. Now, with the old Soviet system in collapse, the survivors who took the reins amounted to the same elites that had operated the Soviet system: a conservative, former Communist *nomenklatura,* supported by the Eurasianist contingent still deeply burrowed into Kyiv leadership. And in the Donbas and south, the same contingent remained closely aligned with Russia.[10] Taras Kuzio, focusing on the postindependence challenges of economic transformation, put it this way:

> [Kravchuk] inherited an economy in free fall with massive *prykhvatyzatsiya* (*grabitization*—as a pun on the word "privatization" and the Ukrainian word for "to grab"), while a culture of rapacious individualism was becoming dominant. . . . Kravchuk adopted economic and political policies that would not disturb those of his allies among the former Soviet Ukrainian elites who had supported the drive to independence.[11]

The nationalists, seeking to preserve the integrity of the country, made a Faustian bargain with the Russified *nomenklatura* that was trying to retain and solidify economic and political power.[12]

Yet the Ukrainian legacy elites were the least likely and most ill-equipped class to undertake market reforms, grow a private sector, or execute any of the radical changes needed to move toward capitalism and integrate with the West. The internal politics of Ukraine would be characterized, throughout the 1990s, by a fitful effort to arrest economic decline, achieve macroeconomic stability, and resist the emergence of actors who might threaten the elites' hold on power. Ukraine, its legacy tethered to Russia, was plagued by a much more robust set of progress-arresting factors than its western neighbor, Poland, to which Ukraine is often unfavorably compared in the context of reform.

Kravchuk himself was especially ill-suited to lead the transformation from a command economy and communism to a market economy and capitalism. His understanding of economics was poor, with a liberal market economy simply beyond his and his advisors' grasp. He and then his even less fully reformist successor, Leonid Kuchma, had no ability to implement anything but modest political and economic changes. As former Communist apparatchiks, their facility for westernization was strictly limited.[13]

The conservative group, the consensus choice of elites for governing Ukraine throughout the 1990s, was thus able to arrest all but weak reforms. This dynamic, operating in the largest country in Europe, closely tied to Russia and the most fully subject to Kremlin influences, made transformation uniquely challenging—and not comparable to the changes in countries like Poland, which seemed to be aggressively transforming into vibrant democracies. Poland implemented a form of lustration, the elimination of swaths of Communist Party bosses from government and industry, and achieved, compared with Ukraine, more revolutionary reform. Ukraine settled on a "little-bit-pregnant" approach, insufficient to realize major transformation. Indicative of this problem is the fact that Ukraine was the last republic to establish a post-Soviet constitution.

Some organized elements in Ukraine did have a strong desire for real change. Yet Roman Szporluk has suggested that "if they thought about it, the leaders of [the independence movements] likely reasoned that their de-facto renunciation of claims to power was not too large a price for persuading all of Ukraine to secede from the USSR."[14] No former Soviet general, Szporluk asserts, would be likely to pledge allegiance to Ukraine if it were dominated by the westernizing Galician elements. Given the challenges of maintaining the territorial unity of Ukraine and authority over

Donetsk, Kharkiv, and Odesa, a government made up of members of the old system might have seemed to nationalists a pragmatic necessity.

President Kravchuk therefore promoted what Kuzio has called "a centrist path of consensus politics that placed greater emphasis on political stability than reform."[15] The president believed he could weave his and his country's way through all opposing forces, never overcommitting to any position, always avoiding direct conflict through sheer adroitness. Kuzio cites an anecdote: "A Kravchuk aide, noticing rainfall, asked the president if he needed an umbrella. Kravchuk replied, 'No thank you. I walk between the raindrops.'" The effect of his endless dodging, and of his recoil from assertive reform, was a sagging economy that made conditions ripe for corruption and oligarchic forms of capitalism and created conditions for arresting Ukrainian economic reforms and Western transformation that persist to this day.

Another effect of having former Communist bosses continue to govern Ukraine, critical to larger regional and global issues, was the divided nature of Ukraine's foreign policy. With Kravchuk still dodging raindrops, the country now existed in a non-bloc status, which gave neither of the two larger blocs, the West and Russia, what they needed.[16] While the largely unreformed Ukrainian economy remained reconcilable with the Russian economic system, Russia saw its foreign policy as insufficiently Russia-aligned to alleviate security anxieties arising from expectations of NATO enlargement and Western integration for former Soviet Bloc countries. The West, for its part, read both Ukraine's foreign policy ambiguity and its failure to achieve political and economic reform as a lack of interest in engaging with European values. Caught in interior east-west power struggles, Ukraine managed to land in neither the East nor the West.

Perhaps no other course was possible in the early days of the newly independent but still Soviet-flavored country. All of the republics had been networked to and dependent on the Russian Empire and the Soviet Union via infrastructure and trade; as the biggest, Ukraine had both the most and the tightest links with Moscow. Because the Ukrainian conservative bent involved loyalty to the Kremlin, even true reformers, compelled to work with the conservatives, accepted a degree of Russia orientation. With such legacies, Ukraine was not yet in a position to follow the kind of reform path that Poland implemented. Reorienting the economy from communism and the East to capitalism and the West involved heavy burdens that the newly independent country could not take up without greater internal resolve and concerted and significant help. Initially, little help was offered. The US was in the midst of a recession; when help did come, assistance was weighted toward denuclearization. The economic support was not sufficient to demonstrate the utility of democratization and market reforms, resulting in a missed opportunity to accelerate societal transformation and European integration.

So Ukraine began its independent existence primed to settle into a state of pragmatic, transactional cooperation with the US, the solo superpower. That cooperation depended on US interests related to the overriding question of what to do with Ukraine's nuclear arsenal.

For the US the effect of these economic, political, and cultural tensions within Ukraine involved some fateful ironies. There was a sense in which the US approach to the Ukraine relationship might seem values-oriented: a general idea prevailed that values-based changes—liberal reform, both economic and political—should serve as a condition for greater US engagement, encouragement, support. Yet the newly independent Ukraine was in no position to institute such reforms quickly or thoroughly. And the US misunderstood the nature of Ukrainian politics, assuming that corruption, for example, was not a Soviet holdover but endemic to Ukraine itself. The kind of help Ukraine needed in order to achieve the desired liberalization did not arrive from the US via any robust bilateral relationship.

Misreading the complexity of the real situation in Ukraine also further confirmed the US in its ongoing tendency to prioritize relations with Russia instead. That tendency was driven not only by, as we have seen, important US interests in Russia but also by a hope for lasting Russian reform and a fear that a devolving relationship with Russia would reopen the unhealed wounds of the Cold War.

ALL OF THOSE issues played into the back-and-forth negotiations over the high-priority denuclearization process that would ultimately leave Ukraine without a nuclear deterrent and see its weapons moved to Russia, which was already bursting with both conventional and nuclear weapons.

The process was intended to achieve nonproliferation and denuclearization—simple and absolute. The United States and Russia had quickly determined that Belarus, Kazakhstan, and Ukraine should turn their nuclear stockpiles over to Russia and purge from their own jurisdictions all military nuclear capability and infrastructure. This doctrine of US-Russia cooperation on denuclearizing, in the weapons sphere, the entire region, and especially on denuclearizing Ukraine, fostered a situation in which the US and Russia became eager to achieve a shared foreign-policy goal—though not necessarily a shared long-term objective—that made Ukraine an object, not a subject, of US policy.

For the Russians, the US approach to denuclearizing Russia's neighbors was very welcome. On the one hand, Russia discerned a mutual interest in cooperating on pan-European security and viewed such cooperation as a welcome sign of US acceptance of Russian superpower exceptionalism: a special, unbound partnership between two world powers to preserve spheres of influence. On the other hand, Russia welcomed the prospect of a freer hand in engaging and coercing its former subjects without the concern of a nuclear deterrent.

The Bush administration implemented a policy of engaging Ukraine bilaterally while encouraging a simultaneous bilateral Russia-Ukraine dialogue on denuclearization. The bilateral US relationship with Ukraine remained tightly limited, focused largely on the nuclear weapons situation. The Bush administration continued to see its bilateral relationship with Russia as the priority and thought the republics, given the growing US-Russia cooperation on the issue, simply had to go along with handing over weapons systems to the Kremlin.

Ukraine, however, had other ideas. Unlike the other former republics, it had suddenly become the site of the third-largest nuclear arsenal in the world. The danger of an irredentist Russia, seen as chimerical by the US, was all too apparent to Ukrainians.

In 1992, therefore, Ukraine's military, defense, and security leaders conducted a secret practical assessment of the possibility of maintaining a nuclear arsenal.[17]

The consensus emerging from those secret deliberations was clear. Volodymyr Horbulin served as a key decision-maker during the talks; he would later become the national security advisor for President Leonid Kuchma, Kravchuk's successor. Horbulin acknowledged that the political cost associated with retaining a nuclear arsenal would have been exceedingly high: Ukraine would have created conflict with the West and been unable to build a broad and deep bilateral relationship with the United States. Vitaly Haiduk, secretary of the National Security and Defense Council of Ukraine from 2006 to 2007, notes that "if Ukraine had changed its position on being a nuclear country and signed an agreement with Russia, what would the US have done? Everything would have been ruined."[18] Immediate logistical issues existed as well. While Ukraine would retain and develop its civilian nuclear energy capabilities, reliant on Russia supplying nuclear fuel, the country didn't have the expertise to become a nuclear military power.

As Horbulin says, "To preserve [nuclear weapons] it was necessary to schedule maintenance checks once every two years. We didn't have the technology for disassembly and demolition, nothing. We made and assembled rockets. A special branch of the ministry of defense in Moscow looked after controls—this was never in Ukraine, and only they could carry out such work."[19]

Ukraine simply did not have ways and means of operating a nuclear arsenal inherited from the Soviets with command and control concentrated, by design, in the Kremlin. Too much of the arsenal was approaching the end of its service life; Ukraine would have been forced to expend major resources to maintain it and thus gain control of even a limited nuclear weapons capability. Retaining nuclear weapons as a deterrent to Russian irredentism and aggression was not a workable policy in practice even if it guaranteed greater security in theory.

The best Ukraine could hope for, it was determined, was to employ denuclearization as a transactional bargaining chip: get favorable terms in exchange for transferring nuclear weapons to Russia.

So while Ukraine did begin transferring tactical nuclear weapons to Russia almost immediately, it balked at transferring strategic nuclear weapons, the ICBMs that had given the USSR the capability to attack the US. To proceed with full denuclearization—the transfer of those most significant weapons systems—Ukraine wanted concessions. It asked for security guarantees to prevent Russian aggression. It wanted compensation by Russia for transferring its highly enriched uranium: the twenty-one uranium caches in southern Ukraine, whose monetary worth, while hard to calculate exactly, was enormous. Ukraine also wanted subsidies and write-offs for the cost of the Russian gas on which it depended and financial support to both cover the high costs of disarmament and help Ukraine's struggling economy.[20]

The US looked with deep disfavor on Ukraine making these demands on Russia and the West in exchange for transferring strategic nuclear weapons. US foreign-policy officials were brimming with optimism regarding Yeltsin, who was in fact keenly interested in eliminating the potential threat of nuclear arsenals in the territories of former Soviet republics; he also seemed to represent a worthwhile investment compared to other Russian leaders, including regressive former Communist apparatchiks antagonistic to the United States. The Bush administration knew too that it had to remain sensitive to Yeltsin's need to placate his own nationalists.

A broader optimism also prevailed. There was hope for a new world order if the United States and Russia, after so many decades of Cold War, could now act together as security partners.

Ukraine's outward desire to preserve a nuclear arsenal as a hedge against aggression—or as a means to extract multiple benefits in exchange for denuclearizing, endangering nonproliferation and denuclearization hopes—gave the US another reason to see Russia as the more stable and responsible player. So the US turned Ukraine's terms around. Preservation of a nuclear weapons program would not be tolerated. No benefits would flow to Ukraine without complete denuclearization, which was to serve as prerequisite and condition for recognition. Only with denuclearization agreed to and implemented would the US consider offering benefits to Ukraine such as a broader bilateral US relationship, along with the economic and military cooperation that might bolster Ukraine's newly realized sovereignty.

The US held that the Kremlin was central to regional arms control and denuclearization. And Yeltsin seemed in a position to make decisions on behalf of the Commonwealth of Independent States, the Eurasian intergovernmental organization that had been formed after the collapse of the Soviet Union.[21] The US therefore made it clear to Ukraine that Russia was central to the overall denuclearization effort. That US position seemed tough, the logic behind it clear.

The outcome, however, was not what the US wanted.

On January 31 and February 1, 1992, Bush and Yeltsin held a summit at Camp David, and the United States and Russia agreed on a host of arms-control measures. Immediately, however, in response to the overt affront and infringement on Ukraine's newfound independence, President Kravchuk announced that Russia did not have the right to speak on behalf of Ukraine. In accordance with that statement, he temporarily halted the transfer even of tactical nuclear weapons to Russia.

Russia responded by asserting that it would remain the regional continuation state for holding nuclear weapons and continue the policies it had agreed to with the United States. This assertion by Ukraine of its sovereignty and by Russia of its exceptional influence ought to have provided the US with a signal of the tensions that would follow, and that a purely Russia-centric approach could be very strategically limiting.

Instead, the incident only reinforced US efforts to work through Russia to implement nuclear threat reduction and denuclearize Ukraine. The results were bumpy. On April 1, 1992, President Bush announced, "President Yeltsin's reform program holds the greatest hope for the future of the Russian people and for the security of the American people as we define a new relationship with that great country." When Secretary of State James Baker met with Ukraine's defense minister, Kostyantyn Morozov, Ukraine at last relented and resumed its transfer of tactical nuclear weapons to Russia. Yet only weeks later, in a memorandum for Secretary Baker, the US showed no awareness of the gains it had accomplished by developing a bilateral relationship with Ukraine but instead doubled down on its Russia-focused policy. The Baker memo noted that when it came to the post-Soviet nuclear arsenal, "Nothing is of more central importance in this process than consolidation of nuclear weapons in a democratizing Russia."[22]

In May 1992, President Kravchuk met with President Bush in Lisbon. The two sides had reached an agreement, and the presidential engagement was the deal clincher. The parties issued a joint declaration announcing Ukraine's agreement to ratify and implement the Strategic Arms Reduction Treaty (START) and the Treaty on Conventional Armed Forces in Europe (CFE), as well as its commitment to renouncing nuclear weapons and joining the Non-Proliferation Treaty (NPT) at the earliest possible time. The declaration also reaffirmed Ukraine's decision to complete the removal of all tactical nuclear weapons from its territory by July 1, 1992, and all remaining nuclear weapons in the subsequent seven-year period stipulated in START.

Then, on May 23, Baker and the Ukrainian foreign minister, Anatoliy Zlenko, joined Russian foreign minister Andrey Kozyrev, Belarusian foreign minister Pyotr Krauchanka, and Kazakhstani state counselor for strategic affairs Tulegen Zhukeyev to sign the "Lisbon Protocol to the Treaty between the United States of America and the Union of Soviet Socialist Republics on the Reduction and Limitation of Strategic Offensive Arms." The protocol was an arms-control landmark. Belarus, Kazakhstan, Russia, and Ukraine, as successor states to the Soviet Union, would assume the Soviet Union's obligations under START; Belarus, Kazakhstan, and Ukraine would accede to the NPT as non–nuclear weapons states "in the shortest possible time" and begin "immediately" to pursue the internal constitutional steps, such as the ratification of laws, necessary to implementing the agreement.

In return for Ukraine's agreeing to denuclearize, the Bush administration rhetorically adjusted its definition of Europe so that it now included Ukraine. Acknowledging in a joint statement with Kravchuk that "the Ukrainian people are now building their own state, one whose independence and commitment to democracy can make a vital contribution to the creation of a new Europe truly whole and free," President Bush announced that "the United States and Ukraine should be not just friends but partners. Ukraine's future security is important for the United States and for stability in Europe."[23] There was no negative response to this statement from the Kremlin. Russia got denuclearization, on its own terms, in exchange for a US rhetorical flourish.

And yet Ukrainians' frustration with the US approach could be heard in President Kravchuk's own remarks, made in that same announcement. Kravchuk highlighted the security risks to Ukraine of denuclearizing. He noted assertions of dominion over Ukraine's Crimean Peninsula by officials in Russia's ministries of defense and foreign affairs.[24] He underscored the need for guarantees by the West to ward off Russian irredentism. He was effectively reviving the Ukrainian security demands that had been rejected in the course of the negotiations.

Meeting those demands remained anathema to the Bush administration. Even as President Bush himself, who had just lost the fight for reelection, brought his term to an end at the beginning of 1993, the issue of a denuclearized Ukraine had been resolved on paper but not in fact, as Kravchuk's remarks might have made clear. Kostiantyn Gryshchenko, later Ukraine's minister of foreign affairs, has noted that "tension was quite high, in both the White House and especially in the State Department." Ukraine did not "intend to use nuclear weapons as weapons," Gryshchenko points out, but in agreeing to giving up Ukraine's ultimate security guarantee, its nuclear weapons, it "needed some kind of compensation and involvement in this process," some significant security improvement.[25]

CHAPTER FOUR

THE END OF HISTORY?

In the US election year 1992, American political scientist Francis Fukuyama published a book entitled *The End of History and the Last Man*, which presented an argument widely interpreted as suggesting that the end of the Cold War and the collapse of the Soviet Union represented not just a major historical shift from one phase to another but something far greater: a grand movement beyond the phenomenon of history itself, if history is understood as a contest among ideologies of government, and as an evolutionary process. History now seemed to be succumbing to the permanent victory of liberal, Western, democratic values. Those values would prevail, in Fukuyama's words, "as the final form of human government."

The book's themes dovetailed with a broader mood of euphoria—mingled with certain key concerns—circulating in the US foreign-policy community at the fall of the Soviet Union. "The age of totalitarianism," Senator Daniel Patrick Moynihan announced, "is over," and mankind would be free to construct a new world order.

Such hopes, in the air since the late 1980s, as Soviet power visibly waned, had been given a boost in 1990, when President George H. W. Bush too proclaimed "a new world order," with prospects for a pan-European security architecture and hopes that Russia might be integrated into the community of nations.[1] Students of great-nation conflict were shifting focus. The new idea was that nation-states had an incentive to cooperate with one another in limiting the power and impact of destructive conflicts—and that non-state actors and rogue states, carrying out and sponsoring acts of terrorism, would now be the main locus of global instability, violence, and conflict.

The new role of the US as sole superpower may have suggested to some at the time, and may suggest to some today, that among its powers was a capability to drive geopolitical outcomes wherever it wanted. In fact, as we will see, the US was not in any such position. Indeed, the end-of-history mood created blinders with long-range effects on US relations with Russia and Ukraine, as well as on Russia-Ukraine relations, that would come to unintended forms of fruition in the twenty-first century.

IN A CAMPAIGN speech on October 2, 1992, presidential candidate Bill Clinton dissented from the foreign-policy approach of his opponent, the incumbent president. "President Bush," Governor Clinton said, "seems too often to prefer a foreign policy that embraces stability at the expense of freedom, a foreign policy built more on personal relationships with foreign leaders than on consideration of how those leaders acquired and maintained their power."[2]

Clinton's criticism went straight to the heart of the transaction-based US relationships with Russia and the former republics that were dominating Bush-administration policy. The candidate seemed to be asserting a new, more idealistic approach, where short-term stability and crisis avoidance were to be superseded by a focus on long-range US values regarding democracy and self-determination. When it came to the denuclearization process, Clinton seemed to be implying that a future administration under his leadership would seek to change course. But in fact, the Clinton administration's progress with regard to denuclearization, to US relations with Russia and Ukraine, and to the Russia-Ukraine relationship would be hampered by a reversion to the short-term, crisis-avoidance approach taken by the previous and, as history would tell, future administrations.

Managing the Russia-Ukraine relationship quickly became an overriding concern for Clinton. Nicholas Burns, then a highly placed staffer on the National Security Council, recalls that "throughout the course of his two terms in office, [Clinton] was involved more in the Russia-Ukraine mix than any other set of issues . . . even more than the Balkans, in terms of his personal involvement."[3] If the commitment was intense, the priorities, in the administration's early days, were familiar: Kremlin-first and Yeltsin-supportive.

Regarding Ukraine, the new president began by continuing to threaten that unless it complied with joint US-Russia agreements regarding the transfer of nuclear weapons, Ukraine would become a pariah state. And Clinton's motives, like Bush's, were understandable. As Eric Edelman, a veteran of both presidencies, puts it, the outgoing Bush administration "kind of left the Clinton administration . . . , I don't think, any real policy towards Ukraine." But Bush's final secretary of state, Lawrence Eagleburger, was blunt in restating the Bush administration's priorities: he advised his incoming successor, Warren Christopher, to moderate the Bush-era policy of a pressure track and instead adopt a coercion-and-enticement approach with Ukraine while focusing on Russia as a high-risk area where success was critical to US interests. Despite hope for Russian reform, however, Eagleburger saw Russian revanchism as a clear and present danger. As Paul D'Anieri has discussed, at a meeting of the Conference on Security and Cooperation in Europe in Stockholm, in December 1992, "Foreign Minister Andrey Kozyrev declared the former Soviet Union 'a post-imperial space where Russia has to defend its interests by all available means, including military and economic ones.' . . . Eagleburger said afterwards that Kozyrev's speech gave him 'heart palpitations.'"[4]

Eagleburger's theory, on leaving office, was that the success of reform in Russia might not in fact assure the success of reform in the other former Soviet states—but failure of reform in Russia would guarantee the failure of reform throughout the former Soviet empire, a disaster for the world as a whole. Warren Christopher himself asserted what had largely been the Bush approach as early as his Senate confirmation hearing:

> [Nothing] is more important than helping Russia demilitarize, privatize, invigorate its economy, and develop representative political institutions. . . . President Yeltsin's courageous economic and political reforms stand as our best hope for reducing the still-formidable arsenal of nuclear and conventional arms in Russia and other states of the former Soviet Union, and this, in turn, permits reductions in our own defense spending.[5]

Yeltsin and Clinton quickly found common ground, both on the broader bilateral agenda and on Ukraine's denuclearization, and because the Clinton administration saw the promotion of democracy as the key to its foreign policy, it was determined to bolster Yeltsin internally against an emerging Russian communist-nationalist coalition. Ukraine continued to waver on denuclearization, a posture that, combined with Yeltsin's promise to deliver on bilateral nuclear arms reductions, confirmed the US bias that the relationship with Russia was the more productive one.

Ukraine's internal politics also inhibited the US from greater engagement. The Ukrainian economic program was transferring most of the nation's economy to the private sector; in the process it was creating a new class of oligarchs closely bound to the presidency while providing limited support to the small and medium business sectors that were driving growth and transformation elsewhere in Central and Eastern Europe. That tendency would corrupt Ukraine's political economy throughout the 1990s and well beyond. Stymieing true social reform, the corruption confirmed the US impression that the new state might make an unreliable partner. Nicholas Burns recalls, "In '92, we were just in a completely new geostrategic position. . . . It was unclear to us what was going to happen . . . to these countries by '93. We felt that there was at least a chance and opportunity for Russia to become a stable, nascently democratic country."[6] Legitimate uncertainty about Ukraine's capability for a strong partnership dovetailed with the preexisting sense of opportunity in Russia, so the US doubled down on its Russia-first approach, especially while the need to get control of nuclear weapons was an active and still unfulfilled US priority for the region.

These rationales, reasonable enough in the context of the day, had the unfortunate effect of making Ukraine, in turn, perceive the US in a way that mirrored the US perception of Ukraine itself: as a partner only for achieving immediate, short-term goals. The US had expressed no interest, so far, in creating any trilateral relationship by which it might directly affect the dynamic between Russia and Ukraine; Russia was dead set against any such arrangement. Burns's explanation reflects the somewhat queasy relation to power that the US found itself in at the outset of the Clinton administration: "We were, in a way, a neutral party, we weren't part of their mix. We had a direct interest; we had a lot of power. We had emerged . . . heavyweight champion in the world in terms of global power in the early 1990s."[7]

Burns's recollections also reveal that in some ways, he and other Clinton officials saw themselves as acting, with Ukraine, on broader bases than simple denuclearization:

> We divided [the former Bureau of European and Soviet Affairs] into a Bureau of European affairs and . . . a new bureau [focused on] the fifteen states. We thought hard about what to call that bureau and Ukraine was very much in mind. A lot of people said "We'll call it the Bureau of Russia and Eurasia affairs," and we finally decided that would diminish Ukraine, that Ukraine was clearly the second-most important of these former republics. So we landed on "Russia, Ukraine and Eurasian Affairs." And that tells you how much we were focusing on Ukraine. . . . So it did go beyond the nuclear issue. . . . We wanted Ukraine to succeed.[8]

Yet Burns also notes the priority of the loose-nukes fear earlier emphasized by the Ungroup and recalls concerns about "the cratering effect it would have if Ukraine dissolved in some kind of revolutionary violence in 1994–1995. So we were trying to think strategically, of course, about the nuclear issue, but even beyond that."[9]

A critical discrepancy was also at work. The fixation on Russia and a Russia-first policy would have been more reasonable had the US begun to enforce a standard of conduct for Russia's behavior regarding the Newly Independent States (NIS), as the former

Soviet republics became known. Russia would soon begin to interfere in regional elections, exercise regional economic coercion, and
foster regional "frozen conflicts," where internal divisions played in
favor of Russian dominance. The US could have condemned Russian misbehavior as violations of fundamental Western values. It
had the power to enforce conditions on Russia's entry into international organizations such as the World Trade Organization.

Yet the US set Western standards of conduct only for the
non-Russian former Soviet republics. The five Central Asian states
and Azerbaijan were held to an appropriately higher standard for
failing to reach political reform and anti-corruption benchmarks,
while Russia got a pass on using force to crush political dissenters
because they were communists, waging a violent war to suppress
separatists in Ichkeria, and supporting the Serbian regime's campaign of ethnic cleansing in the Balkans.

Russia was thus permitted by the sole superpower to conduct
its own fitful transformation, without sufficient criticism or con-
ditioning of aid, engagement, support, and inclusion in reform-
minded Western institutions. US policymakers continued to fear
that criticism would roil Russian elites or give Russian nationalist
reactionaries ammunition for further retrenchment. A principled
US approach, less biased toward Russia and more equitable to the
former republics, would have combined assistance for Russia with
making it clear that Russia, too, would have to adhere to the same
international standards the West was demanding of others.

CLINTON DID MAKE policy changes, though. While unswerving
on the nuclear priority that prioritized and privileged Yeltsin and
Russia, in the spring of 1993 his administration began facing some
stark facts.

Denuclearization remained the priority, but the goal had not been met. That was thanks in part to the US position of uncompromising toughness on Ukraine.

That May, a review of US policy toward Ukraine concluded that the coercive strategy was falling short on delivering both denuclearization and help for Ukraine's transformation. The new administration could see more clearly than its predecessor that even the shortest-term aims weren't being met. The supposedly realist approach wasn't all that realistic in practice. Success would require a change in the relationship.

Some senior figures in the administration hoped to push relationships with the Newly Independent States beyond short-term interests. Daniel Fried, who would become Clinton's ambassador to Poland and assistant secretary of state for European and Eurasian affairs, identified a policy conflict in which "all of those countries gave you the political capital that made the Russia-first position untenable. . . . [The NIS] are Europeanized, and because we want to see them through the prism of Moscow . . . they're little" in the eyes of the US. As Fried explained, the real attitude, veiled to a degree was, "you know, 'Go home, countries.' That's not what people said, but that's what they meant."[10]

Secretary of Defense William Perry, a major proponent of a broad bilateral relationship with Ukraine, seized on the May 1993 policy review to expand beyond the purely nuclear-focused approach:

> My primary concern was seeing Ukraine established on solid footing as an independent democratic nation. And I had that feeling independent of the nuclear issue. . . . And then and now [my views] tend to be value-based rather than realpolitik-based. I really valued the independence of those

countries, and I looked at the history of them. . . . I had a strong, I suppose sentimental reason for supporting the independence of all of those countries.[11]

In using the possibly self-deprecating term "sentimental," Perry was invoking a preference for US commitments of the kind long spurned by the realist school. He wanted longer-term relationships, focused on a range of issues, sensitive to the former republics' historic struggles, and dedicated to helping them build liberal democratic institutions.

In late June 1993, Strobe Talbott, serving as ambassador-at-large and special advisor to the secretary of state on the NIS, was also inching toward a more balanced approach to encouraging Ukrainian denuclearization. When testifying before the Senate Foreign Relations Committee, Talbott expressed a commitment to broadening US relations with Ukraine. He described Ukraine as playing a role in Central and Eastern Europe important to US interests, which he framed in broader and more lasting terms than a simple effort to achieve urgent, immediate goals, arguing that the United States should conduct its relationship with Ukraine independently of its relationship with Russia.[12]

So by the summer of 1993, the Clinton administration was exploring new initiatives. Some at the White House had begun to consider making a sober commitment to taking Ukraine seriously as a partner—despite certain drawbacks in the approach of Ukraine itself. The goal seemed to be to offer Ukraine enough reassurance that it would stop wavering, fully commit to START (which it had signed in 1992), and move quickly toward the goals of the Lisbon Protocol, signed in 1991. Once that was done, Russia would be the only nuclear-armed successor of the USSR.

Yet as the denuclearization process proceeded, the administration continued to make Ukraine policy derivative of Russia policy in ways that, while perhaps sensible at the time, would have long-term effects quite other than what the US hoped to achieve. Because the overriding goal remained to shore up Russian control of weapons systems, the administration continued to pressure Ukraine, in part by rejecting the possibility of a meeting between Presidents Clinton and Kravchuk until after Ukraine ratified START and acceded to the NPT as a non-nuclear state.

And even when progress in the US-Ukraine relationship did, suddenly, emerge, it emerged from an important shift by Russia itself. By July 1993, the inadequacy of bilateral Russia-Ukraine denuclearization dialogue had become inescapable, as Russia played its characteristically domineering role and Ukraine rigidly asserted its sovereignty. Russia was compelled to overcome its reluctance to involve the US directly in that dialogue. At the Tokyo G7 summit, Yeltsin relinquished a long-held insistence on bilateralism and proposed to the United States using a trilateral American-Russian-Ukrainian format to finally secure Ukraine's denuclearization. President Clinton "agreed on the spot, thinking that the trilateral approach would have a higher chance of succeeding if Yeltsin had a personal stake in the outcome."[13]

Fishel speculates that Yeltsin had determined that the Russian desire for a Ukraine with no nuclear arsenal far outweighed the blow to Russian regional exceptionalism represented by American involvement in the talks. To Kyiv, US engagement, no matter how Russia-focused, looked far better than continuing to negotiate one-on-one with Moscow. Talbott and the Russian deputy foreign minister, Georgiy Mamedov, immediately began working on a US-Russian-Ukrainian nuclear accord acceptable to all three nations. For the first time in any significant way, Ukraine was now offered a package of benefits—economic enticements, key leader engagements, and security assurances—as an incentive for carrying out full denuclearization.

Assurances, however, were not guarantees. In diplomatic parlance, security assurances are merely statements of intent, based on trust, with a vague warning of a potential response if the agreement is broken. Security guarantees are provisions, such as those in Article 5 of the NATO pact, which commit all signatories to collective defense, including the use of military force to defend all other signers. The US had never been willing to offer Ukraine security guarantees.

The issue had already arisen during deliberations on the enlargement of NATO to include former Soviet Bloc states. That process had been ongoing since the fall of the USSR, with support from both the Bush and the Clinton administrations—and to the concern of Russia. NATO had even initiated relations with an independent Ukraine, in 1992, during a visit by Kravchuk to NATO headquarters in Brussels and the establishment of the Ukrainian embassy there, though strong opposition to NATO membership for Ukraine also existed.[14] The Czech Republic, Slovakia, Hungary, and Poland—states that had been part of the Soviet Bloc but not, like Ukraine, part of the USSR—feared that a Ukrainian effort to enter the alliance would be far more triggering for Russia than their own efforts and create roadblocks. In 1993, therefore, NATO membership for Ukraine was not on the table (Ukraine nevertheless supported the initiative of Central and Eastern European countries to join the alliance).

The offer of security assurances, not guarantees, was therefore as much as Ukraine was going to get. And the offer was combined with direct pressure, including making a meeting between Clinton and Kravchuk conditional on Ukraine's cooperation. Still, a foundation was being built for a bilateral US-Ukraine relationship that might outlast denuclearization.

EVEN AS THOSE more positive negotiations were ongoing, however, an event occurred in Russia that cast a strange light on Ukraine's role in the denuclearization process. Russia's Duma election of December 12, 1993, saw the election of Vladimir Zhirinovsky and a significant number of other ultranationalists. A founder of Russia's Liberal Democratic Party—it was avowedly anti-liberal and antidemocratic—Zhirinovsky espoused a harshly authoritarian, Russia-centered brand of nativism, loudly anti-US and anti-Israel; he would soon promise that if he were elected, elections in Russia would cease. Seeking common cause with Western far-right movements, including France's National Front headed by Jean-Marie Le Pen, he took to extremes the long history of Russian exceptionalism, especially regarding Ukraine. Twenty years before the 2022 Russian invasion, Zhirinovsky and his followers and allies were claiming Russian dominion over the Crimean Peninsula and other territories. And they were demanding changes in the domestic policies of the NIS to grant ethnic Russians privileged status, including making the Russian language a coequal official language and protecting ethnic-Russian control of the republics' institutions—an unpalatable demand for newly independent states throwing off the yoke of Moscow control.

The election of the Russian ultranationalists—their sights clearly set on ending Ukrainian independence—naturally stoked Ukraine's desire for full-scale security guarantees, not mere assurances, from the West. Yet their rise elicited no US policy change. Still, on January 12, 1994, as a result of the latest agreement,

President Kravchuk did finally receive a US presidential visit. President Clinton made a brief refueling stop in Kyiv, met with Kravchuk at the airport, and commended "his courage and his vision" in negotiating the agreement and praised Ukraine as "a nation with a rich heritage, enormous economic potential, and a very important position in European security."[15]

Two days later, at the Kremlin, Clinton, Kravchuk, and Yeltsin signed the Trilateral Statement on Ukraine's denuclearization. According to the statement, there was to be detailed financial assistance for Ukraine, linked to the process of removal of warheads to Russia. Ukraine was also to be compensated for the value of the highly enriched uranium collected. Some of the assistance to cover costs of denuclearization came in the form of US government Nunn-Lugar Cooperative Threat Reduction funds, which had been earmarked, beginning in 1991, for enabling denuclearization, and some came indirectly, as debt relief and low-enriched uranium for Ukraine's power plants.[16] In 1995, as a result of concluding denuclearization agreements, the United States granted $550 million to Ukraine in general economic and reform support.

Those funds and their purposes might have appeared to reflect a new degree of US commitment to the long-term growth of democracy in Ukraine. So it was a telling moment, at least for Ukraine, when the White House, announcing the success of the Budapest Memorandum and the trilateral statement, assured the American public that no *new* obligations to Ukraine had been made part of the agreement. The fact also remained that the commitments were fully contingent on Ukraine's first carrying out its obligations under the agreement, underscored by Assistant Secretary of Defense Graham Allison, who stated, "Ukraine's security problem will be solved once Ukraine gives up its nuclear arsenal."[17] On the surface, the comment was both naive and counterintuitive. The short-term goal was explicitly given priority over the security issue and the long-term relationship with the United States.

Truly finalizing the security issues—so critical to Ukraine—was deferred until the summit of the Conference on Security and Cooperation in Europe, held in Budapest, Hungary, in December 1994. The Budapest summit defeated, yet again, certain US expectations in ways that presaged later conflicts.

Nicholas Burns clarifies the naivete harbored by US officials regarding the relationships with Ukraine and Russia: "We thought that Budapest would go well. There's no question in my memory and in my mind that the Ukrainians understood completely the difference between security assurances and Article 5 security guarantees. And they understood they were getting security assurances. We went through that chapter and verse ad nauseum with them for months."[18]

In Budapest, the Clinton administration hewed to the security policy established by its predecessor. It was true that, as reported, no new promises had been made to Ukraine: the negotiated solution repackaged existing security assurances, which applied to all of the former republics, into a narrower, Ukraine-specific set of documents, symbolically and politically important to Kyiv, which sought to bolster its sovereignty. But it did not really give Ukraine any special status or protection, despite the growing evidence of Russian irredentism, whether the rise of nationalist parties or the war in Ichkeria.

Burns's and others' expectation that Budapest would go well did not materialize. The Budapest Memorandum, formalizing the security agreement, was indeed signed there—yet many Ukrainian officials eager for westernization felt that the agreement gave Ukraine very little in the way of either security or development in exchange for Ukraine giving up the world's third-largest nuclear arsenal.[19] Kravchuk and others would retain a sharp memory of the pressure that had been applied to them to sign. Some felt that major changes, including EU and NATO membership for Ukraine, should have been at the very least in view.

Yeltsin, for his part, took the Budapest Memorandum as an opportunity not to confirm the positive bi- and trilateral relationship, which had finally realized the shared goal of denuclearization, but to seize the limelight and bridle publicly against what he now abruptly called the domineering, expansive tendencies of the United States. As Burns recalls, "We felt this would be celebratory. But Yeltsin was always focused well beyond the nuclear issue. And he was focused on NATO at that time, and on efforts to think about NATO expansion, and he really laid into President Clinton. He gave the speech that was very obstreperous, and it really soured the Budapest meeting."[20]

Prefiguring a line later taken by Vladimir Putin, Yeltsin histrionically cast Russia as the exceptionally dishonored victim that had exchanged "a Cold War for a Cold Peace." Yet his diatribe didn't involve any real concern: Ukraine in NATO wasn't even in the cards. Yeltsin's concerns were over all NATO moves eastward, despite the fact the enlargement would see no NATO troops permanently stationed in the new territories until Russia's invasion of Ukraine in 2014. Yeltsin was likely responding to the overall affront to Russian exceptionalism and the fact that Russia was no longer able to dictate terms in Eastern Europe, as it had done for decades; he also likely calculated that NATO enlargement would render safe the new member states, neutralizing the threat of Russian force in Eastern Europe. Russia would still have other coercive tools—diplomatic, informational, and economic power—but those tools would not provide Russia with the ultimate coercive power of force that Moscow was too often ready to employ.

Yeltsin's speech nevertheless put Clinton on the back foot. The US president had come to Budapest to take a victory lap; Yeltsin let loose a shotgun blast of vitriol. The sole superpower "end of history" mindset, with its presumption of incentives for American-led cooperation among nations, did not readily acknowledge the potential for Russia taking a stance of outright adversarial conflict with the US. In response to Yeltsin's complaints, the Clinton administration instantly became eager to mend fences. The press and others framed US missteps in familiar terms; Russia always remained at the center of the story. Ukraine was shunted off to the side.

But Ukraine did denuclearize. On May 31, 1996, two trains departed Ukraine for Russia, carrying the last of Ukraine's strategic nuclear warheads.[21] The deadline of June 1, 1996, required by the Budapest agreement, had been fulfilled.

THE SUCCESS REPRESENTED by the Budapest agreement following such a long period of wavering and obstruction might have suggested that the high-pressure attitude of the Bush administration, in which Ukraine policy was relegated to a subcategory of US policy toward Russia, harmed the bilateral relationship with Ukraine and undermined denuclearization goals. The lesson should have been that the Clinton administration's somewhat more direct and expansive engagement, despite its flaws, offered a model that would serve both immediate interests and long-range values for both Ukraine and the United States. Clinton's first-term approach, which can now be seen as the period's high-water mark for the bilateral Ukraine-US relationship, should have been understood at the time as something to build on.

That lesson was not learned. After Budapest, Clinton's Ukraine policy, responding to a variety of ensuing constraints and conflicts, would not differ dramatically from Bush's. For the balance of the 1990s, US engagement with Ukraine was driven by and derivative of Russia policy, with effects that, as we will see, became increasingly dire, both for the region and for the West.

CHAPTER FIVE

A PEACEFUL TRANSFER
OF POWER

The approach to denuclearization taken up by the Clinton administration—enlightened, relative to that of its predecessor, but still casting Russia as arbiter of the process and making Ukraine policy derivative of Russia policy—was becoming increasingly anachronistic. Key leaders in the administration advocated for a more balanced, values-driven strategy for the region, including a greater focus on the newly independent states, but as in the Bush administration, they remained a minority.

There was a viable alternative to the prevailing Russia-centrism. It was not zombie liberal internationalism. It was not neoconservatism, not isolationism couched as restraint, and not morally bankrupt realism—short-term-interest-serving and in that sense purely transactional. A mix of those old forms did govern the denuclearization process and would continue to prevail. The unintended consequence was to put Russia in a position to re-engage in regional aggression and nuclear extortion of the West.

As early as the early 1990s, however, a "neo-idealist" approach could have prevailed instead. Fostering a longer-term outcome, more consonant with American interests, and resulting in greater and more genuine stability for the region and the world, a policy based on neo-idealism would have departed from narrowly defined and immediately gratifying aims and sought effective internationalism through long-term strategies, fostering Western values in a region where significant challenges existed.

In neo-idealism, geopolitics in general is addressed via a framework grounded in "values primacy"—the centrality of values to interests—and a moral commitment to fundamental, aspirational ideals: freedom, human rights, democratic institutions, and self-determination. When necessary, those ideals are consistently and muscularly defended. Where values have primacy, vital interests are not discarded. In the denuclearization process, neo-idealism would still have sought nuclear nonproliferation while supporting democracy and warding off Russian aggression.

Neo-idealism is now emerging as an approach to US international relations in response to thirty years of failure. But the fact is that the START agreement of the early 1990s already contained provisions for reducing nuclear weapons; the goal, therefore, should not have been to transfer to Russia existing nuclear weapons platforms sited in the former republics, with the bulk in Ukraine, making it easier for Russia to meet the treaty thresholds. The goal should have been to entirely dispose of the weapons and systems in Belarus, Ukraine, and Kazakhstan, while reducing launch platforms in Russia. Since 2022, Russia has used not only its own but also some of those same transferred systems to threaten a non-nuclear Ukraine with strategic bombers and nuclear weapons that were once in Ukraine's custody. That situation was brought about by failure to adopt a neo-idealist policy in the 1990s.

Requiring Russia to cooperate in a true and durable threat-reduction effort by neutralizing the weapons—the road not taken in the 1990s—is an example of the tough-minded approach that would be repeatedly avoided, as we will see, in the ensuing series of turning points and climaxes that led to the Russian invasion of Ukraine in 2022. For neo-idealism also rejects a sentimental faux idealism: over-optimistic; comfortable imagining adversaries as potentially cooperative, in the face of evidence to the contrary; making rhetorical claims on Western values while signaling unwillingness to engage in the difficult, sometimes necessarily confrontational action that might establish and foster them.

US and Western missteps in the denuclearization process began a history of veering between those cynically realist and faux-idealistic extremes. While seemingly polar opposites, the extremes share a tendency, ultimately fatal, to crisis-manage instead of clarifying positions; to privilege those with whom the prospect of real gains remains out of reach, instead of those with shared interests and values, where common policy aims might be achieved; and to sell out long-standing ideals, all-important not only to global security but also to liberal democracy itself.

BY THE LATE 1990s, the US continued to find itself unable to create or act on almost any policy for Ukraine that was not derivative of and secondary to Russia policy. Both before and after the Budapest summit held at the end of 1994, struggles with reforms within Ukraine—related to, but not necessarily essential to, the West's and Russia's primary transactional denuclearization arc—negatively impacted the country's relationships with both the US and Russia.

Events would later reveal that the significance of these problems received insufficient attention from both Ukrainian and Western policymakers. The potential for deterring what would reveal itself as an increasingly naked exercise of Russian aggression would have required the West taking Ukraine's struggles seriously as issues in their own right.

The internal Ukrainian issues that came to play a role in geopolitics are naturally better understood in retrospect than they could have been at the time, especially since they center on questions of Ukrainian national identity that were not easily or widely understood in the West. Because the politics of representative government in Ukraine continued to reflect underlying national divisions, it was clear as early as February 1992 that Rukh, the party that had guided the country to independence, had reached a high state of tension. Schism threatened between the more nationalistic and Western-aligned factions, associated with the capital and western regions, engaged in their Faustian bargain, and the old Russian and Russified former Communist *nomenklatura*, favored as the ruling class by many in the business elite that now controlled much of the economy, emotionally and commercially connected to Russia, and accustomed to corrupt, post-Soviet-style operations and practices.[1]

The persistence of corruption in Ukraine, often framed by Western commentators and policymakers as endemic and indigenous, was in fact a natural evolution of practices established during the Soviet period. High-ranking Soviet officials had routinely used criminal networks and personal connections to acquire wealth and smuggle both luxury goods and basic necessities from Europe and the United States. Organized crime was also a tool of the Soviet government: members of the Russian mob in the United States acted as extensions of Soviet intelligence; Russian gangs, with their origins in prison culture, often received instruction and direction from Soviet authorities.[2]

Now new opportunities for corruption blossomed in Ukraine, thanks to the sorry state of the country's economy in the 1990s. After independence, in Ukraine just as in Russia, organized crime networks took advantage of the new condition of institutional instability and economic destitution. Individuals tied to organized crime, former members of the security services, and Communist Party bosses gained control of Ukraine's most lucrative resources in oil, gas, coal, and agriculture via coercion, brute force, and an opaque voucher-privatization process: vouchers for shares of company ownership were issued to each employee, but since those vouchers were not hard currency, necessary to putting food on the table, bosses snatched up most of them for pennies on the dollar, contributing to the creation of Ukraine's first oligarchy.[3] Many "petty" forms of corruption, such as soliciting bribes for basic government services, were normalized in Ukrainian society in this early period of independence. To this day, the 1990s generation of both Russian and Ukrainian leadership blames the West for faltering in shepherding economic reforms: the pressure for rapid privatization and market reforms, it is believed, in the absence of understanding and treating the conditions of the post-Soviet system, precipitated rampant corruption.

To the West, the comparison with Poland looked stark. Poland and Ukraine had similar population sizes, shared a border, and had emerged from communism around the same time. But they'd pursued divergent trajectories for market reforms and democratization, and since Ukraine's economy was larger than that of Poland, Western policymakers found themselves asking why Ukraine was not keeping pace with Poland on reforms and European integration, why it was failing to keep pace with Polish prosperity, and why the Baltic states too were making better progress than Ukraine.[4] Given its legacy of Russian influence burrowing deeply into its society,

Ukraine was able to implement only half-hearted reforms and could not cleanse itself of Communist Party apparatchiks and start anew.

Managing these dynamics posed challenges for Ukrainian presidential leadership, which was also drawn from the older, pre-independence generation of government. In 1994, former prime minister Leonid Kuchma, having resigned his position, challenged Kravchuk for the presidency. Kravchuk had been weak in pursuing political and economic reforms—but not weak enough, in a sense, for the former Communist *nomenklatura*, for the Russified eastern regions, and for the Eurasianist contingent in the Donbas region. To them, he was too much of a nationalist.

Their disapproval focused on his positive attitude toward developing ties with the West. That was despite his strictly limited ability, as a formerly Communist apparatchik himself, to pursue those ties and to pursue serious internal reform. The 1994 election, like all of Ukraine's elections through 2019, was therefore shaped by a stark regional, cultural, and political divide. The center and west of the country favored the more nationalist incumbent. The east and south favored maintaining links to Russia, opposed building ties to the West, and supported Kuchma.

The 1994 Ukraine election also had important resonances for geopolitics. Kravchuk was the candidate preferred by Washington. A known quantity, he had delivered on the nuclear question; US officials had had less contact with Kuchma and were less certain of his views. Yet the US took no public position and only hoped quietly for Kravchuk's reelection. Not publicly taking sides in other countries' elections is indeed the standard approach of US government, but in this case the policy for Ukraine was starkly distinct from the policy for the Russian election, scheduled for 1996, where a decision was already in place to provide full and overt support for Yeltsin.

The 1994 Ukraine election was thereby ranked, in the familiar way of our policy for the region, as far less critical to US interests than Russia's election, where vital national interest rationalized setting aside the policy of noninterference in the elections of other states. And to the degree that the Ukraine election was deemed important at all, its importance was framed as the first reasonably democratic presidential transfer of power in the former Soviet space. This was a weak benchmark, too easily satisfied by the fact that the election was taking place at all, and did not suggest that there was a sufficiently compelling concern for Ukraine in the White House. Ukraine's election proceeded without US involvement, while for the Russian election, two years later, the administration was ready to put a thumb on the scales.

When Kuchma won the election, his victory was indeed seen by the West as a success insofar as it showed Ukraine was capable of a peaceful transfer of presidential power. But the result also represented a rejection of Ukraine's nationalism in favor of closer ties with Russia, and that ought to have alarmed the West, or at least indicated that Ukraine's journey to European-style democratic statehood and fully escaping the influence of its imperial overlord would be long and fraught.[5] Instead, the US was satisfied with the mere peacefulness of the transfer of power and shifted its priorities elsewhere.

Not that Kuchma succeeded in reversing conditions and reverting wholesale to Soviet-era practices. As Taras Kuzio has shown, Kuchma didn't reestablish "the Soviet domination of Ukraine by the 'Dnipropetrovsk mafia'" (the old USSR-aligned *nomenklatura*). His election did shift even more political power to the traditional elites of eastern Ukraine, but then, as Kuzio puts it, "in the manner of Russian President Yeltsin, [Kuchma] balanced and played off regional groups."[6]

Ihor Smeshko, later the head of the Ukraine State Security Service, noted that "Kuchma was a Soviet technocrat. Kuchma even said, 'Tell me what to build, and I will build it in very Soviet fashion.' Government institutions that are strong help limit the influence of overly political actors; instead, we had oligarchizing and poor privatization."[7]

Kuchma would be president for eleven years; to date he is the only Ukrainian president to serve more than a single term. But his leadership was characterized by a queasily fluctuating politics of stasis that did not succeed in encouraging national unity. The country's conservative streak, embedded in the old *nomenklatura*, expressed itself in both a lack of reform and a continuation of the Kravchuk foreign policy that enabled neither the transformation necessary to integrate with the West nor the unified pro-Russia stance that might have, as Ukraine inched farther from Kremlin control, at least partially assuaged Russia's concerns about security on its Western border.[8] Caught in its own internal East-West power struggle, Ukraine landed in neither camp and remained alone, outside either sphere of influence while nevertheless retaining an economy still dependent on the Russian system. Even though some people in Russia believed Ukraine was going too far in breaking free of Russian influence, it never went far enough to strengthen its sovereignty and deter Russian coercion.

Ultimately, Ukraine's decidedly ambiguous policies regarding reform and Western alignment were read by US officials, with too little nuance, as indicating a lack of interest. Throughout 1994 and 1995, various forms of compensation and relief did come to Ukraine under the terms of the denuclearization deal, from both the United States and Russia. Yet US resources for the post-Soviet space as a whole remained relatively paltry. The largest share was sent to Russia on the basis of size and need. Ukraine was subject to the usual Russia-derivative calculations.

Secretary of Defense Perry remained an outlier. Through January 1997, when his service ended, he pushed for a broad, well-grounded bilateral relationship with Ukraine, based on the values of independence, democracy, and self-determination. But much of the Washington consensus was against him.

All of this produced effectively a reversion to a Bush administration policy for Ukraine. Domestically, like Bush, Clinton was focused on reviving a struggling US economy. Like Bush, he saw the success of reform in Russia depending heavily on a single individual, Boris Yeltsin, and therefore invested considerable personal effort in bolstering him.

Domestic party politics played a role, too. In 1996, Clinton was running for reelection. American commentators were comparing progress in Ukraine unfavorably with that of Poland and the Baltic states; polls showed that the US electorate did not support substantial aid for either Russia or Ukraine.[9] To the extent that the eyes of the US public were on the region at all they continued to see Russia first and foremost, and they had not fully thrown off the idea that Russia remained an antagonist, even if the Cold War was officially at an end. In this, the public was more perceptive than some policymakers, even though for those who cared to look closely, widening cracks were becoming visible in the edifice of Russian reform. Those cracks began raising skepticism on Clinton's team about the likely success of Russian democracy and Western cooperation. And skepticism, like the hope it began to replace, played into the bias for doubling down the focus on Russia and overlooking Ukraine.

One factor was the outbreak of Russia's first Chechen war, a brutal anti-independence counterinsurgency begun by Russia at the end of 1994 and carried out through the summer of 1997.[10] The Chechens fought the war to a standstill with Russia's superior-on-paper army. Underperforming and outfought, Russia resorted to the scorched-earth policy of leveling Chechen cities.

Yeltsin also failed to reform Russia's economic system, which resulted in the famous "Wild West" Russian economy of the 1990s. Emerging US skepticism about Russian reform set an unfortunate pattern for future US policy for both Ukraine and Russia—a pattern prefigured, as we have seen, by Lawrence Eagleburger at the end of the Bush administration. Excessive US hope about Russia was suddenly replaced by excessive US fear.

This increasingly reactive approach of the US to Russia had a peculiar impact on Ukraine. Amid a growing US fear of Russian revanchism, and concerns over the conflicts in Yugoslavia, the Clinton administration did expand the bilateral US relationship with Ukraine, including giving critical assistance to the support of market-economy reforms there. A potentially useful effort, the Gore-Kuchma Commission, put the US vice president, Al Gore, in direct contact with President Kuchma on a range of issues beyond denuclearization.[11] That effort was in some ways parallel to—so not, in that sense, entirely derivative of—a host of other vice-presidential commissions to foreign nations, including the Gore-Chernomyrdin Commission, which connected Gore directly with the Russian prime minister, Viktor Chernomyrdin.

Yet even this policy progression in Ukraine was triggered by concerns regarding Russia and Europe: it was thus tactical, still a subplot in the greater Russian policy drama, with no long-term, values-based sustainability. Despite the infusion to Ukraine of much-needed aid, the relationship lacked the nuts-and-bolts policy components that addressed the needs of Ukraine itself. That left the country still operating outside any stable sphere of influence and perennially subject to changes in Russia's status as perceived by the US.

ALL OF THOSE uneasy shifts in the key relationships, with outcomes hazy to all concerned, were occurring in the context of the ongoing and, from Russia's perspective, potentially highly problematic issue of NATO enlargement.

By 1996, after years of pressure from Central and Eastern European states, and after navigating past Russia's presidential elections, Clinton openly supported a rapid and thorough enlargement of the alliance, a policy endorsed by many Republican lawmakers. That year, he announced his desire to see former Warsaw Pact countries and post-Soviet republics—clamoring for the security of NATO as a guarantee against Russian territorial ambitions—become alliance members. Dissent came from a number of foreign-policy thinkers. They included Democratic senators Bill Bradley and Sam Nunn, former secretary of defense Robert McNamara, and George Kennan, the prominent Soviet Russia hand who authored the famous "long telegram," credited with organizing the US Cold War strategy.[12] They argued that Russia represented no external threat to the independence of those countries—that the Clinton administration, at the insistence of the countries themselves, was pursuing a policy of enlargement not justified by concerns of Russian revanchism sparked by the Chechen war but as an anchor to secure Eastern Europe in the Western, democratic, European project. And yet the certitude of these former Soviet Bloc countries about an emerging Russian revanchism was so great that elements of Poland's political establishment were suggesting that if Poland didn't receive NATO protection, Poland would have to develop nuclear weapons of its own.

Clinton's NATO policy may fairly be seen, therefore, as forward-looking, especially given the realities of Russian-exceptionalist ambition later. One consequence, however, was that it soured the Clinton-Yeltsin relationship, adding to US skepticism about Russia, and kept Ukraine in a uniquely difficult position, driven largely by Moscow's insistence on the supposedly unique nature of Russia's historic position. As Robert Gates remembers, "Clinton kept trying to reassure Yeltsin, it was going to be okay, that NATO wasn't hostile, and blah, blah, blah . . . it's not anti-Russian and so on and so forth. And they weren't having any of it."[13]

For Russia, hope and anxiety continued to focus on Ukraine. The hope was of reintegrating Ukraine, reflecting an essentially offensive position of encroachment. That led Russia to mirror-image its own impulses, reading the West as taking an offensive position of encroaching on Russia—via NATO expansion. Anxiety arose from the explicit affront to Russian exceptionalism: incapable now of establishing its own bloc, by either enticement or force, Russia felt the painful lack of a veto power over European affairs, let alone world affairs, that it believed it had inherited from the Soviet empire.

Gates underscores the fact that the very independence of Ukraine remained a sore point with Russia:

At the beginning, Gorbachev was very open about this, before he left office, that any attempt of Ukraine to become independent would be a huge problem, and Yeltsin repeated that line. They had real issues with that, even then. And Yeltsin, because he needed Clinton's help, Yeltsin swallowed it, but he was very blunt with Clinton about the consequences of NATO expansion. And particularly involving Ukraine. And I think that he warned Clinton on several occasions in some pretty specific language that this was a huge strategic mistake.[14]

Within Ukraine, meanwhile, ongoing tensions in the domestic political and cultural situation, discussed above, led to an official attitude about NATO membership that was unusual among former Soviet republics. Given the First Chechen War and other signs of Russian restlessness regarding its former empire, many Central and Eastern European countries were actively pursuing NATO applications with eager support from voters. But in Ukraine, as Klimkin reports,

> it was totally futile to expect Kravchuk to come up with an idea for gaining membership in NATO and EU. All the early functionaries came from Soviet backgrounds. They wasted all of the opportunities presented to them. [It was a] wasted chance: begging for something rather than building a common narrative and unified goal. . . . Political and business elites wanted to use Russia to maintain and develop their business positions. At the same time, they wanted to be quasi-independent, not independent, because they profited from gas prices, commodity prices, and entering into different kinds of relations. This hybrid form of interaction with Russia went on throughout Kuchma's time, with Kuchma steering these relations.[15]

Soon many new countries had joined NATO or were on track to do so. But not Ukraine. It hadn't even applied.

The NATO issue would be revived, as we will see, in Bucharest in 2008, with dramatic effect. At the end of the 1990s, however, a combination of long-standing Russian anxieties, Ukraine's inability to unify around a genuine casting off of Russia's influence, and the US tendency to keep its relationship with Ukraine derivative of its relationship with Russia fostered a situation in which Ukraine on its own, lacking any nuclear trump cards, and receiving only spasmodic, provisional support from the West for addressing its many problems, faced the rapid rise of a new force in Russia's government, a force for which nobody was sufficiently prepared: Vladimir Putin.

CHAPTER SIX

THE WAR ON TERROR

A common misconception about the formulation of Ukrainian national identity emerged in the 2010s in the US. According to this idea, such an identity consolidates itself mainly in response to Russian claims, chauvinism, and threats—in other words, it exists only negatively, in opposition to Russia, not positively, as a function of Ukraine itself. It would be equivalent to arguing that Ireland is best understood as not-British, rather than inherently Irish, or that Portugal is not-Spanish. This misconception—as if the country's political elites, and the population at large, harbor no clear vision of Ukraine in a regional or geopolitical context outside the existential threat of national extinction—contributes to Russia's sense of its own exceptionalism, and the privileging of that exceptionalism in Western Europe.

The reality, as we saw in Chapter 1, is that a distinct Ukraine identity has long existed. That identity has less to do with political orientation than with an ethno-cultural understanding formulated in the seventeenth and eighteenth centuries, reawakened in the nineteenth, preserved through Soviet suppression in the twentieth, and, given unprecedented freedoms, flourishing in the twenty-first. Already well-developed in western and central regions, and well-rooted in eastern Ukraine, the powerful sense of national identity was demonstrated unequivocally by the independence referendum of December 1, 1991. In the years following independence, national institutions, language, culture, and consciousness developed particularly among the young population that knew no other existence and—among the population under the age of thirty—had never experienced the existence of the Soviet Union as adults.

And yet as the twentieth century came to a close, the faulty sense of Ukrainian history that contributes to this now-common misconception continued to warp the relationships among Ukraine, Russia, and the US.

AT THE END of the 1990s, US-Ukraine relations were facing significant challenges, posed largely, as we have seen, by an absence of shared interests and values. Though Ukraine no longer held the United States' attention as a nuclear state, the prospects for a bilateral relationship remained feasible, as long as Ukraine remained aligned with US values. As the decade ended, however, Ukraine increasingly pursued domestic and foreign policies that diverged from Western values: inadequate reforms, obstruction of democratization, and growing corruption.

On the domestic front, the US point of view was colored by a dramatic and widening contrast with the progress of Poland, which, while it has struggled with corruption and antidemocratic tendencies even to this day, was making much bigger strides in westernization than Ukraine, whose corruption was a regular agenda topic of the Gore-Kuchma Commission. Western forays small, medium, and large into doing business in Ukraine—profit-seeking, of course, but also risk-taking investments necessary for Ukraine's development as a market economy—came under constant assault by corrupt Ukrainian businessmen and their government partners.

Kuchma's administration was both unwilling to implement and incapable of implementing reforms within the judiciary, law enforcement, and state security services that would undermine factions critical to the president's power base and wealth. The United States was finding the messy business of democracy-building exhausting; as the corruption expanded and became endemic, it aggravated the US perception of Ukraine as an unreliable partner. The US also had a poor understanding of what President Kuchma was dealing with domestically. While he did exercise significant control over the Rada, both his own bloc and opposing factions often sought to implement their own agendas, arresting reform legislation, undercutting anti-corruption programs, and jockeying to strengthen control over ministries and industries to extract rents. In a government lacking a long history of norms supporting the rule of law, progress was naturally excruciatingly slow. Kuchma continued to represent a country largely stuck in domination by Eastern-minded Russified elites. His fumbling efforts to play various political forces and oligarchs off against each other, along with his government's abuse of administrative tools to punish political opponents, added to US skepticism.[1]

On foreign policy, Ukraine's pursuit of its national security interest—trying to drive hard bargains to extract concessions, security assurances, and financial support in exchange for denuclearization—was interpreted by the US not as an understandably dogged pursuit of national aims but as waffling disingenuousness. In a Western diplomatic system prizing veracity, follow-through, and concrete deliverables, Ukraine was seen as a bad-faith actor. Kuchma also continued his efforts to perform balancing acts with Ukraine's position between Russia and the West, further contributing to the downturn in the relationship with the US.

In 1999, Kuchma set the stage for what would become known as Ukraine's Orange Revolution of 2004. That year, he manipulated the electoral process to allow him to hold on to the presidency, in part by marginalizing one of his toughest likely opponents in a runoff. The death of another top opponent in a car accident, just as the campaign was revving up, also served to improve his chances.[2] The quality of the US relationship, which had reached a modest high-water mark during the first Clinton administration, worsened through the second term; as we will see, more outright tensions would emerge in 2000, amid the final days of the Clinton administration, and persist and develop in early 2001, with the beginning of the presidency of George W. Bush.

The Ukraine-Russia relationship of the late 1990s also played a significant role in the troubles that would develop in the new century. Kuchma attempted to expand relations with the West while maintaining relatively friendly relations with Russia. Retaining economic links with Russia was a reasonable approach: Ukraine's economy, like that of the other former Soviet republics, was oriented on a hub-and-spoke system, with all regional economies directed toward trade with Russia. Kuchma himself described the state of affairs this way: "Ukraine didn't have its own economy, it had a piece of the Soviet economy that didn't amount to a functioning independent, stand-alone economy. As a result, it necessitated ties with the East, the post-Soviet space, and in particular Russia. It is this disposition towards the East that drove my decisions and resulted in my mistakes."[3]

At the conclusion of its first decade of independence, Ukraine thus continued to muddle through its quest for nationhood, developing neither a Russian model, which would have reassured Moscow, nor sufficiently strong ties with the West that would have made it a less inviting target of Russian ambition. With neither Russia's security concerns nor the West's values and interests satisfied, Ukraine was left vulnerable—outside the sphere of influence of either security bloc. It had become an unloved buffer state, with its internal contradictions still unresolved.

On a societal and cultural level, despite the conservatism and the dominance of regional power centers, a competition for a Ukrainian national identity—European and westward-oriented or Eurasian and eastward-oriented—was ongoing. The post-Soviet youth, living in an independent state, were learning the Ukrainian language and history and gaining a greater understanding of Ukraine as a nation. This evolution involved explorations of greater integration with the West, attenuating Russia's grip on Ukraine and slowly consolidating a Ukrainian identity different than that of Russia, even while permitting space in eastern Ukraine for a Russia-friendly orientation.

Still, the emerging political orientation was not moving toward the West clearly enough to overcome Western indifference to the notion of adding a poorly understood Ukraine to the European community. For Russia, meanwhile, Ukraine's slow drift away from the Kremlin was about to become unacceptable.

AT THE CLOSE of the Clinton administration, US hopes for Russia were also undergoing a change. The optimism, sometimes wary, that had developed through two US presidential administrations, largely via cooperation on denuclearization, had receded. The horrific scenes from the First Chechen War, the chaotically unregulated "Wild West" economy, and Russia's aggressive backing of Serbia's campaign of ethnic cleansing in the Balkans contributed to new concerns among US policymakers.[4] Russia still held the front-and-center position in policy considerations for the region, but it was no longer seen as a promising, newly westernizing partner. Russia had started to become a problem again, though not a threat comparable with that of its Soviet past.

Russia, for its part, thanks to its long tendency toward favoring statists and strongmen loyal to the belief in Russian exceptionalism, underwent a major shift that the US was poorly equipped to handle. Fallout from this change, unpredictable at the time, would lead to new and dangerous conditions for the region—and for the stability of the world.

In 1999, after eight years as president, Boris Yeltsin resigned.[5]

Following his reelection of 1996, Yeltsin's effectiveness had markedly declined. He had periods of illness, drunkenness, and absenteeism. At the same time Russia experienced traumatizing economic crises that he was ill-equipped to confront, including the crash of the ruble, even if he had been at peak fitness. His administration also suffered from constant shakeups over administrative and policy failures, and it was known that many key decisions were not in fact being taken by the president but by members of his family and close inner circle.

By 1998, members of parliament had called for Yeltsin's resignation. In May 1999, when the Russian Duma prepared impeachment charges, Yeltsin fired the prime minister and the government and nominated a new prime minister, who was approved by the Duma. But three months later, Yeltsin fired him, too.

Then he nominated Vladimir Putin for the post. An obscure forty-seven-year-old ex-intelligence officer, Putin had risen only very recently in Yeltsin's orbit. He was nominated as prime minister mainly because he could be trusted not to prosecute Yeltsin or retaliate against his family: a former operative of the KGB, the USSR's foreign intelligence and domestic security agency, Putin was a strong central-government statist, mainly seen as a pliable bureaucrat for elites wishing to pull strings outside of public view.

His political career began in 1990, in the administration of Leningrad, which reverted to its pre-Soviet name, Saint Petersburg, in 1995, when Putin was still working in city government as a deputy mayor. He served as an aide to a close Yeltsin associate, Anatoly Sobchak, considered one of Russia's most aggressive reformers; Putin was also a supporter and builder of the Our Home–Russia Party.[6] In 1997, having moved to Moscow, Putin appears to have worked his way up quickly, basically as a fixer, bringing Yeltsin's political opponents to heel: a malleable functionary who could secure Yeltsin's legacy without threatening other dominant political elites then running Russia.

For reasons that Fiona Hill and Clifford G. Gaddy, in *Mr. Putin: Operative in the Kremlin*, call mysterious, Putin was first appointed by Yeltsin to the role of deputy chief of the presidential staff and chief of the Main Control Directorate of the Presidential Property Management Department, which was responsible for Russian assets, both hard currency and other forms of wealth located in foreign countries, and for transferring to the Russian Federation all assets of the former Soviet Union.[7] That put Putin in a position to allocate the resources of a slush fund, established by the intelligence services and state apparatchiks in the late Soviet period, among the various political elites. In July 1998, Putin became the head of the Federal Security Service (FSB), the little-reformed offspring of the KGB.

Then, in August 1999, Yeltsin not only appointed Putin acting prime minister but also announced a preference that Putin succeed him as president. From that position, the acting prime minister, soon the acting president, formerly so little-known—"a colorless apparatchik," says Serhii Plokhy—transformed himself into a charismatic figure.[8] He galvanized major support with remarkable speed, largely, as Hill and Gaddy have shown, by leveraging public reaction to recent events that seemed to signal a growing Russian weakness. They included humiliating bilateral treaties coming out of the Chechen war in 1996, where great Russia was compelled to negotiate with a tiny separatist region and grant it autonomy; the loss of the Baltic states to NATO; and loosened connections to the former republics, especially, of course, Ukraine, where some Russian elites and indigenous Russified elements remained especially concerned about retaining Russian control of the Black Sea Fleet. Putin characterized these phenomena as a trend that was degrading Russian power and identity—which he promised to reverse by applications of new strength.

To personify this, Putin very publicly took personal charge of a massive offensive against the "newly active" Chechen rebels, galvanized by a series of bombings of Moscow apartment buildings that experts think were orchestrated by Russia's Federal Security Service to create a pretext for the Second Chechen War.[9] With the help of allies who controlled Russian media, Putin's public support shot from the low single digits to majority support in a matter of months. He cast his tough-guy stance in relation not only to foreign policy but also to the prevailing domestic social and economic chaos, taking advantage of the public's mounting impatience with lawlessness, a law-flaunting oligarch class, economic hardships, and the general malaise undermining the view of Russia as exceptional. As part of his effort to win the upcoming presidential election, he appealed to the desires of security elites and oligarchs who had influence over elections, promising stability and strength.

Overall Putin established a grand bargain with Russian society. In exchange for centralizing control in his person, he would usher in an assertive conservatism, rejecting democracy and concentrating power, reversing Russia's economic and geopolitical slide. That bargain would remain the basis of his rule until the start of the Russia-Ukraine war in 2014. As Hill and Gaddy put it, "Everything Putin has said on the subject of saving Russia from chaos . . . is consistent with the general elite consensus in the late 1990's. Putinism is a reflection of the conservative faction's political desires of that moment."[10] Putin promised, that is, a return to Russian exceptionalism, and in May 2000, in a climax to his meteoric rise to power, he was elected president.

LATE IN 1999, President Clinton had received a call from Yeltsin, assuring him that, as prime minister, Putin was "a solid man who is kept well abreast of various subjects under his purview."[11] Clinton had also met Prime Minister Putin himself, at an Asia-Pacific Economic Cooperation meeting in New Zealand. He told both Putin and Yeltsin that the critical thing, from the US- and Western-values point of view, was a free and fair election to replace Yeltsin.

But when Yeltsin unexpectedly resigned and Putin slid in as acting president—the anointed successor, in advance of an election—the US administration's attitude became less focused on the democratic principle of fairness. The focus shifted to avoiding violence and instability. A peaceful transfer of power became paramount for the Clinton administration, now in its final year, ahead of what would prove to be a famously contested and protracted US election in the fall.

Ukraine's President Kuchma, for his part, understood Putin's ascendance as a sign that his country would now have to manage a neighbor that would leverage its dominant security and defense apparatus to gain authoritarian control within Russia, expect to extend broad influence over the former Soviet space, and claim a central role in dictating the world order. Yet his keen analysis of the coming challenges with Russia didn't carry over into either hardening Ukraine against the Russia threat or introspection regarding his own shortcomings. Kuchma instead blamed the problems in the US-Ukraine relationship on the US and Russia and presented Ukraine as blameless, though his self-serving conclusions aside, Kuchma was in fact culpable in Ukraine's avoidance of real reform and failure to move forcefully toward the West. In an increasingly challenging period for the Russia relationship, the persistence of conservatism in Ukraine, as perpetuated by Kuchma himself, obstructed the advances in liberal democracy that would have improved the bilateral relationship with the United States.

That fact was dramatized in September 2000, when Georgiy Ruslanovych Gongadze, a Georgian-Ukrainian journalist who had become one of the leading critics of Kuchma and his administration, disappeared. In November, his body was found in a forest about forty miles outside Kyiv. He had been shot in the head and then, in an effort to cover up the crime, decapitated and bathed in acid. Kuchma's own intelligence aide presented substantial evidence that Ukrainian security services had carried out the murder and that Kuchma was implicated.[12] Throughout 2001, the murder would become a national and international scandal, sparking protests within Ukraine, drawing intense criticism from the West, and increasing tensions over the question of Ukraine's place in the group of liberal nations.

In December 2000 the Supreme Court of the United States finally ruled on who had won the presidential election more than a month earlier. The Republican candidate, George W. Bush, governor of Texas, was inaugurated in January 2001; his vice president was Dick Cheney, who had served as secretary of defense in the administration of the new president's father. In its first months, the Bush-Cheney administration focused on using the status of the United States as the sole superpower to conduct a more muscular foreign policy in the developing world, privileging near-peer states and further marginalizing places like the Newly Independent States—except in instances where there was an important, seemingly immediate national security interest. Regarding Ukraine, the already weakened relationship not only languished but actively deteriorated.

The deterioration was mutual. If the US had reason to be skeptical of Ukraine's capability of ever becoming a westernizing partner, Kuchma had reason to be cautious about the ascendance of a second-generation Bush administration. The elder Bush had set the realist policy that had placed the preservation of the Soviet Union far ahead of Ukrainians' desire for self-determination and independence. The younger Bush's national security advisor, Condoleezza Rice, was seen as the author of that pro-Kremlin, anti-Ukraine-independence policy: she had served the elder Bush as senior director of Soviet and East European affairs in the National Security Council and as a special assistant to the president for national security affairs.[13]

As Kyiv nevertheless pushed for high-level dialogue, the Bush White House began dismantling the previous administration's vice-presidential commissions, including those for South Africa, Egypt, and Kyrgyzstan, as well as both the Gore-Kuchma and the Gore-Chernomyrdin Commissions, which had enabled communication on multiple issues between the US and Ukraine and the US and Russia. According to Leon Fuerth, Vice President Gore's national security advisor, bureaucratic infighting among cabinet-level officials made departments and agencies prefer to conduct bilateral policy processes on their own authorities, rather than subordinate their roles to the vice president's staff.[14] Whatever the shortcomings of the Kuchma and Chernomyrdin commissions, they had at least provided a venue to discuss complex problems. At a stroke, that venue disappeared; the momentum of the approach pursued by the former vice president, including regular engagements between key principals, came to a halt. For Ukraine, that meant the already-challenging US relationship, fraught with mutual misunderstandings—stresses driving Kuchma's decision-making, conditions placed by the United States on improved relations—could no longer be ameliorated by a channel that Ukraine had been using to manage political disagreements.

However, although senior Bush policymakers were not advancing engagement with Ukraine, some senior policy staff, including Ambassador Steven Pifer, then the deputy assistant secretary of state, were. Their interest took the form of advancing a NATO open-door policy that included Ukraine. This revived question of Ukraine's relationship to NATO, dormant throughout the 1990s, triggered new dramas. As Pifer explains, official NATO language welcoming new members, though drafted with countries in Central Europe and the Baltic region primarily in mind, applied implicitly to Ukraine, whose military assets might aid in transatlantic security. But "the more difficult question," Pifer says, "turned on Kyiv's readiness to implement democratic reforms to meet NATO standards."[15]

That question was raised by the new president Bush in a speech in Warsaw on June 15, 2001, making clear his administration's interest in Ukraine joining NATO, which Bush declared he was open to. He welcomed

> all of Europe's democracies that seek it and are ready to share the responsibility that NATO brings. The question of when may still be up for debate within NATO, the question of whether should not be. . . . The Europe we are building must include Ukraine, a nation struggling with the trauma

of transition. Some in Kyiv speak of their country's European destiny. If this is their aspiration, we should reward it. We must extend our hand to Ukraine, as Poland has already done with such determination.[16]

The statement demonstrates fundamental contradictions at the base of the Bush-era foreign-policy thinking known as neoconservatism, a philosophy championed by Vice President Dick Cheney, Deputy Secretary of Defense Paul Wolfowitz, and others in the administration, known as neocons. Bush's aspirational invocations in the Warsaw speech load the oratory with values reflecting idealism. But that idealism is combined with a transactional, interest-driven view of relations formed on the basis of power—prioritizing Russia even while seeming to embrace Ukraine in NATO—and foreign adventuring conceived in the absence of any recognition of the limits of US power. Schizophrenically practicing realism and idealism at once would defeat the aims of both.

The day after giving the Warsaw speech, Bush met in Slovenia with Putin and, as Bush put it, "I looked the man in the eye. I found him very straightforward and trustworthy—I was able to get a sense of his soul."[17] The remark landed poorly at home. Reaction suggested that the US president had shown himself to be naively trusting; Bush's stated impression would prove to be well wide of the mark.

And yet the Ukraine-in-NATO question might have offered an opportunity for a degree of constructive tri-laterality. However surprising it is in retrospect, in mid-2001, Russia's official position was not to oppose Ukraine's joining NATO.

"I am absolutely convinced," Putin said in 2002, "that Ukraine will not shy away from the processes of expanding interaction with NATO and the Western allies as a whole. Ukraine has its own relations with NATO; there is the Ukraine–NATO Council. At the end of the day, the decision is to be taken by NATO and Ukraine. It is a matter for those two partners."

Putin had moved very far from the position Yeltsin had taken in the 1990s and was at that moment hopeful that even Russia itself might be able to join NATO. If he was to be taken at his word at the time, no compelling conflict existed between advancing principled US interests and aims with regard to Ukraine's relationship to NATO and maintaining US relations with Russia.

Nevertheless, the window of opportunity for an expanded Ukraine-NATO relationship came and went quickly. By the time the question of NATO membership returned, the world had changed. In this entirely new context, the question of Ukraine and NATO would become explosive.

On September 11, 2001, many of the issues explored in this book so far were swept into a new and unforeseen vortex with both immediate and long-range consequences for all of the relationships involved. The terrorist attacks on the Pentagon and the World Trade Center caused a shift in US policy that shaped relationships with Putin's Russia and Kuchma's Ukraine in new and ultimately highly unfortunate ways.

THE NEW CLIMATE of immense urgency and extremity confirmed and amplified the short-term, crisis-driven approach that has habitually marked US foreign-policy decision-making. In light of much later events, especially Russia's 2014 invasion of Crimea and eastern Ukraine and 2022 invasion of all of Ukraine, the US reaction to the 9/11 attacks can be seen as a characteristic US response to a foreign-policy crisis. The reaction included a global war on terror, a war of choice in Iraq, a concomitant privileging of the Russia relationship, and relations with Ukraine defined almost solely by short-term transactions, not the long-term fostering of Western values. While understandable from the point of view of the moment, the response was never based on a cogent, strategic consideration of long-term ramifications, credible priorities, and relationships appropriate to US values.

When US relationships to Ukraine and Russia entered a new phase in late 2001 and 2002, the American public's focus was firmly on other issues. The terror threats that 9/11 placed front and center punctured a delusion, in a way that state actors never had, that the two oceans surrounding the United States provided impregnability. Eight months into President George W. Bush's term of office, the administration therefore completely refocused its foreign policy on the Middle East and what Bush called the global war on terror. That fixation was to drive US policy for most of the next two decades.

Having to prioritize both their time and the nation's resources, senior policymakers now ranked the war in Afghanistan and the global war on terror as the top priorities, demoting the importance of nation-state threats. Given the unipolar, sole-superpower moment, when nation-state threats still seemed remote, and given the "end of history" view that still held sway, it seemed a reasonable trade-off to downgrade nation-state relations in order to deal with a threat that had brought a catastrophe to the US mainland. Such, at least, was the rationale for the Afghanistan campaign.

And by a strange twist of logic, Iraq under Saddam Hussein was framed as a terror threat of another kind: an authoritarian regime seemingly brandishing weapons of mass destruction. In addition to fighting the "good war"—punishing al-Qaeda for attacking the United States, eliminating international terrorist safe havens in Afghanistan—the United States therefore launched another war, this one a war of choice, in Iraq, and then, with the Hussein regime toppled, proceeded to manifest in Iraq the same insurgency threat that it had gone to Afghanistan to root out. The new goal became democratization through nation-building, along the lines Bush would lay out in 2003 in the Freedom Agenda.

From today's perspective, the long-term engagement in wars of choice in the Middle East, with the aim of confronting enemies that never posed an existential threat to the US or even our allies—and drawing resources away from coping with nation-state actors that might in fact amount to existential threats—should be viewed as a mistake, as the subsequent history of Russia-Ukraine-US relations, and relations with China, clearly shows. Because the neocons' heady aims of defeating terrorism globally, while sweeping into the Middle East and establishing democracy by military force, departed so sharply from the tightly restricted, realist-school approach of George H. W. Bush, those aims did reflect a kind of revived idealism. Yet neoconservative thinking was enmeshed in the delusion that as the sole superpower, the US was in a position to work its will quickly and easily wherever and whenever it chose. The policy ignored historical challenges and eschewed the hard work necessary to build, over time, the kinds of relationships critical to fostering liberal values and democratic institutions. In pursuing a war on terror, and in letting it drown out almost every other foreign-policy consideration, the neocons committed the US not to a genuinely neo-idealistic policy—tough-minded, clear, demanding of allies and opponents alike—but to an over-the-top mood of using American power to achieve a delusory totality of change, with delusory speed.

Other policy objectives were indeed occasionally pursued during the period, at times becoming temporarily preeminent; strategic arms-control negotiations with Russia was one. Yet terrorism and its enablers became the lens through which policymakers obsessively focused on the world throughout the first decade of the new century. When the US took its eye off potential nation-state threats and absented itself from managing them, its two biggest challengers in the international system, Russia and China, took advantage of its distraction and absence.

The US reversion to hope and optimism when it came to Russia may have been encouraged by the fact that the first major world leader to call President Bush after the 9/11 attack was Vladimir Putin, who was sympathetic and shared a loathing of terrorism.[18] Putin's offer of support and cooperation in fighting international terrorism captured the attention of the US administration and reflected a critical effect of the new US policy fixation: emerging powers used the opportunity of a crisis to offer promises of cooperation in combating terror while asserting regional hegemony. They seemed confident that there would be little US backlash or resistance as long as the US was consumed by the idea of the war on terror. As we will see, that kind of self-interested, somewhat cynical calculation on the part of multiple nations would play a negative role in the US-Ukraine relationship as well.

The revived US notion of Russia as a flawed but possibly constructive partner, capable of even greater cooperation, was further reinforced—even advanced—by National Security Advisor Condoleezza Rice, the Bush administration's most senior Russia expert. Speaking on CBS's *60 Minutes*, on March 28, 2004, Rice asserted that it was "a good thing that we [built a good relationship] with Russia, because, after all, our ability to function in Central Asia [to support the war on terror] was very much dependent on that good relationship with Russia." The US wanted a military base in what had been the Russian sphere of influence, and because Russia complied, it was in a position to exploit our gratitude. Or as Thomas Graham, director and then senior director for Russian affairs on the National Security Council staff from 2002 to 2007, explains succinctly, "When the focus shifted to Iraq, obviously, Russia becomes a key player in that, in part because of its seat on the UN Security Council."[19] Needing its support in the UN for the wars in Iraq and Afghanistan, the US wooed Russia.

Framing Russia, despite its antidemocratic and regionally ambitious tendencies, as a great power supporting the United States in a fight against terror naturally gave Russia a higher priority in US thinking than Ukraine, which was experiencing democratic backsliding and proliferating corruption in any event. In hindsight, integrating Ukraine, a critically important state, into the West and the rules-based international order was in the US's long-term national security interests and served both Western values and regional and global stability. At the time, however, that perspective was overwhelmed by the immediate drama unfolding in Afghanistan and Iraq.

Instead, the United States now went out of its way to excuse Russia's undemocratic behavior, even its aggression toward its neighbors. The approach to Russia sought to establish a few areas of cooperation and avoid any degradation in bilateral relations by largely ignoring its undemocratic excesses, which were mounting up. As Russia expert Paul Goble notes, in this case regarding Russia's 2014 invasion of Crimea:

> Moscow is routinely held to lower standards than the others, is subjected to far less criticism than is directed at the others, and is not given the constant improving lectures on how it must behave domestically and internationally if it is to be a partner of the West. . . . Politicians and commentators have gone so far in many cases that they have accepted Russian propaganda and blamed the victim rather than the victimizer.[20]

Long before the 2014 invasion, Ukraine was being asked to meet standards of behavior never required of Russia. The war on terror greatly exacerbated the historic double standard.

Some US officials serving during that period deny the marginalizing of policy fronts other than the war on terror. Nicholas Burns, who served in a number of key positions, described a division of labor between senior government officials, where principals maintained focus on the war on terror, and the principal staff below them focused on next-tier priorities, suggesting Ukraine policy still received keen consideration. He underscored the idea that the US government had the capacity to effectively manage multiple competing tasks. Yet, Eric Edelman provided an equally persuasive and forthright assessment of policy priorities during his tenure in the Defense Department, from 2005 to 2009: "I didn't spend a lot of time on Ukraine when I was USDP [undersecretary of defense for policy], because of the amount of time I was devoting to Iraq and Afghanistan, which were my major preoccupations. Russia [was] a close third, I did pay a lot of attention to Russia, because of my previous experience there and my concern about the direction [of] Putin from the beginning."

Steven Pifer, ambassador to Ukraine from 1998 to 2000, describes the Ukraine relationship this way:

The years 2001 and 2002 proved even more difficult for the bilateral relationship, which went into a steady downturn as new problems arose and few solutions were found. By the end of 2002, the relationship had hit its lowest point since Ukraine regained independence in 1991. It was so difficult that President Leonid Kuchma told a December 2002 press conference in Kyiv that the year's "most difficult thing is the worsening of relations with the United

States. The main task for me as president will be to solve this problem."[21]

It is especially important to keep in mind, when criticizing US missteps in Ukraine policy, that the problem Kuchma is referring to in the Pifer quotation involved a series of uncooperative moves on his own part that contributed to undermining the relationship. On the one hand, in May 2002 Kuchma actively sought entry into NATO for the first time. On the other, he continued engaging with Russia, sending a message that if the West was not prepared to engage with Ukraine, then Ukraine would turn back toward Russia.

Then, at the same moment that Ukraine was asking for NATO membership, it undertook a series of moves that looked as if it were determined to boost America's enemies. In one contentious meeting, US national security advisor Rice asked Ukraine not to provide heavy weapons to newly independent Macedonia, then under threat from Albania. After appearing to agree not to, Kuchma went ahead and provided the weapons anyway. And as the United States ramped up for Operation Iraqi Freedom, Kuchma also agreed to provide Iraq with advanced air-defense systems.[22]

Ukraine was conducting business with other American adversaries as well, including selling arms to Libya and providing turbines for Iran's Bushehr nuclear power plant. In October 2001, Ukrainian armed forces accidentally downed Siberia Airlines flight 1812 en route from Tel Aviv to Novosibirsk, killing all sixty-six passengers and all twelve crew members.[23] Those actions combined with the growing corruption in Ukraine, which directly impacted US business interests, to send a long-declining relationship into outright tailspin.

Three attempts were nevertheless made to organize a Bush-Kuchma meeting—though it was conditional, as always, on Kyiv addressing the issues that concerned the US. But Kuchma did little to fulfill the prerequisites.

The United States and Ukraine shared responsibility for the absence of a common understanding of how to sustain the kind of relationship that might have allowed policymakers to see past Russia, too long the prism for assessing the relationship. With the exception of Condoleezza Rice's stop in July 2001, there was no senior-level administration visit to Ukraine by Bush, by Cheney, or by a cabinet secretary.[24] And while Washington had hosted a visit by the prime minister, President Kuchma had yet to meet with Bush. Kuchma argued that he had to overcome contentious relations with the Rada and other political elites and insisted that he needed a meeting with Bush in order to realize reforms; the Bush administration insisted on seeing the reforms before committing to a presidential engagement. It was a classic standoff.

It was no surprise, therefore, that in his 2002 end-of-year press conference, when Kuchma again denied that Ukraine had sent radar to Iraq, he also decried the worsening of US-Ukraine relations and blamed Russian provocation instead of accepting any responsibility.[25] The beginning of 2003 thus marked two years of virtually steady decline in the US-Ukraine relationship. As Pifer explains, the only factor keeping the relationship out of complete free fall was Ukraine's official support for the overriding US concern, the war on terror:

Since 9/11, Kyiv had offered political support on the UN Security Council for resolutions to frame and enable a broad response to terrorism, supported eleven of twelve international counterterrorism conventions, and increased intelligence sharing on possible terrorist activities. US Air Force flights regularly transited Ukrainian air space (more than 4,500 in the September 2001–October 2002 period alone), and Ukrainian heavy-lift aircrafts had moved humanitarian assistance, as well as German and Turkish troops, to Afghanistan. The Ukrainian military was also helping to re-equip the Afghan National Army.[26]

Then, in November 2002, nearly ten years after the most recent effort to reassess and reset Ukraine relations, the National Security Council initiated a Ukraine policy review. The goal was to define strategic objectives and chart a better way ahead. The review concluded in January 2003, and Pifer describes the result: "[The US ambassador to Ukraine, Carlos Pascual,] shared the results of the review with the Ukrainian government during the second half of January, offering, as well, an illustrative list of issues for US-Ukrainian dialogue. The relationship was in trouble, but Washington sought to leave the door open for improvement. The initial Ukrainian reaction to the policy review seemed positive."[27]

The policy review helped the relationship to improve—but not to be transformed. It was still essentially transactional, now reshaped for the post-9/11 world. Kuchma arrested the declining relationship by going beyond his earlier contributions to US operations in Afghanistan and committing Ukraine to the coalition of the willing being called on by President Bush to help carry out Operation Iraqi Freedom. Ukraine provided 1,800 troops—the fourth-largest contingent—to that operation and to Operation Enduring Freedom, including hundreds of chemical-weapons troops to the forces conducting operations in post–Saddam Hussein Iraq.[28] By firmly supporting immediate US aims, Ukraine started to register with senior US policymakers as a relevant partner.

But the relationship was improving by ignoring the difficult questions that would lead to more substantive alignment between the West and Ukraine—further reforms and anti-corruption efforts— and by elevating important but short-term military benefits for a US policy fixated on the war on terror. But at least the US was paying attention, and members of the Bush administration were actively anticipating the 2004 Ukraine presidential election.

The administration could not know that in the course of that election, partly as a result of interference by Vladimir Putin, Ukraine would undergo a revolution that directly challenged Russian hegemony and challenged the US's Moscow-centric policies. The 2004 Ukraine election and its aftermath would ratchet up the likelihood of new conflicts among all players.

CHAPTER SEVEN

A NON-PEACEFUL TRANSFER OF POWER

Despite Russia's cooperation with the US in the fight against terrorism, a growing sense of unease was developing, both in the region and in the West, regarding Russia's undemocratic—soon antidemocratic—activities, both domestically and throughout the former Soviet space. Yet even as Russia's violent conduct during the Second Chechen War and continued support for Serbian nationalists in the Balkans raised alarms, the US government managed to harbor hope that a durably democratic Russia would emerge.[1] Even Vladimir Putin's attacks on private property and the expropriation of oligarchs' assets in media and energy holdings continued to be explained away, in US policy circles, by the argument that these were compromises required to exert control over the unruly oligarch order in an effort to reduce corruption and ultimately bring about reform. This proved to be a delusion.

To offset any US concerns, Russia appealed to two major US interests: progress in the war on terror and fruitful arms-control negotiations. During the Bush presidency, a contradiction between the American exceptionalist desire to interact with other exceptional great powers, on the one hand, and support for self-determination, on the other, was rationalized by the need to prioritize the fight against terror over diplomacy with multiple nation-states. Efficiency trumped idealism.

This concatenation of US biases and rationalizations amplified Ukrainian skepticism about US and EU seriousness in supporting Ukraine as a unique nation-state with its own identity. Ukraine parliamentarian Hanna Hopko has summarized the view this way: "For all thirty years of our renewed period of independence, the West has never considered Ukraine more than a buffer state. It's all just rhetoric—when Ukraine needed true investment and support [the West was absent]."[2]

Hopko's bluntness is both refreshing and understandable. During three administrations, the United States showed reluctance about countering or directly criticizing Russia's regression toward authoritarianism and irredentism. Even as Russia attacked domestic civil liberties, property rights, and business interests and signaled a more muscular approach to relationships with its neighbors, US thinking continued to be moored both to the naive-idealist hope for a Russia interested in democracy and a pan-European security architecture and to the "realist" concerns about averting and managing crises at all costs. Neither the delusional idealism nor the short-term realism was a viable way to manage our relationship with Russia.

As events would show, the region and the world were changing. The 2004 presidential election would lead to the protests and changes in Ukraine known as the Orange Revolution, which directly challenged Putin's new efforts at reasserting Russian hegemony.

Although Russia remained the dominant priority for the US, one result of Ukraine's tangible commitments to Operation Iraqi

Freedom and Operation Enduring Freedom was that the US had a greater stake in the outcome of the 2004 election. The US "Freedom Agenda" was extended to include a desire to see a free and fair 2004 presidential election in Ukraine. As D'Anieri says, in *Ukraine and Russia*:

> It was widely anticipated that the 2004 election would be pivotal for Ukraine because one of two things had to happen. If the election were free and fair, many believed, Kuchma (or his designated successor) would be defeated, reversing Ukraine's slide toward authoritarianism. Kuchma and his supporters were expected to try to rig the election through tactics including controlling the media, patronage, and fraud. That would consolidate autocracy and likely move Ukraine away from the West and toward Russia. Therefore, well before the election, opposition groups were preparing to run a parallel vote count and to challenge fraud through protest.[3]

Kuchma favored Viktor Yanukovych, a former prime minister with an eastern Ukrainian power base, as his successor. Yanukovych prioritized stronger relations with Moscow, official status for the Russian language, and rejecting closer relations with NATO. As a teenager, he had been convicted and imprisoned for robbery and assault. He acted the tough guy, and this, combined with his Russia-centrism, lent him a certain appeal to some voters, especially in the east. Kuchma, Western governments determined, was preparing to corrupt the electoral process and use the public administration of media to limit voters' exposure to competitors. He hoped to ensure a Yanukovych victory, which would protect the Kuchma faction against corruption investigations that would surely emerge if Yanukovych's leading opponent, a reform candidate, won the election.

Yanukovych's rival was Viktor Yushchenko, also a former prime minister. He had been forced out of office in 2001 after his political fortunes began to eclipse Kuchma's. Ukrainian-speaking, a pro-Western technocrat nationalist, Yushchenko was also a former governor of the National Bank of Ukraine. He was campaigning on ending corruption, fostering liberal economics, and on pursuing a non-Russified Ukrainian nationalism.

To Russia, Yushchenko was an unwelcome demonstration that Ukraine was marching forward as an independent state, fitfully but steadily building a national identity, and most alarmingly slowly shedding its deference to Russia. That fact represented a wound in Russia's sense of its own exceptionalism.

Moscow's hold on "Little Russia" was becoming tenuous anyway. A Yushchenko victory, which seemed possible, would further loosen the hold.

It was clear to Russia that Kuchma's candidate, the pro-Russian heavyweight Yanukovych, was more likely to maintain Russian influence. After meeting with Kuchma on July 26, 2004, Putin, as Pifer says, "effectively endorsed Yanukovych." In fact, Putin did far more than endorse. As the electoral battle began, he poured Russian money into the Yanukovych campaign. "Gazprom and other Russian sources reportedly contributed $300 million to Yanukovych's campaign war chest," according to Pifer.[4]

Putin stage-managed a high-profile engagement to validate his preferred candidate when US national security advisor Condoleezza Rice visited Moscow, in May 2004, and he paraded Yanukovych before her.[5] He was telegraphing to the United States not only that he had picked the next president of Ukraine but also that he would not tolerate a Ukrainian president who threatened to move Ukraine further from Russia and toward the West. In making an overt expression of regional power, impinging on both Western values and the stability of Europe's frontier, Russia had become a US adversary. And the United States didn't realize it.

THE REFORM CANDIDATE Yushchenko fully recognized Kuchma's desire to install a successor who was ready, willing, and able to protect him from the kind of investigations a reform government would be bound to undertake. Yushchenko and his allies laid the groundwork for large-scale protests in the likely outcome that the election was stolen from them by some subterfuge or overt fraud.

Privately, Washington regarded Yushchenko as the candidate who was more pro-Western and better aligned with US interests and values.[6] Yet the administration held to its decision to support a democratic election process, and that meant avoiding any perception of US support for any candidate.

The Kremlin, by stark contrast, had no such inhibitions. As well as openly and aggressively campaigning for its candidate, Russia conducted covert influence operations. As Pifer notes, "Gleb Pavlovsky, a Moscow 'political technologist' who had worked on Russian political campaigns, established a 'Russian club' in Kyiv that aimed its efforts at supporting Yanukovych and criticizing Yushchenko, while Russian electronic media, relatively available in eastern Ukraine, broadcast a steady stream of pro-Yanukovych and anti-Yushchenko messages."[7]

President Kuchma also took a heavy hand in trying to influence the election. Yushchenko's flight clearances for campaign trips were denied and his campaign's access to media was curtailed. Administrative resources were turned to manipulating the election commission and pressuring civil servants to support Yanukovych.

Yushchenko supporters were harassed. Opposition rallies were disrupted. As word of these efforts surfaced, reform supporters became ever more vigilant in organizing to protest what they assumed would be a stolen election.

Then on September 5, Yushchenko fell gravely ill. Rushed to Vienna for treatment, he was diagnosed with dioxin poisoning, which causes extreme skin lesions.[8] The dioxin was later shown to have been made in a laboratory and highly refined; Yushchenko believed it had been slipped to him by government officials at a state dinner. He was unable to campaign for a month, and when he did return to the campaign trail, he was quickly exhausted. His face was disfigured by the toxin. But nonetheless his campaign seemed to have been reinvigorated. The brazenly brutal attack on him only served to underscore the seriousness of the issues at stake.

The US government continued to urge the outgoing president Kuchma to hold free, fair, and transparent elections. In October, Ambassador John Herbst confirmed Washington's readiness to work with whomever the Ukrainians elected while underscoring that the election needed to be honest and transparent. The State Department released a statement expressing the US government's disappointment and added that the disruption of opposition rallies, muzzling of independent media, misuse of administrative resources, and other serious violations cast doubt on the Ukrainian government's commitment to its democratic obligations. The statement urged the Ukrainian authorities to allow a free vote and warned that if the election failed to meet democratic standards, Washington would need to reexamine its relations "with those engaged in election fraud and manipulation."[9] The remark was aimed at Kuchma and Yanukovych.

But the US shied away from criticizing Russia's machinations, even though much of the "fraud and manipulation" was sponsored by Moscow. The concern was that to do so would harm US-Russia relations and disrupt the busy agenda for collaborating on arms control and the war on terror, including maintaining operating bases for Afghanistan throughout Central Asia, where Russia had a great deal of influence. The United States had also been undertaking NATO enlargement, now contrary to Russian wishes, and the Bush administration therefore wanted to conduct US-Russia relations with great delicacy. So throughout September and October, as Russia continued to conduct an influence campaign to deliver a Yanukovych victory, the US would criticize only Kuchma's efforts at election theft, not Putin's illegitimate influence.

Russian advertisements went on endorsing Yanukovych in both Moscow and Kyiv. Playing on some Ukrainians' regard for Putin, Yanukovych and Putin campaigned together in Russia and Ukraine. The Kremlin implemented policies to highlight the economic benefits of a Yanukovych presidency. From October 26 to 28, Putin visited Ukraine to attend a military parade marking the sixtieth anniversary of the city's liberation in World War II and delivered a lengthy speech—widely broadcast on Ukrainian television—praising Russia-Ukraine relations and the work Yanukovych had done as prime minister. And yet, as Fishel reports, when two days before the election, US deputy secretary Richard Armitage published an op-ed emphasizing the importance of a free and fair process, "the op-ed did not reference the negative role being played by Moscow as it worked to skew the outcome in Viktor Yanukovych's favor."[10]

Fishel clarifies another layer of Russia's machinations. Russia would benefit if the US reacted negatively to Yanukovych's becoming president via corruption. "The US threat to review relations with Kyiv in the event of an undemocratic election," Fishel writes, "must have been music to Putin's ears."

THE ELECTION WAS held on October 31, 2004, and the reformer Yushchenko won a plurality of the vote.[11] Because he had not achieved the majority required to avoid a second-round runoff, a second election was scheduled for November 21. The political tension was palpable.

During an October 31 press conference, a US State Department spokesman, pressed on Russian election interference in Ukraine, acknowledged reports of Russian involvement in the campaign and added that the US government "often discussed the subject of Ukraine with officials in Moscow and obviously, consistently urge[d] them to support free and fair elections in Ukraine."[12] He then made the assertion that democratic elections in Ukraine were in Moscow's interest, reflecting the fanciful American hope that the US and Moscow had shared interests.

In the November 21 runoff, election monitors reported massive irregularities: abuse of absentee balloting, ballot stuffing, falsified vote counts. "Some observers were blocked from entering polling stations," monitors reported, "while others reported buses taking voters from one station to another to cast multiple ballots."[13] The next day, Ukraine's Central Electoral Commission (CEC) issued an unofficial report showing that Yanukovych had narrowly won the runoff: 49.7 percent to 46.7 percent. Those results flatly contradicted exit polls showing Yushchenko beating Yanukovych handily: 54 percent to 43 percent.

Analysts questioned the results from the CEC, showing that voter turnout in pro-Yanukovych areas had improved by incredible margins since the first round: some areas in his power base of Donetsk and Luhansk reported turnout up by more than 40 percent.[14] Yanukovych's eastern strongholds also delayed sending returns. All of that combined with the suspect data from the CEC to convince many that election manipulation had occurred.

On November 22, the International Election Observation Mission in Europe, coordinated by the Organization for Security and Cooperation in Europe, delivered a scathing assessment of the vote. The report cited "a higher incidence of serious violations" than on October 31, and that "in Donetsk Oblast, preliminary turnout figures announced by the CEC are so improbable as to cast doubt on whether that [the voters'] choice was always safeguarded."[15] It was also clear that groups of voters whose livelihoods depended on the state had been pressured to support Yanukovych and that citizens mobilizing for other candidates had been pressured to stop.

Essential freedoms had thus been violated. With the falsification of the tally and the means behind the falsification now dramatically exposed, well-organized reform forces went into immediate action throughout Ukraine.

Protesters occupied the Maidan Nezalezhnosti (Independence Square), Kyiv's central square.[16] Other major protests occurred around the country, ultimately involving millions of Ukrainians who were rapidly mobilized, due to the advance preparation by pro-democratic civil-society organizers, to demonstrate nonviolently on a mass scale against both the election theft and Russia's hand in it. The protesters rallied around the leadership of Yushchenko and Yulia Tymoshenko, a former deputy prime minister and his main partner in what was turning into a democratic popular revolution. The goal was to compel the courts to nullify the fraudulent election results and order a new second-round runoff for December.

US decision-makers denounced the rigged election but stopped short of explicitly criticizing Russian interference. On November 24, in response to a question about what the Department of State should do about Moscow's interference in the Ukrainian electoral process, Secretary Powell stated that he "would rather concentrate on how we get out of . . . the difficult situation," adding that "at a later time, one can talk about how we got into this situation." Avoiding explicit criticism of Moscow carried over to President Bush's press engagement on November 26. When asked if "President Putin overstepped his bounds," Bush referred to "a lot of allegations of vote fraud" but made no mention of Putin or Russia.[17]

December 3 saw a great victory for the Ukrainian protests and the cause of liberal democratic reform. Ukraine's high court invalidated the runoff election. A new election was scheduled for December 26. On December 7, during congressional testimony, US ambassador-designate to Ukraine and US deputy assistant secretary of state for European and Eurasian affairs John Tefft finally mentioned Moscow's open support for Yanukovych, but while he noted reports of Russian financial backing for the Yanukovych candidacy, Tefft also stated that the US government would pursue "balanced cooperation" with governments in the region—code for the policy of calibrating between support for Western values and not upsetting Moscow.[18] On December 17, Secretary of State Powell put the policy of balanced cooperation more clearly and yet again underscored the importance of the relationship with Russia above everything else:

> President Putin has taken some steps that we think do not lead toward cementing his democracy properly, and when that has been the case we have spoken to him about it. We have spoken to him about it in the spirit of friendship and in the spirit of asking why some of these actions are taking place. And so, Russia is not going back to being the Soviet Union. The Cold War is not coming back. And we want to encourage President Putin and our Russian colleagues to

keep moving in the right direction to build their democracy on a sound foundation, and that includes free access to
media, respect for human rights, and to keep moving in the
direction they had been moving.[19]

In the Ukrainian presidential runoff on December 26, Yushchenko won decisively. Opposition legislators then reached an agreement to combine the election rerun with constitutional changes to
reduce the power of the presidency. These changes amounted to a
poison pill. Presidential power shifted to the prime minister and the
Rada; the president would now be more reliant on the pro-Russian
bloc of parliamentarians, undercutting Yushchenko's ability to
implement westernizing reforms. Nevertheless, the nonviolent
mass protest movement on behalf of corruption reform, individual
liberty, and a national identity not beholden to Russia had delivered
a fair election result, which placed a Western-leaning reform candidate in the presidency.

Those events became known as Ukraine's Orange Revolution:
Yushchenko's supporters had taken orange as the color for his campaign. It was one of the many "color revolutions" underway in the
former Soviet space on behalf of self-determination and liberal
democracy and in opposition to the persistence of Soviet-era apparatchiks and Russia-leaning elites. These color revolutions were
naturally deeply disconcerting to Putin and the Russian elite, and
Ukraine's Orange Revolution was the most important and disturbing of them all. It wasn't only that Ukraine remained a centrally
important space for Russia, both practically and emotionally. The
revolution there had also been directly precipitated by Russian overreach within Ukraine. Feeding Putin's fears about possible instability in his regime, the Orange Revolution was seen by many, both in

the upper echelons of Russian government and in opposition civil society, as a model for ousting Putin himself.

IN HIS MEMOIR, *In My Time,* Vice President Dick Cheney notes Russia's central role in precipitating the Orange Revolution and writes that he "had long believed that the United States should play a more active role in integrating Ukraine and other former Soviet states into the West."[20] And in the wake of the Orange Revolution, US-Ukraine relations did make tentative steps toward becoming less derivative of Russia policy. Nevertheless, Bush administration policy, as well as the policies of successor administrations, retained its long-standing bias. In *The Limits of Partnership*, Angela Stent writes:

> Like its predecessor, the Bush Administration was divided over how much its policy toward the post-Soviet states should take Russian concerns into account. The Office of Vice President Cheney advocated a tough policy toward Russia, generally supporting Russia's neighbors and expressing suspicion about Moscow's intentions . . . [while others, including the NSC senior director for Russia, Thomas Graham,] advocated a more realist and interest-based policy toward Russia, recognizing the necessity of taking Russian interests into consideration when crafting US policy in the post-Soviet space.[21]

Meanwhile, Russia's efforts at election interference were not publicly condemned by the US, nor were they sufficiently criticized in private by policymakers who remained concerned that such criticism would spoil the possibility of Russia's support for the war on terror. Fishel has summarized the policy toward Russia's role in the Orange Revolution:

> The Moscow factor primarily manifested itself through the Bush administration's conscious and sustained failure to call out and confront malign Russian interference in the run-up to and during the 2004 presidential election in Ukraine, including through explicit support for its preferred candidate during the campaign and by extending its political support once the fraud was committed. Both the Bush White House and the Department of State routinely and consistently declined multiple opportunities to accurately characterize Moscow's clearly negative role in undermining Ukrainian democracy and, therefore, willfully misrepresented election-related developments in Ukraine in order to avoid criticizing Moscow.[22]

The Kremlin's efforts to encourage a crackdown on democracy in Ukraine, to intimidate Ukrainian civil society, and to warn off European intermediaries who tried to keep the outgoing Kuchma administration on the straight and narrow were eventually met with a unified Western response focused on democratic principles and process, but the US role in that response remained muted, in service of the idea of cooperation with Russia that was, in fact, becoming increasingly unlikely in any event.

This muting of US condemnation—the absence of a forceful response to Russian meddling in efforts at democracy—represented a failure to deter Russia's malign influence. The failure to deter enabled and emboldened Russia.

Vitaly Haiduk, former secretary of Ukraine's National Security and Defense Council, has expressed a common Ukrainian view of the US: "What would have been their goal? Orange Revolution did not even affect the interest of the USA/EU. What did they do, even though Ukraine chose Europe? Nothing, nothing happened."[23]

Haiduk's criticism extends beyond the nature of US-Ukraine relations to decry the lack of any US strategic vision for bi- and multilateralism, revealing a deep Ukrainian skepticism about its relationship with the West ever having much utility—or any— compared to its relationship with Russia. Eugene Fishel, though taking a perhaps more balanced and nuanced view, arrives at a similar conclusion:

> The Orange Revolution ultimately became a poster child for President Bush's Freedom Agenda. But Washington did not press its advantage. In fact, the US government redoubled its efforts to engage Moscow, perhaps believing that it was possible to have it both ways, and despite the mounting evidence that Putin's Russia was utterly rejecting the liberal world order as envisioned in Washington. Though the US government went out of its way not to blame Moscow for its irresponsible behavior vis-à-vis Ukraine, the Kremlin clearly did not think this was sufficient when it came to leadership changes in the post-Soviet space, particularly in Ukraine.[24]

Even at critical junctures such as the Orange Revolution, US-Ukraine relations remained derivative of and consequently subordinate to relations with Russia.

And yet, for Putin, the outcome of the Orange Revolution undermined his aims for a Ukraine oriented toward Russia and demonstrated diminishing Russian influence and the lack of a Russian regional hegemony that he had tried so hard to recapture. As

D'Anieri notes, "Russia was vulnerable in a way that it had not realized, it had been humiliated, and it was determined to act. If many Russians had assumed that sooner or later Ukraine would return to the fold, the Orange Revolution raised the prospect that it might be lost permanently, and western interference was seen as being to blame."[25] One unintended consequence of the US policy not only of noninterference in Ukraine but also of non-criticism of Russian interference was that Russia was able almost immediately to declaim, unchallenged, a completely false version of events, in which the unseen hand of the United States had manipulated Ukrainian politics to bring about the Orange Revolution. From the blow to Putin's hopes for 2004, much conflict would now flow.

INSTEAD OF IGNORING Russia's developing narrative of US and EU interference, the United States might have attempted to counter the propaganda and condemn Russia's vilification. Principled support for democracy and democratization could well have been very effectively integrated into the Bush administration's Freedom Agenda and even added substance to that rhetoric regarding the post-Soviet space. Verbal support for a democratic outcome might have been backed up and nurtured by resources and direct attention to Ukraine.

Coming on the heels of antidemocratic moves within the Russian Federation against property rights and oligarchic interests, and following the violent suppression of a civil war in Chechnya and attacks on Russian civil society and opposition groups, the United States would have been sending the message that although undemocratic trend lines in the Russian Federation were internal affairs, and the US was not prepared to interfere in such affairs, it would counter Russia's attempts to export its undemocratic policy to former Soviet states that were seeking to chart a path toward democracy.

That was the road not taken. Instead, the consequences of the Orange Revolution led decisively, if at times circuitously, to the invasions of 2014 and 2022. The Orange Revolution was a more critical juncture in all of the key relationships than has been widely acknowledged. If US policymakers had abandoned, at that critical juncture, the short-termist habit of mollifying Russia as a priority and had insisted on asserting long-standing US and Western values along tough-minded, principled, neo-idealistic lines, the increasingly bold and even extreme moves Putin made later could have been deterred and a number of catastrophic crises forestalled. Instead, further missteps by the US and West, in the wake of the Orange Revolution, put Russia, Ukraine, and the West on a trajectory toward outright conflict.

The lessons that might have altered matters would not be learned over the next two decades—but that doesn't mean they can never be learned. The later they are learned, the more challenging their application; still, even amid the current crisis caused by Russia's disastrous 2022 invasion of Ukraine, US policy has the capacity to bring enduring regional stability.

CHAPTER EIGHT

RUSSIA REVANCHIST

Although it has become clear to me that the period in US-Russia-Ukraine relations beginning in 2005 initiated an inexorable slide toward war in Ukraine, unobstructed by the US seizing the opportunities to prevent it, I had no such clarity at the time. I was sure that we had not reached the end of history—that nation-state actors and great and regional powers still had a role to play in war and peace—but during the early days of the color revolutions and the Yushchenko presidency, I was a junior US Army officer, fully immersed in combat. I'd arrived in Iraq in the fall of 2004. I had deployments in Fallujah and Mosul.

Even while serving in Iraq, and with my work and study as a foreign area officer still ahead of me, I was by no means oblivious to the exciting events occurring in Russia and Ukraine in the early 2000s. I was glued to the reports of the corrupt election of Yanukovych in 2004; the hundreds of thousands who protested in the streets of Kyiv, the city of my birth; and the ongoing power struggles in Ukraine between forces of authoritarianism and democracy. In early 2005, when Yushchenko was inaugurated, I felt I had reason to hope for a Western-leaning democratic future for the country of my ancestry. Soon that hope, along with other career factors, would inspire me to change my Army career, studying Russia, Ukraine, and great-power relations generally. Once I began to gain experience in the region and in policymaking roles, I did come to see the conflict between Russia and the West as inevitable.

As with the George W. Bush administration in general, my own Army career in the early 2000s was driven, day-to-day, by the intensity of US focus on the Middle East, as well as on non-state actors like al-Qaeda and the Taliban, rather than the key threat to global security: Russian ambition and exceptionalism. Some of the US failure to face hard facts and make difficult decisions regarding Russia and Ukraine remains understandable, in light of the daily crises. The urgent overwhelmed the strategically important.

There would come a point, however, where the reality of Russia's aims and tactics regarding Ukraine and the region, and the fatal tendency of the US to apologize, on the one hand, for Putin's authoritarian and expansionist aims and actions and to hope, on the other hand, to crisis-manage them, should have become glaringly obvious to US policy analysts and policymakers. They didn't become obvious, because US officialdom has so often and so long tended to think transactionally and short-term, instead of basing decisions on values and long-term interests. If they had looked harder and negotiated harder, if better precepts—neo-idealist precepts—had guided US Russia and Ukraine policy, the West might have recognized the looming military threat following Russia's invasion of Georgia in 2008, forestalled the Crimea annexation and eastern invasion of 2014, and averted the full-scale invasion of Ukraine in 2022.

IN 2005, AS Serhii Plokhy has pointed out, the intensity of the blow Russia felt it had sustained from the Orange Revolution should have been hard to minimize. Gleb Pavlovsky, the top Kremlin political advisor, described that turning point as "our 9/11."

Putin's attitude had been made utterly clear by the failed effort to control the 2004 election. Given other recent acts of aggression, it was impossible for many Ukrainians to imagine Russia backing off. Vitaly Haiduk, former secretary of the Ukraine National Security and Defense Council, expressed a view representative of many Ukrainians who backed Yushchenko in 2004 and were supporting him as president in 2005. Russia differs from Ukraine, in Haiduk's view, because "Russians . . . were fine living under a Tsar."[1]

That sweeping characterization, reflecting the historic tendency of Ukrainians to cast their national identity in opposition to a supposedly Eastern Russian mindset—a mindset making Russia prone to authoritarian leadership and undemocratic government—played into the Ukrainian public's support for the new Yushchenko regime, which was pro-democracy, openly Western-aligned, and at least notionally anti-corruption. To both the Ukrainian and the Russian leadership, then, Yushchenko's victory represented a rejection of the Russian-backed corruption that had defined Yanukovych's 2004 presidential campaign.

Yushchenko and other Ukrainians were also keenly aware of the historic Russian-exceptionalist mythos regarding Ukraine, embraced by Putin and others, and the threat those beliefs posed to Ukrainian independence. Hence in part Yushchenko's revived drive, beginning immediately upon his inauguration in 2005, to both strengthen Ukraine's national identity internally and to make Ukraine a NATO member, which would end the threat of Russian attack.

The choice seemed to be stark. Ukraine, still operating outside the two available spheres of influence, could seek one of two things: some kind of accommodation with an increasingly aggressive Russia or reliable protection against Russia's obvious hunger to regain control of Ukraine. Although Ukraine's earlier efforts to join NATO, beginning in the 1990s amid the denuclearization process, had not succeeded by 2005, the Yushchenko administration, under no delusions about Putin's long-held dreams of a Russian imperial role in the region, and the critical importance in those dreams of a subdued Ukraine, had good reason to believe that only a full-scale, treaty-driven relationship with the West, backed by military power, could realistically provide appropriate security for an independent Ukraine. Yushchenko began pressing urgently for an invitation to join NATO, via a Membership Action Plan (MAP), a NATO program for providing advice, assistance, and support specifically designed for a nation seeking membership.[2] The MAP program, begun in 1999, had most recently been used in 2004 to admit Bulgaria, Estonia, Latvia, Lithuania, Romania, Slovakia, and Slovenia. That had been the alliance's biggest enlargement yet.

Only weeks after becoming president, therefore, Yushchenko traveled to Brussels and addressed a summit meeting of NATO members' heads of state. He formally announced that he wanted the attendees to see Ukraine as a future member of NATO. He framed the announcement in terms of a strong European and democratic alignment. Invoking the Orange Revolution, he expressed Ukraine's gratitude for the support of NATO's Parliamentary Assembly, which had witnessed, during the recent election, "the fact of falsification" and "contributed to the honest rerun of the voting. Your support," the president said, "has helped the Ukrainian democracy to win."[3] He called the election result a "European choice made by the Ukrainian people" and asserted that the future of Ukraine, which he again called European, was to be "inseparably linked" with NATO.

The officials gathered in Brussels seemed inclined to take the request seriously. In the 1990s, states that had been part of the Soviet Bloc but not, like Ukraine, part of the USSR and the Russian Empire, had feared that their own efforts to join NATO might be undermined by any connections with Ukraine's bid, which had been weak in any event; they'd withheld support.[4] Now, however, they feared having a Russia-controlled Ukraine—or an expanded Russian empire itself—on their eastward flanks and were ready to support Ukrainian membership. Certain key Western states, however, including Germany, France, and the Netherlands, were wary of admitting a country that had not yet successfully liberalized and gained control over corruption and doubtful that Ukraine was prepared to undertake the reforms necessary to align with the European Union and interoperate with NATO.

The entire effort was anathema to Putin. When Russia had earlier expressed openness to Ukraine becoming a NATO member, it had assumed Ukraine was nothing like the Europe-aligned democracy that had emerged from the Orange Revolution, over and against Russia's every effort to prevent such an outcome. Others argued persuasively that Putin's earlier openness to Ukrainian NATO membership was mainly an attempt to get an unreconstructed Russia-style government into NATO: a Trojan horse.

Either way, by 2005, Russia's calculation had changed. While in a press conference following his Brussels speech, Yushchenko called Russia "our strategic partner," and while he assured the world that "Ukraine's policy towards NATO by any means will not be against the interests of other countries, including Russia," the "European integration" he really envisioned was quite clear.[5] Putin could see it clearly. As early as the first month of 2005, the trajectory for conflict between Russia and Ukraine, nearly but not utterly inevitable at the end of 2004, was a step closer to being locked in.

In April 2005, Putin delivered a speech to the Duma—a watershed address. He announced what seemed to many observers a startling new direction for post-Soviet Russia. He didn't only reject, though still implicitly, NATO membership for Ukraine. He also rejected the Orange Revolution and the independence of all the former Soviet republics.

Putin began by revising the recent history of Russia and its neighborhood. "The collapse of the Soviet Union," he asserted, "was the greatest geopolitical catastrophe of the century. . . . Tens of millions of our citizens and fellow-countrymen found themselves outside the Russian Federation." The European twentieth century, it is worth remembering, had included two world wars; the murder of 6 million Jews; Stalin's murders, on a similar scale, of Russians and Ukrainians; the partition of Germany; and the absorption of Eastern European countries into the Soviet empire. Putin nevertheless claimed that as a result of the Soviet collapse, tens of millions of Russians now suffered in exile and oppression, and by implication they needed Russian support, even rescue.

Putin linked the story of the lost states to internal collapse within Russia, invoking the demolition of Russians' savings, the disbanding and, he said, hasty reform of beloved Russian institutions, the supposed capitulation to Chechen terrorism, the oligarchs' unrestrained pursuit of corporate interests, and mass poverty. His response was to announce a thoroughgoing effort to create efficiency in the corporate state: purging corruption, collecting taxes, controlling oligarchs, fighting crime, and stimulating economic growth.

In practice, many of those efforts would involve initiating an antidemocratic domestic policy, which centralized domestic controls in the Kremlin. Outside Russia he offered an international vision of the post-Soviet space, which, as Putin put it in the speech, included security of borders and the creation of favorable external conditions for resolving Russia's domestic problems. . . . It goes without saying that the Russian nation's civilizing mission in the Eurasian continent must continue. Its purpose is to ensure that democratic values blended with national interests should enrich and strengthen our historical commonality.

Also, for us the issue of international support in guaranteeing the rights of Russian compatriots abroad remains highly important. And this is not a subject for political or diplomatic bargaining.[6]

Despite references to democratic values, the message was surprisingly clear.

The speech naturally caused Yushchenko serious concern. "Putin called the collapse of the Soviet Union the worst geopolitical tragedy of the previous century," he later recalled, "so he wants to reestablish an imperial or pseudo-imperial state." Then, invoking the long history of Ukraine's place in Russia's imperial self-conception, Yushchenko added, "That empire needs Ukraine in order to exist."[7] Putin's deeply grievance-filled pronouncements, reflecting Yeltsin's sentiment, also made Ukraine the chief culprit in the Soviet Union's collapse.

US POLICYMAKERS TOOK little note of Putin's Duma speech at the time. It was easy enough to explain it away as presidential oratory aimed at his domestic audience. Plans to create efficiencies, fight corruption, and crack down on oligarchs might even have seemed anodyne. As Eric Edelman, then serving as US ambassador to Turkey, and therefore interested in Russia policy, recalls, "We did not pay enough attention to what was going on domestically in Russia. . . . There was, you know, a big foreign policy side. It was the Orange Revolution, ultimately not Iraq, that ultimately pushed Putin into a really directly adversarial position."[8]

US analysts also largely missed, therefore, the significance of Putin's announcements coinciding with a new development in Russian war doctrine—a development that directly involved the US, in that it looked back to the Cold War struggle between the US and the Soviet Union. While the term *hybrid warfare* was not fully identified and defined before the military analyst Frank Hoffman published his observations in 2007, the doctrine was taken up by Russia in 2005.[9] It refers to a military strategy employing well-synchronized, sophisticated blends of conventional and unconventional instruments of power, with traditional physical assaults on an enemy supported, and even at times superseded, by propaganda, disinformation, and, especially important in Putin's developing view, hidden interference in political processes, all of which can serve as highly effective tools of war and blur lines between competition and confrontation.

In taking up the hybrid warfare doctrine, Putin and his security services and the military were engaging in a process of mirror-imaging: they projected their own motivations on adversaries. Having failed to covertly control the 2004 Ukraine election, they presumed the Orange Revolution could have come about only through the malign influence of the opposing power, the United States. In analyzing the situation, they therefore concluded that the actions they would have taken to orchestrate it had been in play. They identified the protests and succeeding events as aspects of hybrid warfare against Russia, carried out by the US. They responded by taking up the hybrid approach themselves. It was to become Russia's next-generation mode of warfare.

By mirroring, Putin misread the situation. While US policymakers expressed strong interest in a free and fair 2004 election, it was by no means US policy to engineer or even vigorously support a Yushchenko victory. Even amid the fraudulence of the election itself, the Bush administration deliberately declined to criticize obvious Russian interference or express support for Yushchenko. To avoid criticizing Moscow, the US even willfully misrepresented developments in Ukraine. The overarching US goal remained preserving opportunities, however increasingly unlikely, for cooperative engagement between the US and Russia.

Putin, however, didn't just project his effort to fix the election for Yanukovych on the US and invent a US effort on behalf of Yushchenko; he also defined this imagined election interference as a move by the US to resume its old Cold War stance toward Russia. According to Robert Gates—in 2006, he would begin serving as Bush's secretary of defense—Putin believed this supposed US resumption of an old antagonism was a threat not just to his control over Ukraine and other republics but also to the internal stability of Russia itself. He believed the US was interfering in Russian elections, too, with a view toward regime change.[10]

However, because of the intense focus on the global war on terror, little note was taken by US policymakers and Russia experts at the time of this fundamental strategic shift.

Another move in 2005 escalated conflict with Ukraine. In further response to the Orange Revolution and Yushchenko's push for NATO membership, Russia raised gas prices. Reducing subsidies to the former Soviet republics reflected a broader policy, but the treatment of Ukraine was what Serhii Plokhy calls "selective," given the more favorable terms enjoyed by Belarus.[11]

The "gas wars" had started. Russia, as well as the Soviet Union before it, had been using oil, gas, and other commodities as coercive instruments. Now Russia turned to both gas-price hikes against Ukraine, to create internal instability by inflaming the struggling Ukrainian population, and supply cuts to Europe, to induce Europe to pressure Ukraine. By 2006, Russia had accused Ukraine of stealing European gas and used the accusation as a reason to drastically reduce supplies to Europe, potentially alienating the West from Ukraine.[12] Not surprisingly, in the face of all this rising tension, Yushchenko continued to press for a NATO MAP.

Then, in 2007, Putin dialed up his rhetoric to a level impossible for the US to overlook. In February, he addressed the future of Russia and Eurasia at the annual Munich Security Conference (MSC), a long-standing, well-regarded forum for high-level discussion of European and global security issues.[13] At that conference, in a speech often called "fire-breathing," Putin revealed to the world his vision of a newly imperialist Russia with a privileged sphere of influence. He also made known his willingness to use force to preserve that privilege.

Most memorably, perhaps, Putin directly attacked both the United States and NATO. Alleging that the United States had taken advantage of the collapse of the Soviet Union to make itself a unipolar, dictatorial power, he channeled controversy over the US war on Iraq, criticized by some Western powers for being pursued without UN Security Council authorization, into his railing against the US. The US, he said, "overstepped its national borders in every way. This is visible in the economic, political, cultural, and educational policies it imposes on other nations." He linked that criticism to conditions in Eastern Europe, explicitly objecting to NATO enlargement and casting Russia as expansion's victim: "It turns out that NATO has put its frontline forces on our borders. . . . I think it is obvious that NATO expansion does not have any relation with the modernization of the Alliance itself or with ensuring security in Europe. On the contrary, it represents a serious provocation that reduces the level of mutual trust. And we have the right to ask: against whom is this expansion intended?"

The Munich speech in an international forum revealed Putin's hostility to NATO enlargement and the United States, and signaled Russia's course change away even from its fitful efforts to integrate with Euro-Atlantic institutions and the dominant liberal democratic order. Ukraine's efforts to integrate with the EU, pursuit of NATO membership, and departure from Russia's sphere of influence triggered a Russian backlash and planted the seeds of a new Cold War.

Whether Putin believed what he was saying, or was merely using his rhetorical threats as a defensive tactic, is a matter for debate. But whatever confidence he may have had about acting on his assertions could only have been encouraged by the US response to his speech.

The near-complete nonresponse, that is. While Secretary of Defense Robert Gates aggressively defended US policy and criticized Putin's belligerence, a policy shift didn't occur broadly within the US government.

Not that experts and policymakers had no reaction internally. Putin's harsh criticisms of the US, combined with the memory of the April 2005 Duma speech, caused a change not in US policy but in US mood. The uneasy aspirations that had accompanied Putin's first term were now gone. The mood swung not toward a new tough-mindedness, however, but to a policy that former ambassador Nicholas Burns calls "hedging."

NEITHER THE OUTSPOKEN Putin of 2005 nor the assertive Russia he led was really new. Despite Russian leaders' avowed belief in Pan-European security, aspects of Russia's autocratic tendencies went back to 1993. While Putin's first presidential term had involved some authentic overtures to the West, that first term had also seen brutal conduct in the ongoing Second Chechen War, which some credibly argue was precipitated by bombings in Moscow orchestrated by Putin and his security services; the state takeover of Russian oil and gas companies; the subordination of media holdings to the state; the assassination of opposition members; and the continued interference in the internal affairs of the Newly Independent States (NIS). It was an ugly catalog of bullying and worse, and had precipitated the color revolutions against which Russia was reacting so strongly by 2005.

It is striking that during Russia's 2005 to 2008 shift—a shift mainly in the sheer blatancy both of the imperial claims and of hostility to the democratic revolutions and the US—Russia-skeptics in the George W. Bush administration remained unable to instigate any plan for countering Putin's provocations. His declaration of hostility naturally demolished the aspirational US mood about Russia. But as long as the conflict in Iraq went on, the Bush administration had little interest, attention, and muscle left for a robustly idealistic counter-policy to Russia's increasingly obvious aggression.

This strange persistence of a sort of limp realpolitik that was clearly less and less effectual—a situation that should have exposed the ineffectiveness of the realism approach in general—had a number of origins. The war on terror remained a paramount concern. Optimism about the "end of history" and the euphoria of the unipolar moment, with its attendant hubris about boundless US power, did not die overnight. As long as policy was focused on non-state actors, encouraged by the three "Axis of Evil" nation-states, Europe and even Eurasia seemed fundamentally politically stable by comparison, if vulnerable to terrorist attack, despite all of the escalating announcements and actions by Putin strongly suggesting the contrary.

So US policy tiptoed cautiously forward: as Burns puts it, hedging.[14] In his experience, Russia was clearly becoming less cooperative with the US, even in the area where our main interest in partnering with Putin seemed to lie: forming a solid global front against terrorism.

The US wanted sanctions on Iran and a continued concerted international effort in Afghanistan. Amid diplomatic efforts to develop those processes, the Russian counterparts now became what Burns calls "extraordinarily difficult." They began obstructing sanctions on Iran and withholding support for the US presence in Afghanistan. The US had said in 2001 that its efforts in the war on terror would require Central Asian airspace for only about two years, but in 2003 and 2004, US presence had only grown. Russian anxiety regarding control over what it considered its sphere of influence further diminished cooperation regarding the war on terror that the US had hoped for from Russia. At the same time, as Burns recalls, it remained unclear to US foreign-policy officials whether Russia was really in a position to carry out a successful invasion of a country like Ukraine or Georgia. Until that question was answered, in Georgia, the overwhelming US tendency to hedge was extended.

US Russia policy had moved very quickly to flip-flopping between hope and aspiration, however qualified, and fear-driven crisis management. That shift set a pattern for multiple US presidential administrations to come. Fixated on Russia, hoping too much and fearing too much from that country, the US largely ignored Ukraine, where there was much less to fear and far more realistic grounds for hope.

In January 2008, President Yushchenko and other Ukrainian leaders wrote to NATO in Brussels, asking to be approved for a MAP at the NATO summit scheduled for that April in Bucharest, Romania. The letter emphasized democratic values and Ukraine's "identifying itself as a part of the Euro-Atlantic security area . . . willing . . . to counteract common threats to security."[15]

President George W. Bush responded with a positive statement.[16] Robert Gates, however, then serving as secretary of defense, saw NATO membership for Ukraine as what he calls "a step too far" in the direction of guaranteeing Ukrainian security, antagonizing Russia, and risking crisis. While Bush felt the US was not in a position to obstruct Ukraine's desire to join the alliance, the apprehensive mood regarding Russia gave Gates and others in the administration no appetite for supporting and pursuing Ukraine's application. For officials now in crisis-management mode, NATO membership for Ukraine remained a topic to discuss, not an issue to act on.

And even as a discussion topic, the 1990s attitude persisted, as much as fifteen years old now, and far outrun by events: while there should of course be some security arrangement for Ukraine, that arrangement shouldn't be NATO. The attitude persisted in the face of, and no doubt partly because of, Putin's response to Yushchenko's letter to Brussels, which was to make threats cloaked in a tone of pain and regret.

"It is horrible to say and terrible to think that Russia could target its missile system at Ukraine," Putin said, "in response to such installations on Ukrainian territory."[17] Within a decade what was "horrible to say and terrible to think" had become a proven fact of life and death. And almost three years after Russia's full-scale war in Ukraine, the West still cannot bring itself to extend Ukraine NATO membership, fueling the perennial threat of war in Europe's largest nation.

CERTAIN FACTORS ON the Ukrainian side, too, helped drive the hedging, half-measure US approach. The US foreign-policy establishment lacked confidence in Yushchenko himself. According to Stephen Hadley, who replaced Condoleezza Rice as national security advisor in 2005, the US had hoped—despite weak support for his election—that Yushchenko would take a hands-on approach to bringing about change in Ukraine.[18]

Instead, the new president had turned out to be mainly an ideas person. He could rally public spirit, but when it came to policy, he needed a strong, detail-oriented implementer. Yulia Tymoshenko, his partner in the Orange Revolution, appointed prime minister in January 2005, had such capacities; however, Yushchenko dismissed the Tymoshenko government in September 2005, after only seven months, and accused the prime minister herself of causing economic slowdowns and being in the pocket of corporate interests.[19] She criticized him in return. The Orange Revolution coalition was splintering.

Another problem for Ukraine was that despite the success of the revolution, national identity remained in a state of flux, driven by regional differences. Despite the advances promoting Ukrainian language and culture, the east-west divide persisted in Ukrainian elections: the east was seen as pro-Russian, with a strong economic link to Russia, the west as nationalist and pro-Western, embracing what the Russians condemned as radical historical figures like the Nazi sympathizer Stepan Bandera.

The US failure to take Putin's 2005 Duma speech seriously, the decision to respond to the Munich speech with anxiety rather than action, the stalling of Ukraine membership in NATO, and, subsequently, the soft response to the Russo-Georgia War in the summer of 2008 exposed the fundamental flaw that had marked US policy for the region since 1993: an inability to make hard decisions in the face of Russian exceptionalism. Had the US kept values and interests firmly in focus, had it indulged less in ungrounded hope and fear-driven calculation, it would have navigated difficult situations with greater clarity and achieved greater security in the region.

This fundamental flaw in the US approach was borne out yet again in the spring and summer of 2008 at the Bucharest NATO Summit—and then when Russia declared war on Georgia later that year. On both fronts, the Western response only paved the way for further crises to come.

CHAPTER NINE

NATO MEMBERSHIP AND RUSSIA'S WAR ON GEORGIA

As the Bucharest NATO Summit of April 2008 drew near, Ukraine wasn't the only country seeking NATO membership. Other nations applying included Georgia, which, like Ukraine, bordered Russia, was a former Soviet republic, and had a deep history as a bridge between Eastern Europe and western Asia. In 2003 Georgia's own color revolution, the Rose Revolution, had made Mikheil Saakashvili Georgia's president. He had been educated in the US and Ukraine; as a West-aligned liberal leader like Yushchenko, Saakashvili harbored concerns, given Putin's election interference and the Duma and Munich speeches, about Russia's aims regarding his country's independence.

So by late 2007, both Ukraine and Georgia were explicitly asking for a MAP: a path to membership in NATO. The US position on MAPs for both countries, all-important to their success, was outwardly positive: President Bush felt an obligation to agree to a path to membership. Yet no hard push was being made by the US to influence resistant countries. Instead, many of the key officials, on both sides of the Atlantic, were concerned about the Russian response.

By 2008 Vladimir Putin had come to consider NATO membership for Ukraine and Georgia unacceptable. And yet the US position, persistently misreading Putin, remained that Russia could be induced to tolerate a westernizing Ukraine. Condoleezza Rice, then serving as secretary of state, recalls, "We believed that there was a narrow lane in which you could navigate both Ukrainian independence and strength and right and good relations or decent relations with the Russians."[1] Rice was looking to do the impossible. The task of strengthening an independent Ukraine and preserving a relationship with Russia was no longer achievable.

And yet, as Rice also points out:

Putin never bought that, and that really was the source of a lot of our difficulties in the relationship going forward. People say, You had problems with Russians around Iraq. . . . We didn't have a problem with the Russians around Iraq. All Putin wanted was that his oil contracts were secure. And he told me flat out, our problem was that he thought that the Freedom Agenda wouldn't stop at the boundaries of Ukraine, that we were really after Russia. And that's how he thought.[2]

Such was the queasy condition of US-Ukraine-Georgia-Russia diplomacy on April 2, 2008, when NATO officials and heads of state, including President Bush, gathered in Bucharest. Their agenda included the question of NATO membership: bilateral

NATO-Russia talks were scheduled for April 3, the second day of the three-day event. Not surprisingly, Putin too came to Bucharest to engage personally in the talks.[3] He was able to command significant attention not only for Russian positions on various issues between Russia and NATO but also for opposition to alliance membership for the countries on its borders.

The April 2 sessions involved a series of public and private meetings among heads of state and other officials, on a variety of topics, with a major focus on maintaining and improving defenses against terrorism in NATO's sphere.[4] When it came to providing MAPs for Ukraine and Georgia, the proposal was supported by the United States, Canada, Poland, Romania, Czechia, and the Baltic states.

"My country's position is clear," President Bush announced at the summit. "NATO should welcome Georgia and Ukraine into the Membership Action Plan. And NATO membership must remain open to all of Europe's democracies that seek it, and are ready to share in the responsibilities of NATO membership." Meanwhile, Russia's deputy foreign minister, Grigory Karasin, focusing especially on Ukraine, announced that if a MAP were indeed offered, a profound crisis between Kyiv and Moscow would result, damaging the security of all Europe.[5]

As the US had expected, beginning well in advance of the summit, Germany, France, Italy, Spain, the Netherlands, and Belgium dissented from the MAP offers, on various grounds that included significant corruption issues in both countries. There was also a sense that neither country was fully independent of certain influences of the Russia-dominated Commonwealth of Independent States: membership might bring a Russian influence into NATO. With critical countries like Germany and France in opposition, and with the US publicly in favor but internally wavering at best, the outcome was now predictable.

On April 3, the summit invited Croatia and Albania to begin talks that would lead directly to guarantees of membership in the alliance and announced that Macedonia would receive a similar invitation, once a solution to that country's naming dispute with Greece was resolved.[6] The summit did not offer a MAP to either Ukraine or Georgia but committed instead to reviewing that decision at the end of 2008:

> NATO welcomes Ukraine's and Georgia's Euro-Atlantic aspirations for membership in NATO. We agreed today that these countries will become members of NATO. Both nations have made valuable contributions to Alliance operations. We welcome the democratic reforms in Ukraine and Georgia and look forward to free and fair parliamentary elections in Georgia in May. MAP is the next step for Ukraine and Georgia on their direct way to membership. Today we make clear that we support these countries' applications for MAP.[7]

Or, as Robert Gates puts it, "We came up with some weasel wording that basically said, Well, we'll get you on the road at some point and so on."[8]

The half-measure announcement made at Bucharest—it came down to offering something now, and someday NATO but not now—fulfilled the unstated, ongoing policy of a Bush administration in conflict with the president's publicly stated position of support for the two countries' membership. The real policy was to push the issue off, in deference to fear of Russian reaction. The decision to offer membership to Croatia and Albania—countries not cast by Putin as Western-backed threats to its sovereignty—made clear to all concerned that the decision to postpone, at best, offering MAPs to Ukraine and Georgia was a direct concession to Russia.

At the same time, by stating that the bordering countries would indeed be NATO members in the future, the summit's announcement did nothing to assuage Putin's misinformed tendency to believe that the West was involving itself with Ukraine in pursuit of the old US Cold War aims of containing and deterring Russia. Eric Edelman, then serving as undersecretary of defense for policy, remembers his own commitment, in the face of Russia's objections, to a Ukraine-NATO policy of sheer hesitance: "I kept arguing that . . . we needed some other halfway house, because I didn't think either Ukraine or Georgia was ready [for NATO membership]. . . . I thought there was also a chance we would provoke Putin now, somehow."[9]

Yet Edelman also retains a clear view of the fundamental contradiction enmeshed in the Bucharest outcome:

We came out with, to my mind, the worst of all possible outcomes at the Bucharest Summit, because [the summit] didn't give a MAP, but they put into the declaration that . . . we're going to declare today that someday they'll be members. So for about five minutes, the Russians were doing the happy dance and slapping each other high fives, because they stopped MAP, until they read all the fine print in the communique and realized, Oh, my God, the alliance has now just committed to having Georgia and Ukraine in NATO.[10]

Putin's fears were thus further incited, while his own provocations—the expansionist ambitions that, since 2005, he had been anything but subtle about; his mirroring a new doctrine of hybrid warfare; and his threats against Ukraine in particular—incurred no cost to Russia at all. Indeed, the only lesson Putin might logically have taken away from the 2008 Bucharest Summit was that the kind of action he'd been taking, for the preceding three years, would be rewarded by Western concessions.

So when on August 8 of that same year, Russia made war on Georgia—the first European war of the twenty-first century, the first launched beyond its borders by post-Soviet Russia—the invasion might have come as no surprise.

And yet, to the US, it did.

IN APRIL, IMMEDIATELY upon his return from the Bucharest Summit, Putin initiated a conflict with Georgia by formally establishing relations with two regions, South Ossetia and Abkhazia, which had earlier seceded.[11]

The US response was muted at best, media coverage almost nonexistent. The strongest public statement criticizing Russia may have come from US senator Hillary Clinton, then campaigning for the 2008 Democratic presidential nomination. Given her later position as secretary of state under President Barack Obama, who won that nomination, Clinton's 2008 statement, about what she cast as major failures of the Bush administration with regard to Russia and Eurasia, remains especially interesting:

> Several weeks ago I called on NATO to extend a Membership Action Plan (MAP) to Georgia and Ukraine at the Bucharest Summit. I emphasized that this move would be a litmus test for the success of President Bush's leadership of the trans-Atlantic community. . . . I deeply regret President

Bush's inability to convince our NATO allies to take this action.

Now the Russian government has taken advantage of the lack of unity coming out of the Bucharest Summit to further ratchet up the pressure on young democracies on its borders. Moscow's actions this week to strengthen ties with the separatist regions of Abkhazia and South Ossetia undermine the territorial integrity of the state of Georgia and are clearly designed to destabilize the government of President Mikheil Saakashvili. . . .

I also call on President Bush to immediately send a senior representative to Tbilisi to show our support for the government of Georgia. The United States should raise this matter in the United Nations Security Council, in a special 26+1 session of NATO's North Atlantic Council (NAC), and in the NATO-Russia Council. Russia needs to hear a unified message from the United States and our European partners about our shared commitment to Georgia's security and territorial integrity. . . .

I am not advocating, nor do I envisage, a return to a new Cold War with Russia, which I believe ought to remain in the G-8, where the United States and its allies can together address our growing list of concerns with Moscow. But the current Administration's mishandling of Russian relations has contributed to Moscow's belief that it can do as it pleases. America and its allies can and must do better.[12]

Significantly, for the US response to the Russian recognition of Georgia's breakaway regions, this latest escalation by Putin was made amid a changing situation in Russia's internal politics. A presidential election was underway in Russia too, and because Putin was then barred constitutionally from serving a third consecutive term, Dmitry Medvedev, Putin's prime minister, was running to replace him.

The prospect of Putin leaving the presidency sent US policymakers swinging back toward the hopeful, aspirational mood of Bush's first term. Medvedev seemed more liberal and Western-aligned; despite Putin's enormous popularity, his prime minister was running for the presidency on a platform that seemed to many Western observers to reject the aggressive and authoritarian measures Putin had been pursuing.

And yet as early as December 10, 2007, Putin named Medvedev his favored successor. The incumbent president was expressing not just confidence in the prime minister's abilities but also personal trust, and Medvedev, in turn, announced that if elected president, he would appoint Putin prime minister. On December 17, United Russia, the conservative party led de facto by Putin, made Medvedev its candidate, and Putin's endorsement and projected leadership role made Medvedev the overwhelmingly popular choice. In early March, a month before the Bucharest summit, Medvedev was elected by a landslide. It was as a lame-duck president and a prime minister elect that Putin attended Bucharest. In May, Medvedev assumed the presidency.[13]

Putin now began a process of rejiggering the role of prime minister to centralize power in that office, violating both the national constitution and all historical precedent. Over his ensuing term, he would transfer much of the state's authority to the portfolio of the prime minister, undermining the presidency as an office, to the point where nervous Russia watchers had reason to believe— incorrectly, it would turn out—that he would remain in the supposedly secondary spot once his and Medvedev's terms were up. US officials nevertheless continued to hold out hope for a liberalizing

Medvedev presidency—hope that would, in fact, be borne out in a few instances—while doubting the president's independence of Putin, on whose coattails he'd been overwhelmingly elected. The US oscillated daily between hope and fear.

The suspense might have been relieved very early in the Medvedev presidency when, having recognized the secessionist regions within Georgia, Russia dramatically revealed its true intentions regarding its role in the region. On August 1, 2008, encouraged by Russia, South Ossetia began shelling Georgian villages. In response, on August 7, Georgian army units entered South Ossetia.[14] Russian troops had already secretly and illegally entered South Ossetia too. When the Georgian army established fire control over Tskhinvali, capital of the region, Russia declared that Georgia was engaging in genocide against the people of South Ossetia and invaded not just the contested regions but the whole country, by air, land, and sea. It called the invasion a peace-enforcement operation.

The ensuing war lasted only five days: a ceasefire agreement was brokered by France. Yet as brief as it was, the Russo-Georgia War involved significant destruction, including many hundreds of both combatant and civilian casualties and the displacement of nearly 200,000 people, along with the regional ethnic cleansing of Georgians. Georgia lost control of parts of South Ossetia and Abkhazia. Russia expanded a permanent military presence in both regions.

The conflict and its effects exposed just how emboldened Russia was by the timidity of US policy. Not constrained even by its stated military aims, which were entirely disingenuous, Russia exploited opportunity, opening a second front, attacking targets outside the contested areas, and blockading part of the Georgian Black Sea coast. It also employed its new doctrine of hybrid warfare; the use of media- and cyber-war in Georgia in 2008 has since come to be seen as marking an important development in twenty-first-century military conflict. Georgia, for its part, fought back with its own media blitz.[15]

The Russo-Georgia War achieved another critical success for Putin's long-stated goals; it ruled out, for the foreseeable future, NATO membership for Georgia.[16] Given now hot territorial conflicts over the legitimacy of borders, with Russia established militarily in South Ossetia and Abkhazia, the alliance would no longer consider Georgia's membership.

Other non-member former republics saw that NATO would not defend them in the event of Russian attack. It was starkly obvious to Ukrainians, especially, that they were now in clear and present danger. It should have been just as obvious to the rest of the world how far Russia was willing to go to defy the West and pursue Putin's dream of regional dominance beyond Russia's borders. Medvedev and Putin had responded to the Bucharest declaration by putting into action the lessons Russia had learned from US nonresponse to its many provocations. Inaction by the West invited impunity, producing deadly consequences.

THE US WAS caught almost entirely off-guard by the Russo-Georgia War. While the invasion had emerged directly from the Bucharest hedge of dangling but not offering NATO membership—gray zones are a green light for dictators—US officials had not anticipated it. Since 2005, an increasingly anxiety-ridden approach to policy had made it hard for policymakers to process what was suddenly glaringly obvious. Now one of the things the US had long feared—a Russian war of aggression—was a fait accompli not because the US had leaned too hard on Russia but because the US had dithered in a state of short-term, transactional tolerance and reaction, leading to delay and paralysis.

The Russian invasion of Georgia might thus have served as a much-needed wake-up call—an opportunity, however belated, to reassess the vacillating approach to post-Soviet Russia that had marked policies of both the Clinton and Bush administrations. But even with all the bloody evidence on the ground in Abkhazia and South Ossetia, that didn't happen. The US did contemplate various options. Its relationship with Georgia had in fact been far closer than that with Ukraine: President Bush had singled out President Saakashvili for praise; Georgia had deployed 2,000 troops to the war in Iraq; a road in Georgia was named Bush Way.[17] With the invasion ongoing, the New York Times quoted Georgians asking when the US was going to come help them. Saakashvili called Bush with what seemed an expectation of military aid. Sending US arms to Georgia was therefore considered at the highest levels. Bush made a strong-sounding statement of support for Georgia. Relations with Russia were temporarily cut off. When the administration sent humanitarian aid, the New York Times framed the use of US troops to deliver that aid as a major statement of support.[18]

In the end, however, the relationship with Russia, though deteriorating, remained the central issue. Any action that would have suggested to Russia that it would pay a price for its aggression in Georgia was deliberately avoided. Within six months, relations between the US and Russia had reverted to what they'd been before the war. It was as if it hadn't happened.

The US was even then in the midst of a presidential contest in which foreign-policy issues played an important part, especially regarding the war on terror. George W. Bush was term-limited out, and Vice President Cheney had declined to run. The parties' national nominating conventions wouldn't be held until late August and early September, but when the Russo-Georgia War broke out in August, and a US response was being publicly and privately debated, the shape of the general election was already clear.

In March, John McCain, senator from Arizona, had become the presumptive Republican nominee. Chuck Hagel, then a Republican senator from Nebraska, serving on the Foreign Relations Committee and the Intelligence Committee and soon to join the administration of President Barack Obama, recalls that with both major parties internally divided on so many issues, officials who were trying to process the meaning of the Russo-Georgia War felt bombarded by campaign politics. Having run against Bush in the 2000 primaries, McCain remained an outspoken opponent of the president on a number of policy issues, especially the benign view of Russia; still, for 2008, he naturally aligned himself publicly with his party's outgoing incumbent, who just as naturally campaigned enthusiastically on McCain's behalf. Intraparty tension, however, persisted.

On the Democratic Party side, Hillary Clinton, senator from New York and former first lady, had faced an unexpectedly hard-fought primary challenge by Barack Obama, senator from Illinois. In June, Clinton conceded and Obama became the presumptive nominee.

Regarding Georgia, on August 9, Obama spoke to Secretary of State Condoleezza Rice and Georgian president Saakashvili and then released a statement saying, in part:

> I condemn Russia's aggressive actions and reiterate my call for an immediate ceasefire. . . . As I have said for many months, aggressive diplomatic action must be taken to reach

a political resolution to this crisis, and to assure that Georgia's sovereignty is protected. Diplomats at the highest levels from the United States, the European Union, and the United Nations must become directly involved in mediating this military conflict and beginning a process to resolve the political disputes over the territories of South Ossetia and Abkhazia. . . . Russia cannot play a constructive role as peacekeeper. Instead, Russian actions in both South Ossetia and Abkhazia appear to be intended to preserve an unstable status quo.[19]

Obama's call for a ceasefire, humanitarian aid, and a diplomatic solution was very much in line with the policy the Bush administration was in fact pursuing, which would impose no noticeable cost on Russia. Despite campaigning as the candidate of change, the nominee of the party opposing President Bush departed very little from the long-prevailing, largely bipartisan approach to issues in Eurasia, in which policymakers of both parties continuously centered Russia. While Russian aggression was condemned rhetorically, supporting the principle of self-determination of the Georgian Republic, Obama's Russia position differed from Bush's only in calling for more positive and cooperative mutual engagement. Meanwhile Clinton, who had been virtually alone in calling out the Bush administration for dangerous failures at Bucharest, was by August campaigning for her former rival and said nothing in public to challenge the Democratic nominee.

It was John McCain, the Republican candidate, who called for a total change of direction in US policy for Russia and the region.

Regardless of the fraught politics of the election year, McCain made a major statement that stuck ruggedly to his long-standing opposition to the Bush administration's approach to Russia and the region. Looking back from 2024, and the disasters in Georgia and Ukraine, McCain's statement of August 11, 2008, is worth reading in full as a rare example of an official departing from the precepts of foreign-policy realism. It avoids any fuzzily unrealistic faux idealism, and instead lays out a values-based neo-idealist vision, supported by concrete calls to action:

> Americans wishing to spend August vacationing with their families or watching the [Beijing] Olympics may wonder why their newspapers and television screens are filled with images of war in the small country of Georgia. Concerns about what occurs there might seem distant and unrelated to the many other interests America has around the world. And yet Russian aggression against Georgia is both a matter of urgent moral and strategic importance to the United States of America.
>
> Georgia is an ancient country, at the crossroads of Eastern Europe and Central Asia, and one of the world's first nations to adopt Christianity as an official religion. After a brief period of independence following the Russian revolution, the Red Army forced Georgia to join the Soviet Union in 1922. As the Soviet Union crumbled at the end of the Cold War, Georgia regained its independence in 1991, but its early years were marked by instability, corruption, and economic crises.
>
> Following fraudulent parliamentary elections in 2003, a peaceful, democratic revolution took place, led by the US-educated lawyer Mikheil Saakashvili. The Rose Revolution changed things dramatically and, following his election, President Saakashvili embarked on a series of

wide-ranging and successful reforms. I've met with President Saakashvili many times, including during several trips to Georgia.

What the people of Georgia have accomplished in terms of democratic governance, a Western orientation, and domestic reform is nothing short of remarkable. That makes Russia's recent actions against the Georgians all the more alarming. In the face of Russian aggression, the very existence of independent Georgia and the survival of its democratically-elected government are at stake.

In recent days Moscow has sent its tanks and troops across the internationally recognized border into the Georgian region of South Ossetia. Statements by Moscow that it was merely aiding the Ossetians are belied by reports of Russian troops in the region of Abkhazia, repeated Russian bombing raids across Georgia, and reports of a de facto Russian naval blockade of the Georgian coast. Whatever tensions and hostilities might have existed between Georgians and Ossetians, they in no way justify Moscow's path of violent aggression. Russian actions, in clear violation of international law, have no place in 21st century Europe.

The implications of Russian actions go beyond their threat to the territorial integrity and independence of a democratic Georgia. Russia is using violence against Georgia, in part, to intimidate other neighbors such as Ukraine for choosing to associate with the West and adhering to Western political and economic values. As such, the fate of Georgia should be of grave concern to Americans and all people who welcomed the end of a divided Europe, and the independence of former Soviet republics. The international response to this crisis will determine how Russia manages its relationships with other neighbors. We have other important strategic interests at stake in Georgia, especially the continued flow of oil through the Baku-Tbilisi-Ceyhan pipeline, which Russia attempted to bomb in recent days; the operation of a critical communication and trade route from Georgia through Azerbaijan and Central Asia; and the integrity and influence of NATO, whose members reaffirmed last April the territorial integrity, independence, and sovereignty of Georgia.

Yesterday Georgia withdrew its troops from South Ossetia and offered a ceasefire. The Russians responded by bombing the civilian airport in Georgia's capital, Tbilisi, and by stepping up its offensive in Abkhazia. This pattern of attack appears aimed not at restoring any status quo ante in South Ossetia, but rather at toppling the democratically elected government of Georgia. This should be unacceptable to all the democratic countries of the world, and should draw us together in universal condemnation of Russian aggression.

Russian President Medvedev and Prime Minister Putin must understand the severe, long-term negative consequences that their government's actions will have for Russia's relationship with the US and Europe. It is time we moved forward with a number of steps.

The United States and our allies should continue efforts to bring a resolution before the UN Security Council condemning Russian aggression, noting the withdrawal of Georgian troops from South Ossetia, and calling for an immediate ceasefire and the withdrawal of Russian troops from Georgian territory. We should move ahead with the resolution despite Russian veto threats, and submit Russia to the court of world public opinion.

NATO's North Atlantic Council should convene in emergency session to demand a ceasefire and begin discussions on both the deployment of an international peacekeeping force to South Ossetia and the implications for NATO's future relationship with Russia, a Partnership for Peace nation. NATO's decision to withhold a Membership Action Plan for Georgia might have been viewed as a green light by Russia for its attacks on Georgia, and I urge the NATO allies to revisit the decision.

The Secretary of State should begin high-level diplomacy, including visiting Europe, to establish a common Euro-Atlantic position aimed at ending the war and supporting the independence of Georgia. With the same aim, the US should coordinate with our partners in Germany, France, and Britain, to seek an emergency meeting of the G-7 foreign ministers to discuss the current crisis. The visit of French President Sarkozy to Moscow this week is a welcome expression of transatlantic activism.

Working with allied partners, the US should immediately consult with the Ukrainian government and other concerned countries on steps to secure their continued independence. This is particularly important as a number of Russian Black Sea fleet vessels currently in Georgian territorial waters are stationed at Russia's base in the Ukrainian Crimea.

The US should work with Azerbaijan and Turkey, and other interested friends, to develop plans to strengthen the security of the Baku-Tbilisi-Ceyhan oil pipeline.

The US should send immediate economic and humanitarian assistance to help mitigate the impact the invasion has had on the people of Georgia.

Our united purpose should be to persuade the Russian government to cease its attacks, withdraw its troops, and enter into negotiations with Georgia. We must remind Russia's leaders that the benefits they enjoy from being part of the civilized world require their respect for the values, stability and peace of that world. World history is often made in remote, obscure countries. It is being made in Georgia today. It is the responsibility of the leading nations of the world to ensure that history continues to be a record of humanity's progress toward respecting the values and security of free people.[20]

One of the most notable elements in McCain's position was its focus on the future of Ukraine. Another was his referring to the war's perpetrators as "President Medvedev and Prime Minister Putin," giving the lie to the daylight that many imagined they discerned between the two leaders. Critically, McCain framed the conflict as ongoing: not a flare-up to be settled in the short term but an underlying problem that, in the absence of the West changing direction immediately, would only get far worse.

And like Hillary Clinton earlier in the year, McCain blamed NATO's withholding a MAP from Georgia for giving Russia a green light for invasion. He defied the fear-based approach, demanded the deployment of international peacekeeping troops in South Ossetia regardless of Russian reaction, and expressed willingness to put a reconsideration of NATO's relationship with Russia on the table.

Most importantly, McCain invoked values-based goals and long-term US and global interests. If Putin was envisioning a return in US policy to Cold War standoffs, the true purpose of what was often called McCain's toughness regarding Russia was to remove options that had incentivized Russia to act aggressively in the first place and induce it to accept its place as an independent nation in a liberal world order.

Neither McCain's warnings nor his aspirations gained any traction with the foreign-policy establishment in 2008. The realist school, operating across party lines throughout the Clinton and Bush presidencies, was quick to deride the statement as nothing but chest-beating provocation. According to McCain, Henry Kissinger, the father of foreign-policy realism himself, called him to say the speech had gone too far. As reported by the *New York Times*, Charles King, a professor of international affairs at Georgetown University, encapsulated the objections, blaming rhetoric like Mr. McCain's for encouraging "Georgia to try to push maximalist positions—'We've got to get this territory back at all costs, and if we get it back, the United States will support us.'"[21]

That viewpoint yet again made Russia the exceptionally critical player in the region, casting aspiration for sovereignty by the bordering countries as an unrealistic overreach. Revealingly, *New York Times* reporting also asserted that Obama and McCain were more or less on the same page on the issue. This was wrong. Chuck Hagel, noting that "you didn't have a particular leader in the Congress . . . that was really focused on these things except McCain," also recalls that McCain's statement was seen "as political, because he was running for president" and that most US foreign-policy experts remained "consumed with terrorism."[22]

The so-called realists yet again prevailed. McCain's cogent and pointed advice was not taken in 2008 and 2009—either by the outgoing Bush administration or by the incoming Obama administration.

On assuming the presidency, Obama did, however, announce a major change in US relations with Russia. He framed it as a move beyond the tension caused by the Russo-Georgia War, now supposedly resolved. The new policy, known as "Reset"—a symbolic mutual pushing of a button, shifting both sides instantly back to a starting point—in fact became a kind of US charm offensive on Russia.[23] If there was a reset, it was really in US mood, which swung back to the earlier aspirational hopes for a more liberal and cooperative Russia, a belief in Medvedev as a liberalizing force, and a resumption of a partnership in denuclearization and US efforts in Afghanistan.

Such, in any event, was the public face of the policy. Internally, watchers remained in suspense, both about Medvedev's independence from Putin and Putin's possible moves at the end of Medvedev's presidential term. Tellingly, few expected anything other than that Putin would resume the presidency at the earliest legal opportunity: no one expected Medvedev to be allowed to serve a second term. With the Obama presidency underway, the hope-fear wobble resumed. The US remained at once hopeful for unlikely improvement and poised to react, to reduce conflict, at all cost, emerging from whatever Russia might choose to do next.

WHAT WAS BADLY needed, in 2009, was not a "reset" of the relationship with Russia but a fundamental alteration of the US's entire approach to the region.

To some it was obvious that at each juncture leading up to and away from the Georgia war, the US operated under a misconception. In 2008, Putin had complied, pro forma, as we have seen, with the constitutional limit on his presidential term and was elected prime minister. But he never yielded and never intended to yield power. It quickly became clear to observers that he was the epicenter of state power in Russia, whatever his title, and that he intended to remain in that position.

The effects were keenly felt in the former Soviet space. By the beginning of 2010, with the Russo-Georgia War and the blowback from Western sanctions in the rearview, Putin's Russia operated with a growing sense of impunity. The rejection of its attempt to gain NATO membership had left Ukraine more vulnerable than ever to the ambitions of Russia, which now saw the NATO membership attempt itself as an ongoing insult and security worry, which could be terminated through military force. It should have been clear to US policymakers by now that Ukraine was critical to Putin's vision for regional hegemony—and that Russia was an opponent of the United States.

A true reset, in 2009, would have redefined the nature of American interest. In a long-range, values-based view, the Russo-Georgia War should have triggered not a charm offensive but durable condemnation and action, combined with an open, active, decisive effort to form far closer US relations with, specifically, Ukraine, as well as the other developing democracies struggling to break free of Russia's influence. Russia had no intention of following a path to become a "normal country," as Thomas Graham puts it—"a country lacking an empire." Critical to Russia's aspirations for a viable exceptionalism remained, above all, control over Ukraine.[24]

Ukraine meanwhile continued to serve as the principal geographical, military, and cultural bulwark against Russian aggression in the East. By 2009 it therefore ought to have been obvious that the real US interest, an independent Ukraine, was in urgent need of military and political support, not just eloquent rhetoric, as the stability of Europe on its Eastern flank was now under threat.

Instead, the Obama administration made a major effort to clarify that the Russo-Georgia War had changed nothing substantive in the US approach to the region. Though the Reset policy quickly proved meaningless, US policymakers continued to behave as if it was still the early 1990s and grounds for optimism existed about a newly democratic, post-imperial Russia. It was a fever dream.

Thus undeterred, Russia began making new moves, which would lead to a new regional crisis far greater than the Russo-Georgia War.

CHAPTER TEN

THE REVOLUTION
OF DIGNITY

One of Putin's key ambitions was the development of an integrated regional economic system, modeled on the EU. Putin's version was the Eurasian Economic Union (EEU), a project intended, as Serhii Plohky has written, "to bring most of the former Soviet republics under the leadership of Moscow," using economic, political, and military might to rebuild a Russian-led Eurasian power. Ukraine was "the cornerstone" of Putin's vision.[1] The EEU was intended to undergird a revival of Russian power and help Russia establish a Russian-Eurasian pole in the emerging multipolar world.

As early as 2003, under President Kuchma, Ukraine had signed an agreement to enter a Eurasian economic space.[2] Soon, however, as a result of the Orange Revolution, under Yushchenko, Ukraine had pulled out of that deal and was aspiring to join the EU, as was Armenia. The question of economic integration—should Ukraine go EU or EEU?—began to drive politics both within and between Ukraine and Russia.

The issue became especially heated leading into and coming out of Ukraine's 2010 election, whose outcome Putin had urgent reasons to want to go his way. In an effort to control that election, he would adopt revealing new tactics, whose effects were unintended, to say the least.

I CLOSELY MONITORED the 2010 Ukraine election, mainly as an observer and supporting planner for a large international and American monitoring mission based out of the US embassy. Even as a combat officer, I'd begun paying attention to the Ukraine-Russia relationship. Now I had an official foreign-affairs role, serving in the US embassy in Kyiv. In 2008, my focus had intensified sharply, as matters in Eurasia did too, given the armed conflict between Russia and Georgia, and I'd made a decision to change the trajectory of my Army career: I would compete to become a Foreign Area Officer (FAO), taking on the obligation to become a subject matter expert for a particular region and serve as a soldier-diplomat and strategic advisor to senior government officials for that region. That's how I began to gain a hands-on education in the nature of great-power conflict, especially with regard to Russia and Ukraine.

FAOs are drawn from all branches of the military to serve as experts in the political-military operations of, as well as conduct security cooperation for, specific foreign regions—hence "area," both in the geographic and the academic sense. As soldier-diplomats, they are trained academically and operationally to integrate all strategic, political, cultural, sociological, economic, and geographic considerations for US policy for their region. China looked, at the time, more benign than it does now, and with things changing so fast, and with the US-Russia relationship heavily fraught, I identified the major challenge in Eastern Europe, Russia, and Eurasia.

I spoke Russian and had both a facility for languages and an affinity with the history of my family's country of origin and the region generally. Conveniently, the US Army had just launched an in-resident FAO program for Ukraine, which I was selected for.

In 2008, I studied the Ukrainian language at the Defense Language Institute. I also began studying the history of the region, which would lead me to examine the nature of great-power conflict, especially with regard to Russia and Ukraine. By 2011, I had completed a master's degree in Harvard's heralded Russia, Eastern Europe, Central Asia studies program (REECA).

Equally important to my understanding was the regional immersion in 2009 to 2010. I was based in Kyiv in my role as an attaché to the US embassy in Ukraine. This was the first time I had set foot in the land of my birth since my family's flight from the USSR in 1979, when I was four. I traveled from Kyiv throughout the country, throughout the whole former Soviet space, and even to Turkey and China. The effect was life-changing.

Now I was monitoring the 2010 Ukraine election, on which Putin placed, yet again, such high hopes for the future of Russian regional hegemony. Going into that election, Ukraine seemed an unhappy shadow of what, as recently as 2005, at the outset of the Yushchenko administration, had looked like a country filled with exciting potential for democracy and anti-corruption reform, emerging from the Orange Revolution. The public was still both culturally and politically unified and divided in all the ways discussed earlier. The people's relationship to the government, however, was in a state of decline, based in large part on the failure of reform. That disaffection would have an impact on the election and the climactic events that ensued.

I saw that a major factor of the unwinding was the deteriorating relationship between Yushchenko and Yulia Tymoshenko, once his partner in the Orange Revolution. As president, Yushchenko—largely a big-ideas figure for Western alignment and liberal democracy—was an inspiring leader who rallied the spirit of a people but struggled to implement transformational reforms. Harnessing the spirit of the Orange Revolution for real change necessitated granular implementation, which was not among Yushchenko's passions and not easily accomplished from the office of the presidency.

The 2004 constitutional changes, a prerequisite for rerunning the election, had been specifically designed to undermine Yushchenko's ability to implement transformation, the result of another tragic Faustian bargain between pro-Western nationalists and pro-Russian factions. They devolved the presidential power necessary to implement reforms to a Rada and prime minister less apt to act and less bold in seeking reforms. And like the preceding bargains of the 1990s, they became a time bomb, blowing up the true reforms promised by the Orange Revolution.

Since Yushchenko was term-limited, Tymoshenko was the obvious 2010 presidential nominee to carry on the bruised, internally divided legacy of the Orange Revolution. She faced a serious challenge—and so, therefore, did the revolution's legacy—in the form of Putin's old 2004 candidate, Viktor Yanukovych. In 2004, he had run on his strongman Russia orientation, backed by Russian money and influence, and had tried to steal the election, triggering the revolution that brought in Yushchenko. In 2010, Yanukovych, again Putin's candidate, took a different tack. He hired Paul Manafort to direct his campaign.

A prominent US lawyer and lobbyist, Manafort had advised a number of Republican candidates for the US presidency. He would go on to serve as Donald Trump's campaign manager in 2016 and be pardoned by Trump in 2020 for convictions of fraud and witness tampering. In 2005, when he began working for Yanukovych, Manafort already had a long international history, beginning in the 1980s, of advising dictators; in the five years between the Orange Revolution and the 2010 election, he'd aided Yanukovych in consolidating the Putin-backed Party of Regions.[3] Beloved by the old, Russified business elites of Ukraine, Manafort brought experience with American electoral processes to coaching the sometimes thuggish Yanukovych in reshaping his image: new clothes, new hair, even elocution lessons. The aim this time was to win, not steal, a democratic election.

At least as important to the rebranding was Manafort's repackaging of Yanukovych's foreign policy. Where in 2004, the candidate had run more or less blatantly as a Russian-type tough, Manafort made him a changed man. The thug had become a reformer. He now offered a "balanced" policy of seeking economic prosperity for Ukraine through relations both with Russia and with the West.

So regarding the key issue of the day, economic integration, Yanukovych was not, on the surface, running against the possibility of a Ukrainian place in the EU; nor was he rejecting on general principles a place in Putin's EEU. That false transformation of Yanukovych was in fact an old and unhappy one for Ukraine, a repetition of the waffling of Kuchma, now in the far more volatile climate of sharply heightened regional tension following the collapse of NATO membership and the Russo-Georgia War.

The real electoral strategy for 2010 was simply to appeal to a slice of the center. For his efforts in developing and implementing that strategy, Paul Manafort was reportedly remunerated off the books by the Russia-backed Party of Regions to the tune of almost $13 million.[4]

It paid off. Yanukovych beat Tymoshenko—and it was clear to me and other election monitors that the 2010 election process was essentially legitimate. The win was narrow. The electorate was divided east-west, but the center was split, in part because the promise of Yushchenko had, in the eyes of many voters, failed. Given the lack of sufficient real progress on democracy and reform, enough central-western Ukrainians had grown disillusioned and apathetic. The liberal turnout fell. On the right, turnout was high, and as planned, just enough of the center went for the rebranded Yanukovych.

Despite Yanukovych's narrow success on a supposedly balanced but in fact Russia-centered policy, the momentum caused by the Orange Revolution was still propelling many Ukrainians toward a Western orientation unacceptable to Russia. Not surprisingly, therefore, given his background and his connections to Putin, the new president quickly put in place a repressive, highly corrupt, Russia-focused Ukrainian regime. He manipulated the legislature into shifting the focus of power back to the presidency. NATO aspirations were publicly renounced. Ukraine gave Russia's Black Sea Fleet a new twenty-five-year lease for its base in Crimea. The eastern, Russia-facing factions retained primacy and pilfered at will. Public funds were moved into the secret bank accounts of Yanukovych's family and friends. His palace, costing many hundreds of millions of dollars, was possibly the most flagrant example of his corruption. The country would soon verge on economic collapse, and to drive home his political point, Yanukovych had his electoral rival Yulia Tymoshenko arrested and imprisoned.[5]

One significant policy of the Yushchenko period survived, however: negotiating with the EU for a closer economic connection to the West. That continuation supposedly reflected Yanukovych's policy of East-West balance, but in fact the new president's supporters in his home region in the south—many were metallurgy oligarchs—wanted better access to European markets for their products. The EU was demanding political and market reforms as a price of developing relations with Ukraine; the oligarchs would have none of that. The EU also wanted Tymoshenko released from prison.[6] These conflicts soon had Yanukovych in a bind.

In October 2011, meanwhile, Putin had presented his economic vision for Eurasia in a widely read article, in which he claimed that new members would by no means have to choose between the EU and his EEU: membership in both organizations would make it possible to integrate all of Europe.[7] This was a mirage: the two systems were not reconcilable. Putin was envisioning Russia as the leader of a powerful economic union capable of competing both with the EU and with China. In March 2012, he was elected to a new term as president, and having regained the office, he restarted the constitutional clock and lengthened its term. It was clear that Russia would be led by Putin for the foreseeable future.

His priority had become achieving his economic integration plan, particularly with regard to possibly reluctant countries like Armenia and, especially, Ukraine, where he expected cooperation from his long-favored candidate, Yanukovych.

IN 2012, AMID these rising conflicts, I arrived in the heart of Putin's operation, Moscow. I had a new FAO assignment: assistant army attaché to the US embassy in Russia, under Michael McFaul, President Obama's ambassador to Russia from 2012 to early 2014, and then his successor John F. Tefft.

An attaché to an embassy observes and reports on the military and political activities of the host country and passes it up the line. I was therefore under constant surveillance and would have to track my trackers. In an authoritarian society, surveillance can be quite in-your-face: Russia's Federal Security Service (FSB), a successor to the KGB, will bug your residence and can enter it at any time. In preparation for the assignment, I'd been trained at the Defense Intelligence Agency's Joint Military Attaché School in attaché trade-craft. In Moscow I reported to Brigadier General Peter Zwack, a career intelligence officer and Russia expert.

One phenomenon took no tradecraft to see clearly. My first visit to Moscow had been in 1997, during Russia's wildest decade. Even on a brief visit to Moscow in 2006, when I was stationed in Germany, the city had been a scene of civic chaos: beat-up Ladas going the wrong way in traffic, cars parked four deep, wildly inflated prices. Order had since been restored. Returning for my fourth trip to Moscow, this time with my wife Rachel and our one-year-old daughter, we were relieved to find day-to-day life far calmer. Putin had made undeniably impressive improvements, reining in oligarchs and high-rolling criminals and establishing a sense of stability. His bringing the Chechens to heel gave much of the public a feeling of day-to-day security, amplifying his strongman reputation, adding to his domestic popularity, and easing resistance to his dangerous ongoing personal assumption of all state power.

Serving at the embassy, I found myself in the midst of Putin's increasingly emboldened policies for both Russia and the region. I also began to get my first sense of the effects of long-standing US policy toward Russia and Ukraine, as it was playing out in diplomatic and intelligence circles. Despite everything, that policy remained marked by transactionalism and buy-in to Russian exceptionalism. The year I arrived in Moscow saw a US presidential election that pitted the incumbent president Obama against Mitt Romney, the Republican former governor of Massachusetts. In March 2012, Romney told CNN's Wolf Blitzer, "Russia . . . is, without question, our number one geopolitical foe. They fight every cause for the world's worst actors." In the third presidential debate, Obama mocked Romney's depiction of the importance of Russian hostility: "When you were asked, 'What's the biggest geopolitical threat facing America?' you said Russia. Not al-Qaeda; you said Russia. And the 1980s are now calling to ask for their foreign policy back, because the Cold War's been over for twenty years."[8]

A little more than a year later Romney would be proven right, and Obama would look complacent. In 2013, however, once Obama was safely reelected, the old ways prevailed.

The US view of Putin and Russia was starker now, of course. Hopes for collaboration with Medvedev around the Arab Spring uprisings in the Middle East had been laid to rest. Putin had come back into office and was visibly consolidating power.

The idea, therefore, was to carry out another round of the "reset": more wishful thinking. My boss at the time, Ambassador McFaul, President Obama's reset architect—and a leader and scholar I deeply admire—was one of the leading proponents of the school of policymakers that continued to be governed by hopes and fears and driven by the Moscow factor. He is now a leading advocate for supporting Ukraine toward victory and managing the relationship with Russia conditionally, based on concrete actions taken by Russia to normalize relations with the West. McFaul may describe the evolution differently, but I perceive him as a convert to neo-idealism's adherence to the centrality of values to interests and the importance of navigating toward long-term policy aims. Having shed delusions regarding the direction and the automaticity of change in Russia, some policymakers are beginning to better understand how to prioritize the defense of our values in the US and in Ukraine, and how to spread them—and where not to, for now.

Amid the ongoing "reset" mode of the day regarding Russia, the US had no high hopes for Yanukovych's Ukraine, for obvious reasons. The fact that Yanukovych's electoral victory had resulted in part from the West not having made Ukraine a priority during the Yushchenko presidency played no role in US thinking; the administration continued to pursue the relationship based on the familiar hierarchy of interests: Russia number one, Ukraine lagging far behind. It's clear now that in 2013, while the US was pursuing its short-term, largely fear-driven policy for Russia, it was missing a crucial opportunity to assert Western values, bring about a genuine reset in policy for both Russia and Ukraine, and thereby obviate a series of disastrous events that, while they could never have been predicted with perfect accuracy, had become inevitable in the absence of such an assertion. After the Second Chechen War, the Orange Revolution, the blocking of the NATO MAP, and the war on Georgia, among many other missteps, it should have been evident that Putin's ambitions would make Ukraine the central issue.

For years, there had been reasons, possibly understandable if highly unfortunate, for the US to delude itself. Now the delusion, and the resulting failure to act, fostered what I have since come to see as malpractice.

Could the US have acted in 2013 to forestall the military aggression on the horizon? It may already have been too late. A change in policy from years of continuous drift to a genuinely assertive defense of Ukraine, which might have included military aid, was too bold a transformation in too short a time. Because time in a crisis is always short, the question was not even seriously addressed.

THE FLASH POINT for the decisive 2013 failure of US policy for Russia and Ukraine turned out to be the progress of Ukraine's EU association agreement negotiations. This time, the consequence of failure were more severe than ever.

Well into that year, Yanukovych had continued his throwback "balanced" policy of engaging in economic talks with the EU. Establishing a relationship with the EU was broadly popular among the Ukrainian people—and not only among Yanukovych's Western-facing opponents—who saw Europe as the path to prosperity.[9] The debate on the issue between the Russian-leaning and Western-oriented factions, and between Russia and Ukraine, was intense and highly public. In September 2013, while the talks were ongoing, my wife and I took a weekend trip from Moscow to Kyiv, where I was struck by the sight of a "babushka" in central Kyiv: seemingly a near-stereotype of the kind of pensioner who remained nostalgic for the days before the fall of the USSR. And yet she was carrying an EU flag to express her support for Ukraine's Western economic alignment.

The flag-waving was more than symbolic. Ukraine's Rada had overwhelmingly approved the progress toward joining the EU economy. In November, Yanukovych traveled to the EU summit in Vilnius, Lithuania—ostensibly with the purpose of signing the economic agreement.

Instead, he refused to do so. The talks broke off for good.[10]

Putin had used what Plokhy describes as a carrot-and-stick approach to get Yanukovych to end his relationship with the EU and join the Russian EEU instead: threatening Ukraine with an economic blockade while offering $15 billion not to sign the EU agreement.[11] Yanukovych told his entourage at Vilnius that Putin had told him that Russia would not allow the EU or NATO to share a border with Russia and that it would occupy Crimea and southern Ukraine if Yanukovych signed.

Putin's strong-arm tactic should not have come as a surprise to the West. Armenia had also been in negotiations with the EU and expected to sign at Vilnius until, in September, Putin bribed Armenia to drop the talks and then pressured the country to join the EEU instead.[12] By now, the US and the West as a whole should have been able to read Putin's designs and tactics clearly; the EU should have seen what was coming.

To most Ukrainian citizens, Yanukovych's sudden withdrawal from the EU agreement at Putin's behest came as a complete shock. Their leader had blatantly abandoned them in favor of the thug next door.

Instantly a robust and durable protest movement began.

Known as the Euromaidan protests, this movement mobilized thousands, soon tens of thousands, and ultimately hundreds of thousands of people in Kyiv and other major cities.[13] It began in Kyiv's streets and Maidan (Independence) Square and quickly spread. The protests continued, as not all protests in the region do, straight through the below-freezing months of winter. They represented a powerful challenge to Yanukovych's presentation of himself as a strong man.

Putin was pressuring Yanukovych, too—to crack down hard on the protesters. So he did, with a violent police occupation of Kyiv and Independence Square.

In response, what had begun as peaceful protest became a violent resistance. In the Maidan, protesters erected barriers with any materials at hand. Buildings burned; armed standoffs occurred. The cobblestones from the square, civilian vehicles, furniture, and tires became makeshift fortifications. Yanukovych directed riot police to disperse the crowds, and as police attacks and protesters' counter-attacks reached a crescendo, snipers opened up on the crowd.[14] Yanukovych had issued instructions to the security services and law enforcement to kill. One hundred people died at the hands of sharpshooters.

That only led to a further explosion of protest, which became the Revolution of Dignity: a full-on opposition not just to the president's rejection of the EU but to the entire Yanukovych administration and the Russia-inspired backslide from the Orange Revolution. Yanukovych and his inner circle, government ministers, and members of the pro-Russian bloc in the Rada were now in outright flight from the country. Power in the Rada therefore shifted, enabling a legislative revolution and the establishment of a caretaker interim government. The EU entered the scene to negotiate a settlement. New laws pulled police out of Kyiv, prohibited the crackdown on protesters, and, on February 21, removed Yanukovych from office.

That night, he fled for Kharkiv; there he briefly tried to pretend he was conducting a presidential tour of factories and said he planned to return to Kyiv. On February 24, however, Putin, though disgusted by what he saw as Yanukovych's weakness in cracking down and by his flight from Kyiv, sent Russian helicopters uninvited into Ukrainian territory to exfiltrate the Ukrainian president to Rostov-on-Don in southern Russia.[15]

The new Ukrainian constitutional settlement shifted power away from the presidency and into the Rada. Oleksandr Turchynov, a protest leader, took over the presidency temporarily. Elections were called for 2014.

And yet the armed forces of Ukraine, already enfeebled by decades of underinvestment and lack of reform, and then by Yanukovych's cuts and corruption, were now at their weakest: on paper they numbered only 70,000 personnel, one-third the size of when Yanukovych became president in 2010.[16] And the country was exhausted by turmoil.

Putin saw the opportunity he had spent many years waiting for.

He had long since made up his mind what his next move would be: military invasion.

CHAPTER ELEVEN

LITTLE GREEN MEN

Putin, both goaded by and taking advantage of the Revolution of Dignity, had likely decided to invade and seize Crimea well before he sent the helicopters to Ukraine to remove Yanukovych. The ensuing operation had all the hallmarks of an off-the-shelf plan, which may have existed ever since the collapse of the Soviet Union. The Ukrainian people's rejection of Russia's heavy-handed influence—and support for closing the gaps with the EU—provided the excuse; the civil upheaval severely degraded Ukrainian security forces; and chaos within the interim Ukrainian government created the opportunity. Putin seized his chance.

The Russian constitution prohibits the annexation of other nations' lands. While ten years later, Putin would openly and axiomatically define all of Ukraine "not a real country" and part of Russia, in 2014 he still felt a need to veil his ultimate goals and give himself a measure of deniability. He therefore tried to justify an annexation of Crimea using the same rationalization he had employed during the Russo-Georgia War of 2008. When South Ossetia declared independence from Georgia, Russia recognized the independence and then supported it militarily in supposed protection of the self-determination of an oppressed people. The ploy had masked Putin's true interest in Georgia: destabilizing a former Soviet republic, creating frozen conflicts and/or annexing its territory, exploiting chaos to increase influence, and terminating any possibility of NATO membership. It should have come as no surprise that Putin used a similar cover story in Ukraine in 2014.

While Crimea remained the only part of Ukraine with a majority ethnic-Russian population, all engineered by the Soviet Union, no Crimean movement to separate from Ukraine had been operating there for decades. The oppression of ethnic Russians in Crimea was totally fabricated. As far back as 1991, more than 54 percent of the population of Crimea had voted to separate from the USSR. Yet Putin built the cover story and pursued his irredentist objectives with such logistical adroitness and barefaced narrative falsehood that the US and the West yet again found themselves on the back foot. Putin conjured a sense of direct threat to the Crimean population by Ukrainian ultranationalists, thereby justifying a supposedly protective maneuver to safeguard a supposedly endangered people who "took to their weapons," in light of the removal of Yanukovych, Putin said, and "looked to us."

Another propitious factor, for his purposes, was the provisional nature of the temporary Turchynov presidency of Ukraine. Since elections were not due until later in 2014, Putin was able to suggest that the government in Ukraine lacked legitimacy. And division between the Ukrainian security services, so recently at war with the protesters, and a new government led in large part by those very protesters helped to further alienate the Ukrainian security apparatus, critical for an effective response to foreign military aggression, from the new and temporary political leadership.

Putin would soon even introduce claims that President Obama himself had betrayed an agreement to resolve the Euromaidan protests. He also said the US had instigated the protests and that the ejection of Yanukovych amounted to a coup, carried out with covert US support.[1] He was mirroring: attributing to the US the exact course of action that he would have instigated himself.

Characteristic of the Russian effort to take Crimea were the "Little Green Men," as they became known, who entered and took control of the parliament building in the Crimean capital, Simferopol, on February 27, 2014. Armed with Russian Kalashnikov rifles and wearing Russian military kit, they wore fatigues with no identifying insignias—hence their nickname.[2] The operation was highly professional, fully planned, and impressively efficient, especially at first.

That same day, legislators were rounded up from around town, forced into the parliamentary chamber, and required to vote on a measure to approve the installation of Sergei Aksyonov as the new prime minister of Crimea. Under the gun, the legislators elected Aksyonov, a career criminal and head of the Russian Unity party, which had won only 4 percent of the recent Crimean parliamentary vote.[3] To shouts of "Russia!" from outside the building, produced by crowds created and paid by Russia, the legislators also passed a call in favor of holding a referendum on fostering greater autonomy for Crimea from Ukraine.

That too was part of a necessary fiction for Putin. He wanted to make it seem that there was a local demand, begun apparently organically, for increased independence from Kyiv. Outright separation of Crimea from Ukraine was not yet publicly revealed as a goal. Russia meanwhile quickly engineered an independence movement, designed to seem grassroots, in a number of Crimean cities: a rally in Sevastopol for the return of that city to Russia, a rally in Kerch calling for the secession of Crimea if Ukraine were not federalized. Seen by Russia as a poison pill against coherent and effective government by Ukraine, federalization would devolve on each of Ukraine's twenty-six states all manner of authority, from legislation to tax collection to law enforcement.

The operation coordinated organized crime networks; compromised local police, SWAT, and paramilitary forces; and paid protesters to obstruct loyal local law enforcement. The goal was to paralyze any response to what was being represented as a spontaneous independence movement. As early as February 28, men in unmarked military attire, though clearly Russian special forces, seized the airports in both Simferopol and Sevastopol. All of this was accomplished quickly and effectively in the early days by plentiful Black Sea Fleet–based Russian security and intelligence services without, at first, open Russian military invasion.

Critical terrain had thus been seized, effectively by Russia, before Kyiv could mount any response. The impressive mix of planning and daring made it instantly clear to Ukraine's interim president Turchynov that Russia was sizing up the situation for the outright annexation of Crimea. The insight was confirmed when, meeting with his security council on February 28, Turchynov was interrupted by a phone call from Putin's ally Sergei Naryshkin, the longtime head of Russia's foreign intelligence service, then the head of the Russian Duma. Naryshkin directly threatened Turchynov: if Ukraine tried to suppress the uprising in Crimea, Russia would invade other parts of the country.[4]

The Ukrainian president and his security council also reasoned that the Russian-installed new officialdom of Crimea was acting on the orders of the Kremlin and its intelligence and security services, as well as coordinating with the Russian military, which had 40,000 troops and the big Black Sea Fleet massed in the peninsula. Both the Ukrainian army and navy were demoralized. Ukraine had only 15,000 troops stationed in Crimea, mostly recruited locally;

the extent of their loyalty to the government in Kyiv was compromised by the fact that their families and everything they owned were now under Russian occupation.

Turchynov and the Ukrainian security council held out hope for Western support. A US frigate, the USS *Mount Whitney*, was in the Black Sea, its stated mission to provide security for US athletes in case of a terrorist attack during the 2014 Sochi Olympics, recently held in the Russian coastal city. The US might be induced to send *Mount Whitney* into Ukrainian waters as an act of deterrence against Russia.

But such a move—assertive, from one point of view, precipitate from another—remained alien to US policy. *Mount Whitney* and other US ships stayed in the Black Sea, but they did not enter Ukrainian waters; by May, they would all leave the region. The idea was to avoid any chance of accident or miscalculation that might trigger a US-Russia confrontation. During the invasion's early days, Ukraine's top leaders reported American and German officials had expressly asked Ukraine not to use military force to defend Crimea.[5] Ukrainian officials ascribed this to a belief that Russia would take such resistance as an excuse to invade all of Ukraine; the West did not want that fight.[6] It was a foolhardy delaying of the inevitable, again giving Putin reason to believe that his boldness would be rewarded by empty European protests and little or no action. Serhii Plokhy explains the stark reality: "Without nuclear weapons, NATO membership, or an army to speak of, Ukraine had no way to stop the aggression."[7]

It's not as if Ukraine had wanted nuclear weapons. It had wanted the security against Russian aggression that such weapons' deterrent power would have provided. Ukrainians would have gladly traded away every warhead for the means by which they could have quashed their neighbor's imperial impulses: Western support.

But the denuclearization process of the 1990s had been followed not by a compensatory show of strength from the West on which Ukraine could count but by the drawn-out NATO-membership process of the 2000s that went nowhere, a consequence of the Russia-prioritizing habits of every US administration throughout the period.

Russia's 2014 invasion of Crimea thus exposed Ukraine's disarmament as a tale of great powers haggling over a vulnerable nation's fate in the face of that nation's protests and legitimate concerns about regional security. With fewer nuclear weapons, the world had been made slightly safer—yet parts of the world, their nuclear shields removed, were left far more vulnerable. That led to a scenario in which Russia waged empire-building projects that the West could not accept and must resist. Confrontation with Russia was merely delayed.

Because this escalation-averse, risk-sensitive approach is inspired by the existence of the nuclear arsenal that distinguishes Russia from non-nuclear authoritarian aggressors, the West has encouraged the idea that a nuclear arsenal is the ultimate security guarantee. Among vulnerable borderline democracies and authoritarian regimes alike, the denuclearization of Ukraine, permitting Russian aggression and making the West a victim of nuclear extortion, has only increased the desire to establish nuclear weapons programs, eroding Western nonproliferation efforts.

AT THE EMBASSY, I had a close-up view of what was going on in Russia. It was clear to me, and to others on the ground there, that the conflict in Crimea was not organic or spontaneous, not driven by genuine local concerns, but rather an operation plotted and manipulated by Moscow. The men in unmarked olive drab had been assembling as an invasion force months before they crossed the border.

From Moscow, I was also getting a close-up view of how the policy community in Washington was processing this new conflict. My duties as an attaché included focusing on all aspects of the Russian military, national security, and defense sectors. So it was my job to report my observations of the Russia-Ukraine conflict from within the Russian Federation. Everybody was shocked by the degree of violence involved in the invasion, and as events moved quickly and quickly became complicated, my reports were going to officials in Washington eager for on-the-ground assessments of Russian activity and behavior.

In early March, Putin engineered a referendum in which the Crimean people and their parliament asked Russia to adopt Crimea as Russian territory; on March 18, he asked Russia's legislature to approve a measure annexing Crimea and the city of Sevastopol. He was determined to secure Crimea for Russia while continuing to deny, for some time, that Russian conventional forces and matériel were directly involved in the separatist moves. And yet, putting forth a vision of "New Russia," Putin had begun the military effort to divide Ukraine that he would pursue for the next decade and exploit through full-scale invasion of the whole country in 2022.[8]

When the interim Ukrainian government got its bearings and recognized that Russia would not limit its snatch and grab of Ukrainian territory to Crimea, it regrouped, and Ukraine's elite Twenty-Fifth Airborne Brigade responded with force to separatist threats in the Donbas region of eastern Ukraine. The lead elements of the Twenty-Fifth were at first overwhelmed by paid protesters and forced to disarm; the next elements to deploy, better prepared for Russia's hybrid tactics, used force to disperse the crowds intended to impede Ukrainian forces and moved to secure critical infrastructure and government buildings. Ukrainian civil society resisted the invasion too, quickly moving to make up for the shortfalls of the Yanukovych-depleted Ukrainian armed forces, via material support and hastily assembling fighting units such as the Azov battalion. The population of Ukraine could clearly see the existential threat where much of the West did not. As in Paris in World War I, as in the British retreat from Dunkirk in World War II, the local people provided private vehicles, bicycles, body armor, anything else that might aid the war effort. Beginning in March and well into the summer, Ukraine managed to roll slowly forward against the Russian onslaught in the Donbas.

I had started taking weekly trips to the Russia-Ukraine border to observe what I could of Russian movements. I studied the maps and learned both the crossing points and quickest ways out. My operation was lightweight—usually just me and one other person. Under constant surveillance by both police and the Security Service, we would find a place to eat, sit unobtrusively, and look from Russia toward Ukraine.

What was I looking for? A smoking gun. I wanted to catch the Russian convoys of equipment and military advisors that I knew had to be crossing the border somewhere in support of the supposed separatists who were fighting Ukrainian forces in the Donbas.

One day I identified a good stakeout spot at a crossing where I thought we might have some luck: separatist forces were in total control right on the other side of the border, guarding the crossing. We waited and waited there. Finally, seeing nothing unusual, we gave up and started driving out of the area.

And there it was, rolling the other way down the busy two-lane road: a full Russian military convoy of troop transports, infantry fighting vehicles, and logistics vehicles with their lights off, heading for the area's main border crossing. We'd caught them. A Russian convoy was about to enter separatist-controlled Ukraine to participate in the fighting there.

But to really nail the discovery and to document what we saw, I had to photograph the trucks as they crossed the border. I was at the wheel, and as we drove past the oncoming convoy, I slowed way down, thinking of the police presence. If I started speeding, they'd have an excuse to pull us over. At a very slow, very legal speed, I pulled up, turned around, and started to follow the line of trucks.

Heavy traffic was moving quickly in both directions on the two-lane road. We knew the police were somewhere following us, and we could track the military convoy's movements not far ahead. To catch up, I was using the few breaks in the oncoming traffic to pass—slowly and legally—and move up, getting closer to the convoy.

I was executing one of those passes when a Security Service car appeared beside us in the right lane, staying alongside, refusing to let me back into the lane, forcing me to drive straight at the rapidly oncoming traffic. The driver was setting up a head-on collision, even possibly a deadly pile-up.

Before I could become a "regrettable accident," in the face of the oncoming vehicles' fast approach, I gunned the engine as hard as it would go, accelerated past the Security car, and swung back in line, right behind the Russian convoy. The Security car dropped back.

I thought we were out of the woods. But by dropping back, the Security car driver had shrewdly forced us into another dangerous situation—with far broader implications even than a terrible car crash. Moving at high speed, right behind the convoy now, traffic behind us evaporating, we were rolling straight toward the border and into an active war zone. If our front tires crossed as much as a fraction of an inch into Ukraine, we would be stopped by the separatists.

They wouldn't just question us. They would detain us. They would parade us as US spies. We would become an international incident.

At the last minute, I veered off the road into an empty parking lot and slammed on the brakes. We jolted to a halt.

I photographed the column of Russian military vehicles speeding off on the road into Ukraine. We had found the smoking gun.

IN MY REPORT, I included the photographs of the convoy heading into Ukraine. I'd been told that my observations were getting high scores, meaning they were considered valuable in Washington. More than once, they were included in the briefings to the president and national leadership.

By now I could identify a stark contrast between the intensity of the military activity I was tracking on the ground and the US diplomatic response. A crisis-management mentality still prevailed in the Obama administration. No great powers were to be inflamed; the US was not going to get precipitately entangled in a distant conflict. During Obama's presidency, a premium was put on thoughtfulness and contextualization, and Putin's claims might seem to have at least some historical legitimacy: Might Crimea really be rightly Russian? Was the 1954 Khrushchev transfer of sovereignty illegal? There was the referendum for Crimean independence. . . . All of that historical narrative, thoroughly engineered by Russia, was bogus. But it was diverting, and it made the US pause.

The fear factor played a role too. Putin indicated he would be prepared to defend Crimea with nuclear weapons.

So now we had reached a point where the West, as a direct result of prioritizing denuclearization in the 1990s, was threatened with nuclear war. The excessive focus on a potential threat posed by loose nukes had led to a situation in which ranks of Russian nuclear weapons were pointed at a poorly defended former Soviet state and the collective West. The weapons and delivery systems that had been transferred from Ukraine to Russia had never been neutralized; some of the heavy bombers that Ukraine transferred to Russia were now attacking Ukraine. The "realist" approach for achieving security through denuclearization had not brought about a real threat reduction but was only subjecting Ukraine and the West as a whole to a new kind of nuclear extortion.

If this was realism, then surely it was time to abandon it. The invasion of Crimea, a flagrant breakdown of all post–World War II norms, is precisely the point where, despite all earlier missteps, the West could have preempted the Russian invasion of all of Ukraine in 2022, an event whose likelihood was made substantially higher by the 2014 Western policy failure. As soon as the Crimea invasion began, confirming every tendency that Putin had been both announcing and carrying out since 2004, it should have become crystal clear—at very long last—that a drastic change in US policy for Russia, Ukraine, and the region was immediately required, if further Russian-irredentist disaster was to be deterred.

That didn't happen.

The difficulty the Obama administration faced was of course by no means entirely of its own making. That was precisely the problem. Acceptance of Russian chauvinism and imperialist, expansionary exceptionalism and the preference for transactionalism, which had begun with the administration of George H. W. Bush and in fluctuating ways transcended partisan divides throughout the three administrations preceding Obama's, created a powerful inertial force in favor of a policy approach that seemed, delusionally, the least dangerous. Obama tended to frame his political positions in idealistic terms; his presidency itself reflected an American ideal of progress in reckoning with and overcoming the toxicity to the body politic of the long legacy of slavery and American racism. With regard to Russia, Eurasia, and Ukraine, his gifts for speaking idealistically, and indeed for embodying idealism, did not foster a policy any more truly idealistic than that of his predecessors. The technocratic-sounding "resets" never came to anything.

A true neo-idealist approach requires not only a rejection of the anti-idealistic school of foreign-policy realism but also a rejection of the language of idealism when unsupported by the difficult, pragmatic actions necessary to effect real change and foster a more genuine and enduring stability. The West offered consideration; Russia brought guns. The US approach was duplicated by Angela Merkel, the prime minister of Germany, the leading power of continental Europe. That made it harder for the US to make a rapid and decisive policy switch equivalent to tearing up a quarter century of minute-to-minute crisis management that predated even Helmut Kohl and George H. W. Bush: Germany and the US reinforced each other's timidity in the face of Russian violence. Whatever risks may have been involved in jettisoning realism in favor of a muscular, assertive policy grounded in American values, we can easily see in retrospect that those risks have only drastically increased since 2014.

Inaction favored the tyrant. It made him look stronger.

So what would a neo-idealist approach suggest we should have done back in 2014? Practically speaking, the first move, that spring, should have been to severely sanction Russia and start arming Ukraine by sending weapons systems. Then the US and NATO should have started to adjust the force posture in Eastern Europe, signaling that the West was serious about taking steps to stabilize the declining security environment in Europe. Support for that policy should have prevailed in the Obama administration and throughout the West—a flat refusal to view developments in the region through the Russia lens.

And yet for literally years to come, all discussions of aid for Ukraine would focus exclusively on everything except giving the country the means to defend itself militarily. From the Ukrainian perspective, all the US did was take weapons away from them.

THE US AND the West did start to change policy toward Russia after the annexation of Crimea and occupation of Ukraine. Despite the failure to supply lethal aid to Ukraine, the annexation of Crimea and invasion of eastern Ukraine did expose the adversarial nature of Russia's relationship with the US. In 2013, as a military attaché, I had observed Atlas Vision, the last-to-date joint military exercise with Russia, conducted alongside a designated Russian peacekeeping force that, since the 2022 phase of the Russia-Ukraine war, has committed atrocities in Ukraine. In 2013, the US was still prepared to believe that Russia might be a benign power. In 2014, everything unraveled.

US embassy attachés, no longer just under heavy surveillance, now came under regular harassment. Ambassador McFaul himself was endlessly harassed by hostile, in-your-face news crews. There were tit-for-tat drawdowns in diplomatic personnel.

Then, in July, as violence in Crimea crescendoed, the passenger flight Malaysia Airlines 17 was shot down by Russian forces.[9] To a degree, this event served as a very belated wake-up call for the West regarding the seriousness of the military situation in Ukraine. Had the West and the US not been credulously clinging to the notion that conditions in Crimea reflected a local and limited rebellion—all reports from the ground to the contrary—civil aviation authorities would certainly have routed air travel around Ukraine.

They didn't, and with no warning, Russian forces shot down a passenger jet with an anti-aircraft missile, killing all 283 passengers and 15 crew. Russia denied any active involvement.[10] The US-Russia relationship further deteriorated. And yet despite this latest alarm, there was still no appetite in the West for providing Ukraine with anything but humanitarian aid. The response even to an event like the Malaysian Airlines 17 downing was simply to try to prevent a bigger blowup.

Meanwhile, the Russia-orchestrated and Russia-supported separatist rebellion was now underway in the Donbas region of eastern Ukraine, where the fighting was to go on for years. In order to combat a strong Ukrainian effort effectively liberating Russia-controlled territory, regular Russian troops, no longer disguised, entered Ukraine in the many thousands, prevailed over the still-reeling Ukrainian forces, and gained control over swaths of eastern Ukraine. On September 14, 2014, following talks held in Minsk, Belarus, Russia dictated to Ukraine an agreement for simmering down conflict in Crimea and eastern Ukraine, with leaders of France and Germany serving as mediators.

The US was conspicuously absent from the Minsk talks. The agreement was then followed up, also in Minsk, on February 12, 2015, with a so-called ceasefire based in part on Ukraine conceding self-government to certain eastern areas of Donbas.[11] Again, the talks went on without US participation, and with the ceasefire never materializing, the Donbas suffered eight years of hot war between 2014 and 2022.

Both of those hastily signed agreements were made when Ukraine was in a deeply vulnerable state; both lacked clarity regarding how Russia and Ukraine were supposed to implement the agreements' many tenets. US policymakers, having neglected responsibility, tried to explain away their absence on the grounds that the crisis was in Europe's backyard. Russia, alone at the Minsk table with secondary players, the real superpower not present, was further emboldened. It acted as the regional superpower; the US looked indecisive and weak. The French and German mediators, seeing Ukraine as a flyover country, took an even more extreme Russia-centering attitude than the US did.

With Ukraine having clearly signed the ceasefire terms under pressure, the flawed agreements led to a long series of further negotiations that would finally break down fully in 2020. In the meantime, Russia believed it had ensured that Ukraine would be a failed state, incapable of integrating with the West and eventually susceptible to returning to Russia's orbit.

AND SO THE point of no return came, in 2014, for all three of the key relationships: US-Ukraine, US-Russia, and Ukraine-Russia. Certainly, further important events occurred. The eight years between Putin's annexation of Crimea and his invasion of Ukraine saw Russian efforts to continue to divide Ukraine. The period saw further missteps by the US, compounded by the sheer policy chaos and grift fostered by President Obama's successor, President Trump.

Still, 2014 was decisive. Russia's military aggression threatened the vital US interest of preserving European security and stability. At that moment, the West faced an undeniable moral choice, unequivocally clear: a sovereign nation's territory had been stolen by a tyrannical neighbor; inaction was inexcusable. If the West really had an ethical worldview and wanted to sponsor a system of values in support of democracy, self-determination, and human rights, the 2014 invasion demanded that those values be backed up by strong deeds. Instead, nothing happened, and Putin won another round. US failure in 2014 presaged and contributed to the reduction in global security that would become more apparent with every passing year.

And yet, while historically climactic, the interests and values collapse of 2014 did not have to be absolute.

The final chapter of this book tells the story of a post-2014 laboratory, in which I was intimately involved, for making a dramatic change in US policy, not just for Russia and Eurasia but for the globe. The year 2015 saw the beginnings of a prototype for neo-idealism in US foreign relations.

How that policy was developed, and how it was not, in the end, effectively implemented with regard to Russia and Ukraine, leading to a failure to forestall the 2022 invasion, offers urgent lessons for the United States, as it faces the consequences of its long neglect of Ukraine and its own moral conscience.

CHAPTER TWELVE

NEO-IDEALISM MEETS PRESIDENT TRUMP

My deployment in Moscow ended in June 2015. Rachel and I bought a house in the northern Virginia suburbs—sight unseen, as military families often must—and we and our daughter moved in that month.

I had received an order to come home and serve as political-military advisor to the chairman of the Joint Chiefs of Staff, Joseph Dunford, at the Pentagon. The Joint Staff, directly supporting the chairman of the Joint Chiefs, the highest-level staff in the military, is made up of the most talented leaders of all branches of the armed services; the chairman directly advises the president and the secretary of defense. Neither a home posting nor an office job had been on my wish list, but the army, not the officer, decides where a serving soldier is needed.

This assignment turned out to be the best thing that could have happened for my professional development and my understanding of overall tendencies in US foreign policy that led to the missteps regarding Russia and Ukraine, fostering the disaster in the region that will require generations to repair. I took an official role, for the first time, in analyzing and trying to correct those tendencies, for the benefit of improving policy not just for Russia and Ukraine but for US relations globally.

At the Joint Staff, I joined a team of intellectually high-powered military officers and civilians helping shape military strategy and operations for US-Russia policy. Having come straight from Moscow, from Putin's invasion and capture of Crimea, and from the newly open hostility in the US-Russia relationship, I already had ideas. But only now was I truly in a position to begin developing the analysis that underpins this book.

So blatant was Russia's most recent violation that it opened up the possibility for new thinking in the US—indeed, it made new thinking essential. The military evidence of incursion, which we understood all too well, cut through some of the delusions that had marked diplomacy for so long. At long last it was plain that, in order to create a cogent strategy for dealing with escalating danger to our allies in the region, and thus to the US itself, we needed a new and better understanding of Russian motivations, goals, and psychology: a highly informed answer to Russia's naked aggression. Arriving at that understanding, and putting it into operation, became the most important part of my job.

The US-Russia relationship had settled in a place of deep mistrust. The US goal was to resolve mistrust and stabilize conflicted relationships as quickly as possible and move on to seemingly more pressing and salient issues in Europe and around the world—especially as the US was still attempting to extract itself from decades of war in the Middle East. It was now clear to me and others that stability can be a laudable goal, but not when purchased at any cost. Delusory deals based on false premises had led, it was finally obvious, to greater and greater instability. The US had been doing many things wrong.

In part that had come about by refusing to see what was before our eyes.

Russia does not by any means share US goals. For years, and again in the Crimea invasion of 2014, Putin had been using his trademark hybrid approach—traditional warfare combined with information warfare, propaganda, disinformation, election interference, economic coercion, assassination, and sabotage—to undermine core Western institutions and erode confidence in democracy itself. Just as he had engaged in projection and "mirroring" when blaming US interference for unwelcome election results in Ukraine, we too were projecting and mirroring. We presumed the Russians shared our interests. From that it followed that centering the Russia relationship, whether hopefully or fearfully, would lead to greater Russian cooperation in a rules-based order. It didn't.

The need for a total change in US thinking about Russia and the region became even more painfully clear in September 2015, just as I came to the Joint Staff. To further its self-promotion as the chief global opponent of the US, and to bolster the one regime in the Arab world friendly to its aims, Russia intervened in Syria.

So Russian and US troops were now operating in the same theater, not by proxy but directly, for the first time since the occupation of Germany after World War II, when we were allies. And the imbalance of US and Russian goals in Syria was dramatic. The US was there with the short-term aim of fighting the Islamic State (ISIL), while implicitly supporting Syrians demanding regime change from the despotic dynasty of the Assads; Russia was there to prop up the brutal regime, assert its influence in the Mideast, and obstruct the US. To further complicate matters, the US and Russia did have one shared aim in that theater: combating terrorist activities by ISIL. To that end, the US had to collaborate with Russia, which was simply weird: we were deconflicting military operations with a country that was now obviously an antagonist.

In November 2015, I was promoted to lieutenant colonel and took up an assignment given to me by Chairman Dunford, who wanted a national military strategy for the entire globe. My role in that project was to analyze the US approach to competing with and defeating Russia across the entire spectrum of conflict; put together and lead dialogue among the expert, cross-functional, cross-departmental teams required to develop and write the strategy; and then put the strategy into effect, encompassing scenarios from mere competition with Russia to outright conflict.

Every expert at the Joint Staff and at other levels, both civilian and military and across all branches of the armed services, was tapped for their knowledge. It was in gathering, coordinating, and analyzing the massive amounts of research involved that the themes I have been underscoring in this book emerged.

The analyses and strategies I put together in 2016 and 2017, based on my years of study and experience in Europe and Eurasia, and leveraging extraordinarily high-level input by so many experts, began to put an end to "end of history" thinking, which in the 1990s had replaced the significance of conflict between nation-states with the threat of terrorism and its rogue-state sponsors. It was time to put nation-state actors back at the historical forefront, in a new "four plus one" threat paradigm: Russia, China, North Korea, and Iran, along with non-state actors. For years, the National Military Strategy (NMS) had become a broad, public-facing document that offered anodyne strategic guidance for the military. The new NMS was to be different. Most of the document was classified. It provided clear guidance on the global threats facing the US military.

By the end of 2016, the NMS had identified Russia explicitly as the chief threat to the US for the following decade.

Theory now needed to move to practice, and the vehicle for that, in military jargon, is a Global Campaign Plan (GPC), holistic and comprehensive, embracing air, land, sea, space, information, electronic, cyber, and all other domains of warfare. To that end, with the encouragement of my superiors, I put together a team to look at the entire spectrum of our Russia relationship. We delved into how Russia fights, its military psychology, its use of hybrid warfare, and its long- and short-term goals. We gamed out scenarios from quasi-peacetime hybrid war all the way through nuclear war.

This project—a total rewrite of US military strategy for Russia—began in the latter days of the Obama administration, when we created the NMS, and continued after President Donald Trump succeeded President Obama in January 2017; the work was percolating upward even while still under development. In "the Tank"—meetings convened by the chairman of the Joint Chiefs to thrash out the biggest national security issues—I set it all out for General Dunford and others and prepped him for discussion on strategy with four-star generals.

General Kenneth McKenzie was then the director of J-5, the elite group at Joint Staff that proposes strategies, plans, and policy recommendations to the chairman to help inform his advice to the executive and representative branches of government; both General McKenzie and Chairman Dunford supported the new strategy. Soon the work made it up to President Trump's secretary of defense, General James Mattis, who marked it up approvingly.

When I was asked to brief highly placed members of the National Security Council (NSC), the coordinating body for security policy, the work came to the attention of Fiona Hill, then serving at the NSC as deputy assistant to the president and senior director for European and Russian affairs. She, along with General H. R. McMaster—Donald Trump's national security advisor—and General Jim Mattis and the Department of Defense counterparts to NSC staff, approved the new, hard-nosed approach. The work of the Joint Staff team and all its expert contributors had become the driver of strategy for both the Defense Department and the NSC.

In the summer of 2018, Dr. Hill brought me out of the Pentagon and into the White House to serve at the NSC, tasked with implementing the policy, which by now had been very well established in the bureaucracy of government. The National Military Strategy and the Global Campaign Plan had official approval from the entire national security apparatus, the Joint Chiefs of Staff, and the four-stars; the Department of Defense riffed off the NMS and GCP, drafting the National Defense Strategy; and the NSC used my work to draft the National Security Strategy and integrated plan for Russia. Such institutional "nesting," from macro to micro, signed off by all relevant agencies and departments, and made explicit in NSC documents, means a plan has the concurrence of the president regarding both the strategy and implementation.

We had achieved a genuinely fundamental alteration of US policy regarding Russia. The new policy rejected Russia's narrative of exceptionalism that had long enabled it to keep us in a fluctuating stasis of fear and hope. The policy instead promoted long-term US interests and Western values, with a view to ending the long, unhappy record of attempting to manage crisis after crisis while selling out the institutions of liberal democracy. Critical to the new approach was actively preparing for further Russian aggression. In 2018, when batches of Javelin anti-tank missiles were delivered to

Ukraine, the US was at long last providing that country with defensive weaponry.

However, it was clear that President Trump, though he had signed off on the National Security Strategy, likely hadn't read it and became by no means keen to challenge his Russian counterpart, Putin. At the NSC, I was the director for Eastern Europe and Russia, a portfolio that included Moldova, Belarus, and, crucially, Ukraine, a position I'd been given in part because I had presented Dr. Hill with a way of carrying out the aims of the policy that Trump had officially accepted. My strategy did not in fact necessarily depend on a direct confrontation. Instead, I proposed hardening the periphery: strengthening the independence and sovereignty of Belarus, Moldova, and Ukraine and deterring Russian aggression.

I GOT BELARUS wrong. My goal was to drive a wedge between Belarus and Russia, and I thought that might be accomplished by encouraging a policy of suspending US sanctions against Belarus— before attaching any conditions for reform. What I proposed was really a version of the old false-hope-and-excessive-fear paradigm: the hope was to entice Belarus; the fear was of a Belarus absorbed into Russia under a State Union Treaty. It was a classic use of a transactional approach—exactly what I had criticized and sought to expunge from our Russia policy. I was working ultimately for NSA director John Bolton, an exponent of the old realist school. He seized on this strategy for Belarus, and the outcome was of course not at all what we'd wanted. US policy sacrificed advancing democratization for an immediate benefit that failed to materialize, and Belarus engaged in violent suppression of democratic protests. By taking a realist approach that, yet again, didn't work, we got the opposite of what we wanted.

Vladimir Putin has a notable talent for reading the characteristic tropes and leanings of his Western counterparts and ruthlessly exploiting the hopes and fears that to him reflect nothing but timidity, indecision, and weakness. So in 2019, he must have relished the chaos that developed when the US process of arming Ukraine, which had hardened the Russian periphery for the first time since denuclearization, was abruptly thrown into utter disarray.

President Trump did not revert to the transaction-oriented, Russia-centering "end of history" approach. Instead, he and some of those closest to him stumbled into entirely new territory, unmapped by his strategic advisors or the NSC.

It seemed at first an inexplicably random move by the president to put a hold on nearly $400 million in US security aid earmarked by Congress for the defense of Ukraine. The hold was 180 degrees out from the stated US policy that the entire government supported, precisely contrary to US national security interests in the whole region, and contrary to Trump's own National Security Strategy. It also exposed Ukraine to an immediate, direct threat, further encouraging both Putin's opportunism and his belief that he could do whatever he wants as regards Ukraine.

So ended, at least for a moment, our brief effort to implement the mere beginnings of a neo-idealistic US foreign policy. That end, in 2019, was farce—it came not with a bang but a grift—but what followed, in February 2022, was tragedy.

I have written in my memoir, *Here, Right Matters*, and elsewhere about ensuing events both political and, to me, personal: Trump's impeachment for the high crime of abuse of power in using US aid to extort a foreign leader to interfere in our domestic politics; my testimony in that impeachment proceeding; the harassment, reprisals, and retaliation that forced my discharge from the Army, just as I was offered promotion to colonel. While those events were wrenching and disturbing, their importance to the case made in this book rests on the fact that throughout that period, no credible sense existed in US government that any policy for Russia and Ukraine, regardless of it having been signed off on by the president of the United States, was going to be followed at all, let alone imaginatively pursued by the president himself.

For Putin, this collapse signaled confirmation of his most baleful view of the United States and Western liberal democracy as a whole: weak, vacillating, untrustworthy, certainly nothing for authoritarianism to fear. The implosion of US policy under Trump involved a more base and chaotic failure than anything that had come before, but to Putin, the mayhem caused by Trump only ripped off the mask of high-mindedness and revealed endemic US hypocrisy. From the denuclearization carried out by George H. W. Bush and Bill Clinton to George W. Bush's global war on terror, from Obama's empty reset through Trump's low-life effort to trade US interests for personal benefit—transactionalism at its most literal and venal—Putin received the same signal over and over again. America's two political parties—Republicans the supposed realists, Democrats the supposed idealists—never really differed in any way that mattered to him.

Under Trump, a proponent of the most vulgar kind of grotesque transactionalism, US policy metastasized into something positively appealing to Putin. That a US president, and the entire Republican political establishment, was willing to forgive—sometimes even invite—Russian aggression all but eliminated any chance that, should Russia initiate a full-blown onslaught against Ukraine, the

US would do anything but acquiesce. The collective West would be the mouse that roared. While it would take time to organize an invasion of Ukraine—he wanted to get past the Beijing Olympics anyway—Putin was not about to pass up the opportunity the US was giving him.

JOE BIDEN WAS inaugurated president in the bitterly divided America of January 2021. In June, at a decidedly sedate summit between Biden and Putin, held in Geneva, Biden asserted that he would stand firm on defending democratic values, protecting the free press, and seeking justice for American citizens wrongfully detained by the Russian government.

That was a major rhetorical departure. The US president was signaling a muscular response to any further Russian attacks on the United States, including retaliation against future cyberattacks. He also seemed to be setting conditions that might constrain Russia's behavior.

Tough talk and reference to placing conditions on the relationship represented a decided improvement over the criminal incompetence of Biden's predecessor. Still, it remained unclear that the United States and its allies would remain united and clear-eyed in the belief that Putin was fundamentally an adversary who needed to be kept in check via unwavering toughness.

And just by holding the summit, the US once again elevated Putin to the world stage. That enabled him to burnish his credentials as a world leader. The US could have backed up Biden's rhetoric with new arms sales to Ukraine and other aid to the government in Kyiv. In 2021, all Ukraine got was a negligible number of Javelins and some Stinger tactical air defense missiles. By that December, Putin had meanwhile done two things: raise the tenor of anti-Ukraine propaganda and assemble nearly 200,000 military personnel along Ukraine's border, as well as tanks, artillery, and all manner of military equipment. The message was clear. We had been here before—with Crimea—and this was far bigger.

Undoubtedly, the US response could have been far worse—and would have been, had former President Trump been reelected. Biden made consistently powerful statements of US commitment to the safety of US citizens abroad, to defending NATO's eastern flank, and to Ukraine's rights of sovereignty, territorial integrity, and self-determination in the international system. The administration also marshaled unity among US allies. Biden spoke with Putin directly and told him the United States was prepared to impose punishing economic measures to protect Ukraine's sovereignty.

But Russia had amassed a $620 billion war chest, enough to weather the harshest sanctions.[1] Putin also had reason to expect that the penalties wouldn't be enforced, either by the Republican elected officials then cheerleading Russia and damning Ukraine or by the Democrats wavering because US allies in Europe would be hurt by them.

He'd heard it all before, and he'd never heard anything to suggest he couldn't with impunity repeat the bloody opportunism he showed when annexing Crimea and fighting in the Donbas region. Only preemptive sanctions, the posturing of forces in Eastern Europe, and the major transfer of weapons to Ukraine might have given him the signal not to act.

No such signal was given. One year into Biden's first term, Russia invaded Ukraine.

CONCLUSION

A NEW US FOREIGN POLICY

U S policymakers' faulty Russia-first approach to US-Ukraine relations has not always been defined by seeking purely transactional benefits (there have been successful nuclear arms treaties) or avoidance of harms to US interests (the West intervened to inhibit Russian support for genocidal regimes in the Balkans). The faulty policy has emerged from a more general perception, a prevailing fantasy that there was potential for Russian progress on everything from constraining rogue states to cooperation on climate change, despite a largely consistent pattern of Russian obstruction and a limited tally of successes.

So when US policy experts debated whether a condemnation of the Russian interference that resulted in the Orange Revolution might affect Russian support of the ongoing mission in Afghanistan, their deliberation was framed within the pattern of aspirational hopes and fears vis-à-vis the US relationship with Russia. The Ukraine policy team advocated for an appropriate response— but in the hierarchy of policymaking priorities, the Moscow decision-makers' voices carried the arguments. The lingering mood of Russian exceptionalism—focusing on Russia's sheer size, its nuclear arsenal, its military, its history, its Soviet legacy—meant that Ukraine policy was always derivative of Russia policy.

The bias toward Russia is thus deep and comprehensive and sustained by a general foreign-policy illusion in which great-power relations are reassuringly unchanging; Russian power, including its nuclear arsenal, is fearsome; and cooperation with Russia on a host of US policy priorities is within touching distance. In US-Ukraine relations, the bias is not just a bug but a foundational feature.

Nor has the magnetism of Moscow been the only influence on US-Ukraine policy. A general US conservatism with respect to change, especially concerning regional hegemons, has played a significant role. Only briefly, in the 1990s, did US interests regarding arms control, democratization, and regional stability for both Russia and Ukraine moderate the gravitational pull to Moscow and enable US policy toward Ukraine to be conducted on its own merits. Then, in the 2000s, the George W. Bush administration again gave the Moscow factor greater weight, in part because of the degraded US-Ukraine relationship, but largely because of those unreliable emotions, hope and fear: hope for good, productive relations with Russia with regard to the global war on terror, fear of US-Russia relations devolving toward a revival of the Cold War.

Consequently, just as Russia and Ukraine started to pull apart—evident in Ukraine's Orange Revolution and Russia's backlash revanchism—US policymakers missed the opportunities to bolster Ukrainian democracy against Russian irredentism and warn off Russia's increasingly malign influence, the precursor to Kremlin military aggression. In hindsight, policymakers failed to note vital clues: too many analysts excused Russia's growing aggression as the product of a status quo power just trying to hang on to its international and regional standing. In reality, Russia, if not in the 1990s, certainly by the 2000s, was a revisionist if not yet a revanchist power, lacking the strength to live up to its Soviet and imperial past yet retaining its nationalist elites and security apparatus, clinging to notional greatness, and biding its time until conditions were favorable to again subdue its neighbors.

The German chancellor Helmut Kohl recognized this in the 1990s. So did much of Eastern and Central Europe. Many states' security policies were designed to secure themselves against Russian aggression. Ukraine, by contrast, failed then to make the hard choices that would have allowed it to better integrate with the West and defend itself. Its history, as a vassal of the Soviet Union and the Russian Empire, meant it was not ready to pursue political reforms with the energy of Poland. A decade of independence, clarity over national identity, and external pressure from Russia were needed to diminish Ukraine's conservatism and propel its willingness to transform its politics. But as long as it was treated as something other than Europe, and as part of Russia's sphere of influence, Ukraine was vulnerable to Russian aggression.

Thanks to the delusional indulgence of Russia by US and Western policy, which began even before the fall of the Soviet Union, Russia was not meaningfully encouraged or incentivized to find a place in the liberal international order and was insufficiently discouraged from pursuing regional aggression, especially regarding Ukraine.

The bloody consequence was a European war that has already lasted longer than its nineteenth-century predecessor in Crimea.

If the US had begun deploying the tenets of neo-idealism thirty years ago, what would be different now?

There were of course no easy solutions. The hopes of the post–Cold War moment warranted an effort to embrace the post-Soviet Russia. Still, under a neo-idealistic approach, US-Russia policy and relations with the region as whole would have been governed, from the beginning, by closer attention to reality and some tough love. US and Western engagement would have been implemented on condition of reform and friendly steps: the more aggressive the reforms, the greater the support and access to Western resources.

A neo-idealist United States, recognizing the limits of its power and understanding that the orientation and stability of Russia and Ukraine would be determined by internal factors mainly beyond US control, would have better managed its many hopes and fears, instead investing in both willing and viable partnerships. This neo-idealist format for foreign relations would still have allowed for progress on critical national security needs like arms control: on that issue, both parties were agreeable. Such an approach would have nurtured a democratic Ukraine and warded off Russian aggression, serving both US interests and Western values.

Neo-idealism would also have proposed a different path in the Putin era. Russia's democratic backsliding and aggression abroad would have drawn a harsher response. In the aftermath of 2008, the neo-idealist perspective would have argued that embracing Ukraine in NATO would close the door on restive Russian military aggression. Even without NATO membership, the 2008 Georgia war and the aggression of 2014 demanded a hard-nosed response to Russia, as well as a significant investment in Ukraine and Georgia. A major investment in Ukraine after 2014, as well as a newly resolved effort to deter further Russian aggression, could have averted the geopolitical earthquake that is the Russia-Ukraine war. In 2016, the unclassified top line of the neo-idealist Russia strategy I authored set an objective: countering Russian malign influence and deterring

Russian aggression. Had that approach survived the chicanery of the Trump administration, we might be in a different position today.

The 2022 earthquake may, however, be just a warning sign of a much more significant rupture to come. What that might look like is terrifying: a proliferation of nuclear states and nuclear weapons, as the authoritarian world decides that the ultimate security guarantee is a nuclear arsenal; and Russia's continuing expansion—after realizing its trinity of a reunited Russia, Ukraine, and Belarus—making its next targets Moldova, Georgia, and Kazakhstan. The most dangerous challenge to the US will emerge if Russia is then prepared to test the integrity of NATO and attack the Baltics.

In the Middle East, the upheaval could see Iran with a nuclear arsenal emboldened to engage in a vicious proxy war, attack its neighbors, and threaten Israel with Armageddon. In the Pacific, China, having noted the lack of resolve by the West in support for Ukraine, could judge the US either incapable or simply unwilling to win a war and decide to use military force to realize its One China policy. Within only a couple of decades, the world's democracies, increasingly brittle from internal divisions, surrounded by a surging authoritarian world, could be drawn into an unavoidable military conflict from a position of significant weakness.

There's the catastrophe.

Such a catastrophe can still be averted. But old habits die hard.

Despite making democratic renewal a cornerstone of its domestic and foreign-policy agendas, and despite the fact that there could be no better way of demonstrating democratic resolve than by defending US values and interests in Ukraine, the Biden administration has repeatedly faltered. NSC officials sought to limit US military support for Ukraine, and their justifications sound pain-fully familiar. Amid the Russian war on Ukraine, the senior lead-ership of the US National Security Council under President Biden might as well have been a revival meeting of the Ungroup of 1989.

The overriding initial concern was that assertive US military support would be futile, as Russia was destined to win its war with Ukraine quickly. After that proved false there was still hope of a quick return to normalcy and fear that support to Ukraine would escalate tensions with Moscow and upset remaining hopes of rela-tions with the Kremlin, risking escalation to a Russia-NATO war. Just months later, after Russia withdrew from Kyiv and was kicked out of Kharkiv and Kherson, Biden's NSC believed that if Ukraine won too much, the war would pose significantly greater risks to the United States, and to global stability, than if Ukraine lost. Through-out the war, US officials have remained eager to avoid the collapse of Putin's regime—a throwback to preserving the stability of Gor-bachev, but this time with a Russian dictator who it's hard to imag-ine being replaced by a more harmful or dangerous Russian leader: the Ungroup's hope of achieving stability through support for the devil you know.

So even as President Biden pledged to give Ukraine all the sup-port it needed to win the war, his administration blocked the trans-fer of Soviet-era jets to Ukraine; declined to provide Ukraine with sufficient long-range air defenses to clear the skies of Russian planes; withheld the quantities of long-range rocket systems and munitions needed to destroy Russian targets within the theater of war; and halted discussion of the transfer of manned and unmanned air-craft required to neutralize Russian long-range attacks on Ukraine's cities. Fearing the same threats that the Ungroup identified three decades ago—nuclear proliferation, loose nukes, and civil war—and seeking to reduce the likelihood of a bilateral confrontation between the United States and Russia, the US greatly overstated the probability of both conventional and nuclear war between the US and Russia.

At the Aspen Security Forum in 2023, Jake Sullivan, Biden's national security advisor, put it this way: "While a key goal of the United States is to do the needful to support and defend Ukraine, another key goal is to ensure that we do not end up in a circumstance where we're heading down the road towards a third world war."[1]

Again we see the long shadow of excessive concern over how Russia might react to US policies. In fact, US-Russia relations have hit an all-time low. Nevertheless, the possibly of an active, deliberate confrontation doesn't really exist. War serves neither state's interests and risks mutually assured destruction. The real risk—courted precisely by the excessive concern that Sullivan expresses—lies in buckling to Russian nuclear extortion and a slide toward a bilateral environment ripe for accident or miscalculation, opening pathways to an unplanned and undesired confrontation.

While planning for contingency is of course the responsible way to manage national security threats, US action should not be determined by trying to avoid the least probable worst-case scenario. Obsessed with off-ramps and face-saving measures, the Ungroup's successors perpetuated indecision at the highest levels of the Biden administration regarding the Russian war on Ukraine. The time wasted on worrying about unlikely Russian responses to US actions would have been better spent resupplying our allies' weaponry, training Ukrainians on Western capabilities, and hastening arms transfers to Ukraine. To state what should be obvious: the US must do better with its strategic assessments and conduct more accurate forecasting and planning, so we aren't wrong so often, and our actions don't end up being a day late and a dollar short.

Some things have changed since the war began. The United States is slowly coming around to providing more of the right capabilities—but not in the necessary quantities, and not before US torpor degraded Ukraine's ability to hold and reclaim territory in southern Ukraine and the Donbas. In the prelude to war, where military support could have deterred Russian aggression, the NSC and the Department of Defense accepted the Russian narrative that resistance was futile and rejected my and many other former policymakers' counsel to supply Ukraine with weapons. Even after the war started, the NSC and the Department of Defense delayed and blocked support during the critical period when Russia was still reeling from a series of stunning defeats. In the second year of war, the Biden administration belatedly began to speak about a policy of Ukrainian victory on the battlefield but stopped short of backing up that rhetoric with the requisite military support.

By 2024, the administration had pledged or transferred weapons to Ukraine, but the assistance has been coming in dribs and drabs, with the administration dithering at every turn on the types and quantities of weaponry necessary to adequately support Ukraine. After months of deliberation, the Biden administration finally agreed to transfer high-mobility artillery rocket systems known as HIMARS, but until the spring of 2024, it refused to provide the longest-range munitions needed to hit deep military stockpiles. In the spring of 2022, Congress passed a Lend-Lease Act for Ukraine, reviving a World War II–era program that gives the president enhanced authority to lend or lease large quantities of defense hardware, but the Biden administration didn't make use of that authority before it expired in the fall of 2023. By the summer of 2024, the US was still conducting a crippling policy of providing weapons to Ukraine while only repairing and maintaining that foreign equipment, which was never before in Ukraine's inventory, in Poland. Ukraine is the largest country in Europe: a vehicle damaged at the front had to travel 1,000 kilometers to be repaired, the equivalent of transferring a car broken down in New York to Chicago for repair. The US should have led the effort to establish logistical and sustainment centers in Ukraine, as close as possible to the eastern and southern battlefields. A fundamental shift may yet start to take shape. In the spring of 2024, NATO member states, including the US, started permitting the use of Western-donated weapons against military targets in the Russian Federation. This is a significant step away from historical patterns driven by hopes and fears. However, major steps toward a neo-idealist approach, like drawing Ukraine into the EU and NATO, remain out of sight. There is no more important action that the US and the collective West can take to secure Ukraine and deter Russia than welcoming Ukraine into the EU and NATO. A Ukraine in NATO, in particular, closes the door on Russian military aggression.

And yet the West, still tethered to Russian exceptionalism and subject to fears of escalation, cannot seem to conceive of taking this bold step, mistakenly assessing the risk of escalation to an imminent conflict as too high. As long as the West remains plagued with these misplaced fears, the reality of a gradual march toward an inescapable long-term confrontation will exist.

THE FACT THAT six US administrations have succumbed to the same foreign-policy shortfalls might suggest that we are destined to keep repeating the same mistakes, leading to a global catastrophe. But that outcome is by no means inevitable.

Neo-idealism proposes a new path, based on a new idea: values are part of interests; interests derive from values; and accepting the primacy of values can provide the continuity that informs policies based on short-, medium-, and long-term interests.

History shows that neo-idealism suits the United States. Crisis seems to clarify the mind: FDR was able to pursue a Europe-first strategy even though it was the Japanese Empire that attacked the United States. Harry Truman was able to chart a course during the Cold War in recognition of the fact that our World War II ally of convenience had become a generational adversary. The Cold War and its existential threat of nuclear Armageddon resulted in a focus on long-term policies that cut across Republican and Democratic administrations.

But since the end of the Cold War, we have seemed to lack the kind of galvanizing, clarifying crisis that drives the focus to the long-term. But that's a delusion: we are in the midst of just such a crisis—the struggle between authoritarianism and democracy, between autocrats and democrats.

In failing to recognize this crisis for what it is, our senior policy-makers have neglected a critical opportunity to assert and act on our core values—to harden developed democracies, encourage developing and struggling democracies, and nurture democratic values and institutions more broadly. Distracted by the old fears, they've missed the fact that a Ukrainian victory would limit Russia's capacity for future military aggression and cement democracy's foothold in Eastern Europe, offering a powerful lesson to would-be authoritarian aggressors and democratic nations alike. By the same token, a Ukrainian loss would see an acceleration of the wave of authoritarianism and democratic decline.

The Russia-Ukraine war can be considered a world war. A large portion of the world, counted by landmass, is locked in a hot war between the largest country in the world and the largest country in Europe. War between Russia and NATO is being diligently avoided by both parties—but the risk remains that an accident or miscalculation could see a spillover. Either way, the overall risk to the post–World War II rules-based international order is the highest it has been since 1945. Allowing Russia to succeed in Ukraine will only hasten the more serious confrontation with Russia and China that the United States is hoping to avoid. The authoritarian world is watching this latest test by Russia closely; its consequences are likely to reverberate from the South and East China Seas to Taiwan and the Middle East. Noting a lack of Western resolve in defending vital national security interests, most notably Euro-Atlantic security, authoritarian regimes would continue to use salami tactics to eat away at security, expanding the terrain for day-to-day hybrid warfare and moving closer to threatening interests the United States would have no choice but to defend or risk ceding what it stands for.

There are certain places, partnerships, and relationships that offer a clear and sound logic for significant US involvement. A strong case can be made for US support to Ukraine. To any American, those fighting for freedom and democracy have natural appeal: the United States lives up to its values by supporting Ukraine. Even from the realist point of view, an affirmative plan building on strategic relationships, including the one with Ukraine, is the best basis for long-term success in great-power competition.

But there is an even more important neo-idealist justification for far-reaching US support to Ukraine. Ukraine is an agent of change. A prosperous Ukraine makes an illiberal, undemocratic, and authoritarian Russia unviable in the long-term. The Kremlin recognizes that a successful Ukraine imperils Vladimir Putin and Putinism itself. An independent, prosperous Ukraine also undermines the Kremlin's strategic goals and rhetoric. Without Ukraine, Russia cannot sustain an imperialist, revanchist narrative of the so-called unity of the ethnic-Russian and Russian-speaking peoples. An example of a successful democracy in the cradle of eastern Slavic

culture, history, and orthodoxy could induce Russia's general population, if not its elites, to see a framework for democratic transition
applicable and palatable for themselves.

The historian Timothy Snyder, of Yale University, has defined
the stakes in the Russian war against Ukraine in the starkest terms.
"Russia, an aging tyranny, seeks to destroy Ukraine, a defiant
democracy," Snyder writes.

> A Ukrainian victory would confirm the principle of
> self-rule, allow the integration of Europe to proceed, and
> empower people of goodwill to return reinvigorated to
> other global challenges. A Russian victory, by contrast,
> would extend genocidal policies in Ukraine, subordinate
> Europeans, and render any vision of a geopolitical European
> Union obsolete. Should Russia continue its illegal blockade
> of the Black Sea, it could starve Africans and Asians, who
> depend on Ukrainian grain, precipitating a durable inter-
> national crisis that would make it all but impossible to deal
> with common threats such as climate change. A Russian
> victory would also strengthen fascists and other tyrants,
> as well as nihilists who see politics as nothing more than a
> spectacle designed by oligarchs to distract ordinary citizens
> from the destruction of the world. This war, in other words,
> is about establishing principles for the twenty-first century.
> It is about policies of mass death and about the meaning of
> life in politics.[2]

BOTH THE REALIST-SCHOOL, interest-based approach, which sacri-
fices values, and the naive, liberal-idealist, rhetorically values-based
approach, devoid of interest, have proven disastrous for US foreign

policy. Hence neo-idealism's call to action: face the reality of our current crisis, with its potentially catastrophic ramifications, and utterly reverse the long, disastrous tendency that has brought us here.

This call to action is categorically different from others, because neo-idealism departs from both foreign-policy realism and naive liberal idealism in focusing neither on the cynicism of short-term transactions, nor on the mirage of hope, nor on the despair of fear, but on achieving what is achievable. Now is the moment to shed our hubris—the belief that sheer US power and force of will can overcome the absence of a willing partner and allow us to pursue aims and advance interests anywhere we choose. We must shift from an aspirational policy to an outcome-driven policy, prioritizing relationships with willing partners. We must assess risk on longer time horizons and avoid making the short-term decisions—risk-reducing yet interest-harming—that destabilize strategic relationships.

The reality is that our adversaries and our friends have agency. They may even have the final say on how our bilateral relationships unfold. The US has been on the one hand too certain of success in the absence of good partnerships, on the other hand deeply reluctant to run ahead of allies. When Germany and France rejected inviting Ukraine into NATO, in Bucharest in 2008, we did not vigorously push our agenda; we followed their lead. The US should be prepared to lead—to advance our own and collective interest, pushing not toward autonomy but toward consensus.

We should assess relationships with adversaries over both the short and the long term. Given that Russia has been, is, and will continue to be an unwilling partner, and even an obstacle to achieving US national security interests, the West must be prepared for a new era of containment. At some point in the downward trajectory of the bilateral relationship with Russia, the United States should have prioritized its relationship with Ukraine above its relationship with Russia. We have an opportunity to make that correction now.

We also have an opportunity to make new investments in other parts of the world, based on the lessons learned from the Russia-Ukraine experience. Russian exceptionalism kept the West from engaging with and advancing the sovereignty of Ukraine. The lesson of that failure should be applied globally. If the US is to advance interests with existing and struggling democracies that share our values, not with authoritarian regimes unlikely to reconcile their worldview to ours, that will mean pivoting, now, toward relationships that the United States has historically deemed of lesser importance but in fact offer opportunities to significantly advance our national security interests. The US should not, for example, be meeting with the Chinese just for the sake of meeting. Russia and China have successfully used salami tactics—taking small slice after small slice—to erode security and advance aggression. A US priority for the next seven to ten years should be greater cooperation on strengthening South Korea, Japan, and Taiwan.

Many other applications of foreign-policy neo-idealism can be made in the service of strengthening liberty and democracy and fending off the tyrannical impulses now stalking our century. The history of missteps in US policy for Russia and Ukraine demonstrates the folly of realism, and while it is now very late to abandon our folly, it's still not too late.

A RECKONING FOR THE LIBERAL WORLD ORDER

The dawn of this second Trump administration marks a somber turning point for America and the world. The America First doctrine is poised to solidify into a chilling, isolationist creed. The Trump administration's withdrawal from global responsibilities, coupled with its relentless fixation on short-term gains, signals a deliberate dismantling of the liberal, rules-based order America once upheld. What remains is an opportunistic, unrestrained form of "realism" that bears little resemblance to the tempered pragmatism of the past—a new policy that abandons allies, disregards shared values, and undermines partnerships painstakingly built over decades.

The America that was once a stabilizing presence on the global stage looks to retreat into a fortress, closing its doors to the world and inviting a dark vacuum to form in its wake. This vacuum left by the absence of any credible, benign power will almost certainly be filled by ruthless authoritarian regimes eager to carve out spheres of influence through military force and political subversion. Nations that once relied on the United States for security and support now face a bleak future, negotiating with regimes unsparing in their ambitions and unbound by principles of restraint. Russia and China, in particular, stand ready to reshape the world in their own image: a world where power is absolute, dissent is crushed, and borders are redrawn at the whims of the strong.

Trump's vision is not merely a rejection of the neo-idealism that seeks to elevate values in US foreign affairs; it is an embrace of calculated chaos. While Trump's policies may appear impulsive, they are deliberate in their disavowal of any coherent strategy beyond transient, transactional benefits. These decisions shatter the foundational tenets of American foreign policy that have held sway since World War II. The previous six administrations, for all their flaws, believed in some measure of containment and support for allied nations. Even the most restrained realists saw value in engagement and recognized the necessity of America's role in the world as a check against authoritarian expansion. Today those checks are vanishing, replaced by a doctrine that prioritizes immediate returns—often serving Trump's own personal or political gains—over the survival of a stable global order.

Yet there are elements of Trump's approach that may, paradoxically, yield unintended benefits. His temperament, an implicit embrace of "madman theory"—a strategy that portrays him as unpredictable and potentially willing to escalate at any moment—may introduce a measure of deterrence against adversaries' adventurism. The prospect of engaging with an erratic, volatile US leader could dissuade states like Russia or China from testing the limits of aggression. This form of deterrence comes with significant risks, including the potential for miscalculation or escalation based on misinterpretation of intent, which could spiral into broader conflicts. And adversaries cannot fail to notice that Trump, operating with a simplistic conception of avoiding conflict, is often eager to appease powerful rivals.

Meanwhile, Europe will face mounting pressure to take its defense into its own hands. US withdrawal from its traditional leadership role could prompt European nations to allocate greater resources to defense and deterrence, warning off an aggressive Russia emboldened by American isolationism. A coalition of the willing may emerge among European states, doubling down on their support for Ukraine's war effort. This coalition could go beyond existing commitments, potentially establishing an air defense zone over eastern Ukraine to counter Russian missile and drone strikes, as well as deploying Western trainers on the ground to bolster Ukraine's operational capacity. While these measures may not compensate fully for the loss of direct US involvement, they signal a recognition of shared responsibility in the face of Russian aggression.

The Biden administration's deeply flawed Ukraine policy of incremental support—always a day late and a dollar short, dominated by misplaced caution and fears of escalation—left Ukraine vulnerable and emboldened Russian aggression. But Trump's doctrine, stripped of even that minimal sense of responsibility, takes the missteps to an entirely new level, actively undermining US alliances.

This is not a recalibration. It is a repudiation of America's role in the world and a clear signal that deterrence of aggression is no longer a goal—perhaps not even a consideration.

The consequences of this approach are dire. A hostile order dominated by autocratic regimes will rise in place of the one America leaves behind. Allies who relied on American support will be forced to fortify themselves against an onslaught of new threats. Europe's nascent security initiatives, which gained momentum after the first Trump administration, may evolve into a more robust collective defense architecture independent of NATO. In East Asia, where a revanchist China asserts itself with growing confidence, new coalitions may emerge to counter its aggression—alliances that form without US leadership and perhaps even without its participation.

While these developments may offer hope for regional resistance to authoritarianism, they also underscore the long-term damage inflicted on America's credibility. Rebuilding trust with allies will require navigating a world where these new coalitions have grown in America's absence. The next administration will inherit not just a fractured global order but also allies wary of America's reliability, forcing future leaders to reconcile with alliances forged out of necessity rather than shared values.

As we weather the storm ahead, we must consider how American foreign policy might evolve after the second Trump presidency. A return to neo-idealism may serve as a guiding principle for piecing together a broken world. The neorealist approach, rooted in the belief that our values are our interests, offers a way forward not only consistent with America's highest ideals but also essential for long-term stability. Future leaders will need to demonstrate a clear commitment to alliances, the rule of law, and collective security, rebuilding what has been lost and forging a new path that transcends the transactionalism of the present.

A personal note: as someone who served in the heart of America's foreign policy apparatus, I have seen firsthand the strength of alliances built on trust and shared values. Watching these bonds fray under the weight of isolationism is profoundly disheartening. Yet history shows that leadership can rise even from the ashes of self-inflicted wounds. The task before us is daunting, but it is not insurmountable.

The story of American foreign policy has always been one of reinvention, learning from failures and striving toward a vision of a better, more stable world. Let us hope that, in the aftermath of this dark chapter, we find the courage to once again lead with purpose, principle, and resolve.

ACKNOWLEDGMENTS

My family originates from Ukraine. While we are unsure how far back that family history goes—two world wars, a revolution, and the Soviet regime effectively destroyed the history of the region's Jewish peoples predating 1917—our family history indicates several branches of my family settling in Ukraine after fleeing Eastern Europe's oppression of Jews sometime in the second half of the nineteenth century. My dad, my older brother Len, my twin brother Eugene, my maternal grandmother, and I fled Ukraine—then a part of the Union of Soviet Socialist Republics—as refugees in the summer of 1979 when I was three years old. Family lore puts us on the last flight out of Kyiv prior to the Ukrainian Soviet Socialist Republic's cancellation of Jewish refugees' flights in response to deteriorating US-Soviet relations following the USSR's invasion of Afghanistan.

None of this work would have been accomplished without the critical contributions from family, friends, and mentors. To start, I want to offer a general thank you to my colleagues that, throughout my career, contributed to this thesis. This includes people I have served with in and out of uniform in military assignments, in postings to the embassies in Kyiv, Ukraine, and Moscow, Russia, and in the White House on the National Security Council. Thank you, Povilas Strazdas, Taft Blackburn, and Generals and Admirals Zwack, Manero, McClintock, Wood, Tarsa, McKenzie, Clarke, and Dunford. Thank you for your continued service, George Kent and Laura Cooper, you are amazing public servants. Scott Roenicke, Matt Dimmick, the NSC Europe team, and the many people at the Department of State, thank you, your impact on my professional development has been immense. A special thank you to Fiona Hill, a model scholar and senior policymaker, I very much appreciate your mentorship and friendship. I hope I've made you proud. Thank you to the amazing scholars Paul D'Anieri, Ambassador Steve Pifer, Professor Serhii Plokhy, and especially Dr. Gene Fishel for your foundational scholarship on Ukraine. Thank you to international relations scholar Ben Tallis for your groundbreaking work on the theory of neo-idealism. I'm glad that my thesis could in some way add to that work. Thank you to the distinguished public servants that I've had the privilege to work with, Ambassadors Fried, Herbst, and Vershbow. Thank you to all of the interviewees, in both the United States and Ukraine, for your contribution to this work and for your distinguished public service. An enormous thank you to all of the readers of this book, your feedback greatly improved the work. Dr. Jane Vaynman, representing the smarter portion of the family, you have been invaluable counsel to my efforts and helped demystify academia and the process of writing a dissertation. Dominic Cruz Bustillos, Adam Stein, and Justin Tomczyk, my research assistants, thank you for helping organize interviews and coordinating schedules, especially during the field work. Thank you also to Kurt Campbell and all of the other benefactors of my studies and Eliot Cohen without whom my studies at Johns Hopkins, in the School of Advanced International Studies (SAIS), would not have been possible. Thank you to Jon Young and Professor Matt Kocher. Matt, I am enormously grateful for your support, professionalism, and guidance. Of course, thank you to Johns Hopkins and the SAIS Foreign Policy Institute, where I have been both a student and faculty for the last few years. Thank you to Ben Wittes and David Priess and the entire Lawfare team for welcoming me as a Senior Fellow, you all were lifesavers. Thank you to Jennifer Pritzker, the Pritzker Military Foundation, and the Pritzker Military Museum and Library for supporting my work. Thank you to my distinguished thesis committee, Professors Hal Brands, Michael McFaul, and Mary Sarotte. You are all amazing scholars and offered not only suggestions and advice, but patience and understanding. This work would not be what it is without your guidance. Ambassador McFaul, thank you for your many years of service, your contribution to understanding Russia, and for encouraging me to pursue my desires to serve on the NSC. I've likely missed key contributors and inspirations to this book, my apologies, but also a big thank you for your contributions. A special thank-you to my dad for pushing me and to my twin brother for his support. Lastly, and most importantly, thank you to my wife Rachel and daughter Eleanor. Thank you immensely! I will now be more available to you!

SELECTED LIST OF INTERVIEWS

UKRAINE

Presidents

Leonid Kuchma (1994–2005): written responses to interview questions; Kyiv, Ukraine; August 18, 2022.

Viktor Yushchenko (2005–2010): recorded in-person interview; Kyiv, Ukraine; August 27, 2021.

Oleksandr Turchynov (acting president, 2014; secretary of the National Defense and Security Council, 2014–2019): recorded in-person interview; Kyiv, Ukraine; September 9, 2021.

Ministers of Foreign Affairs

Kostiantyn Gryshchenko (2003–2005, 2010–2012; ambassador to Russia, 2008–2010): recorded in-person interview; Kyiv, Ukraine; August 25, 2021.

Pavlo Klimkin (2014–2019): recorded in-person interview; Kyiv, Ukraine; August 30, 2021.

Vadym Prystaiko (2019–2020): recorded Zoom interview; September 21, 2021.

Secretaries of National Security and Defense Council

Volodymyr Horbulin (1994–1999): recorded in-person interview; Kyiv, Ukraine; August 30, 2021.

Vitaly Haiduk (2006–2007): recorded in-person interview; Kyiv, Ukraine; August 25, 2021.

Konstantin Yeliseiev (2016–2019): notes from in-person interview; Kyiv, Ukraine; August 26, 2021.

Oleksandr Danylyuk (2019): recorded in-person interview; Kyiv, Ukraine; August 27, 2021.

Head of the Security Service of Ukraine

Ihor Smeshko (2003–2005): recorded in-person interview; Kyiv, Ukraine; August 27, 2021.

Others

Ostap Kryvdyk (senior policy advisor to the speaker of the Verkhovna Rada, 2016–2019): recorded in-person interview; Kyiv, Ukraine; August 26, 2021.

Hanna Hopko (chair of the Committee of Foreign Affairs, Verkhovna Rada, 2014–2019): recorded in-person interview; Kyiv, Ukraine; August 30, 2021.

UNITED STATES

President

Bill Clinton (1993–2001): recorded Zoom interview; July 8, 2022.

Vice President

Al Gore (1993–2001): recorded Zoom interview; December 17, 2021.

Secretary of State

Condoleezza Rice (2005–2009; national security advisor, 2001–2005): recorded Zoom interview; October 11, 2021.

Secretaries of Defense

William Perry (1994–1997): recorded in-person interview; Kyiv, Ukraine; September 27, 2021.

Robert Gates (2006–2011): recorded Zoom interview; December 1, 2021.

Chuck Hagel (2013–2015): recorded in-person interview; Kyiv, Ukraine; December 1, 2021.

Assistant to the President for National Security Affairs (APNSA/National Security Advisors)

Stephen Hadley (2005–2009): recorded Zoom interview; November 15, 2021.

Jim Steinberg (deputy national security advisor, 1996–2001; deputy secretary of state, 2009–2011): recorded in-person interview; Washington, DC; December 14, 2021.

Undersecretary of State for Political Affairs

Nicholas Burns (2005–2008; National Security Council, 1990–1995): recorded Zoom interview; December 8, 2021.

Undersecretary of State for Arms Control and International Security

Rose Gottemoeller (2012–2016; assistant secretary general, NATO, 2016–2019; assistant secretary of state for verification, compliance, and implementation, 2009–2014; director for Russian affairs, 1993–1994): recorded Zoom interview; October 12, 2021.

Undersecretaries of Defense for Policy

Douglas Feith (2001–2005): recorded in-person interview; Kyiv, Ukraine; August 27, 2021

Eric S. Edelman (2006–2009): recorded Zoom interview; November 17, 2021.

Assistant Secretary General, NATO

Alexander Vershbow (2012–2016; assistant secretary of defense, 2009–2012; US ambassador to Russia, 2001–2005; senior director, National Security Council, 1994–1997): recorded Zoom interview; December 13, 2021.

Assistant Secretary of State for European and Eurasian Affairs

Daniel Fried (2005–2009): recorded Zoom interview; December 6, 2021.

US Ambassadors to Ukraine

Steven Pifer (1998–2000): recorded in-person interview; Palo Alto, CA; August 28, 2021.

John Herbst (2003–2006): recorded Zoom interview; December 20, 2021.

Others (NSC Staff, Senior Directors, Russia or Ukraine Experts)

Thomas E. Graham (special assistant to the president and senior director for Russia on the National Security Council, 2004–2007; director for Russian affairs, 2002–2004): recorded Zoom interview; January 4, 2022.

Leon Fuerth (national security advisor to Vice President Al Gore, 1993–2001): recorded Zoom interview; December 17, 2021.

Toby Gati (senior director for Russia, Ukraine, and Eurasia for US National Security Council, 1993; assistant secretary of state for intelligence and research, 1993–1997): recorded in-person interview; November 19, 2021.

NOTES

INTRODUCTION: A NEW WAY

1. Brzezinski, "The Premature Partnership," 76.
2. Kuzio, *Russian Nationalism*, 156; Suny and Martin wrote how Russian identity was tied to religion, shifting and growing territory, the state, and the union of "great," "little," and "White" Russians. Ronald Suny and Terry Martin, *A State of Nations: Empire and Nation-Making in the Age of Lenin and Stalin* (Oxford: Oxford University Press, 2001), 36, 38.
3. Sarotte, *Not One Inch*, 127; Kuzio, *Russian Nationalism*, 36, 38.
4. Tallis, "Neo-idealism: Grand Strategy"; Tallis, "Rise of New Idealists."

CHAPTER 1: FROM THE COSSACKS TO CHERNOBYL

1. "Chernobyl Accident 1986."
2. "Chernobyl Accident 1986"; Bendix, "Real-Life Characters."
3. "In 1987–1988, Ukrainian dissidents were released from the Gulag, and they returned to Ukraine to take up the process of democratization that they had championed during the third historic cycle. In championing democratization, they believed they were supporting Gorbachev's policies that could be readily seen in the name given to the Ukrainian Popular Movement for Restructuring (Perestroika). Released dissidents refounded the Ukrainian Helsinki Group (UHH), which they renamed the Ukrainian Helsinki Union (UHS), that allied itself with the cultural intelligentsia to launch Rukh. The KPU prevented Rukh from holding its founding congress until September 1989, the same month that Shcherbytskyi resigned as KPU leader. He passed away a year later." Kuzio, *Ukraine*, 41.
4. Plokhy, *Gates of Europe*, chaps. 3–4.
5. Plokhy, *Gates of Europe*, chaps. 3–4.
6. Snyder, "Making of Modern Ukraine," class 5.
7. Plokhy, *Gates of Europe*, chaps. 3–5.
8. Snyder, "Making of Modern Ukraine," class 6.

9. Plokhy, *Gates of Europe*, chap. 3; Plokhy, *Gates of Europe*, part II.

10. Snyder, "Ukraine Holds the Future."

11. "What Does It Mean to Be Ukrainian? The Life of Taras Shevchenko."

12. Communism gained in strength when more than two-thirds of Ukraine was incorporated into the Soviet Union. The eastern territories of modern Ukraine were known as the Ukrainian SSR during World War II. Plokhy, *The Gates of Europe*, 229; Hill and Stent, "The World Putin Wants"; Martin, *Affirmative Action Empire*, 75–122.

13. Plokhy, *Gates of Europe*, chap. 4; Martin, *Affirmative Action Empire*, 325–335.

14. Szporluk, *Russia, Ukraine, and the Breakup*, 50.

15. Plokhy, *Gates of Europe*, chaps. 4–5.

16. Kuzio, *Ukraine*, 49.

17. Plokhy, *Gates of Europe*, chap. 4.

18. Among Yushchenko's last acts as President was to bestow the title of "Hero of Ukraine" on the World War II–era figure Stepan Bandera, who had been a leader of the Organization of Ukrainian Nationalists. It would be hard to think of a more divisive step. To many, it was inconceivable that he could be praised, let alone made a "Hero of Ukraine." The historiography of Bandera and the Ukrainian Insurgent Army is among the most bitterly contested issues in Ukraine and feeds the notion in Russia and the West that those most committed to Ukraine's independence are fascists or are tolerant of fascists. Yushchenko's decision was a godsend for those, like Yanukovych and the Russian government, who wanted to paint pro-Western politicians as extremists. To this day, the identity narratives that Russia uses to claim Ukraine as the belligerent and Ukrainians as the aggressor against ethnic Russians rely on drawing propaganda from the USSR's Banderites struggle. Plokhy, *Gates of Europe*, 280; D'Anieri, *Ukraine and Russia*, 171–172; "The Poison Pistol."

19. Plokhy, *Gates of Europe*, chap. 5.

20. Soviet nationalist policies and the influx of Western Ukrainians had progressively Ukrainianized Kyiv from the 1950s, ensuring that it would become the center of dissident and cultural movements in the 1960s and late 1980s. Kuzio, *Ukraine*, 27.

21. "Thanks to Shcherbytskyy and his associates, Moscow has succeeded in cultivating a following of loyal 'Little Russians' in Ukraine, who are willing to subordinate the republic's interests to those of the centre." Kuzio, *Ukraine*, 36.

22. As discussed in the acknowledgments section, family lore places my nuclear family and me on the last flight out of Kyiv before this action was taken.

23. Kuzio, *Ukraine*, 41.

24. "All nationalist movements have radical and moderate wings, and Ukraine was no exception to this rule. Pro-democracy dissidents and former prisoners of conscience and cultural activists concerned about Soviet assimilationist policies formed the moderate Rukh that became the main group within

the Democratic Bloc that fielded candidates in the March 1990 republican elections. Radical nationalists organized the Ukrainian Inter-Party Assembly and other nationalist formations, some with links to the émigré OUNb (the wing of OUN aligned with Bandera), and they boycotted the 1990 Soviet republican parliamentary elections. Describing Rukh and national democrats as 'moderates' needs to be placed into a comparative perspective because their programs are those typically supported by moderate Center-Right parties in Europe. At the same time, Russophone eastern Ukrainians have, until the Euromaidan, perceived not only nationalists but also Ukraine's national democrats as nationalists that reflected the deeply ingrained legacy of Soviet tirades against the all-encompassing term of 'bourgeois nationalism.'" Kuzio, *Ukraine*, 41.

CHAPTER 2: UNGROUP

1. Vindman, "Stop Tiptoeing Around Russia."
2. Gates, interview with author.
3. Goldgeier and McFaul, *Power and Purpose*, 26–27, 34.
4. Gates, interview with author.
5. "It was also in this speech that President Bush made it clear where Europe ended: at the putative Soviet border. While referencing the re-unification of Germany and the fall of communist regimes in Central Europe, he announced that 'Europe has become whole and free.' This framework clearly left nations like Ukraine and others still subject to Moscow's domination on the wrong side of the artificial dividing line." Fishel, *The Moscow Factor*, 41.
6. Wilson, "President Bush Had 'the Vision Thing.'"
7. D'Anieri, *Ukraine and Russia*, 27; Fishel, *The Moscow Factor*, 36.
8. "Not everyone in the administration shared Scowcroft's view. . . . Secretary of Defense Dick Cheney and his top advisers saw the devolution of power and potential independence for the Soviet Republic of Ukraine as significantly advantageous for the geostrategic interests of the United States." Goldgeier and McFaul, *Power and Purpose*, 23; "This position was consistent with Cheney's view that the United States should be 'pushing for the breakup of the Soviet Union.'" Goldgeier and McFaul, *Power and Purpose*, 35; Fishel, *The Moscow Factor*, 37–39.
9. Fishel, *The Moscow Factor*, 37–39.
10. Gates, interview with author.
11. Goldgeier and McFaul, *Power and Purpose*, 26–27, 34.
12. Goldgeier and McFaul, *Power and Purpose*, 26–27.
13. Pifer, *Eagle and Trident*, 33.
14. Fishel, *The Moscow Factor*, 41.
15. "New Union Treaty."
16. Graham, interview with author; D'Anieri, *Ukraine and Russia*, 31.

17. Bush, "Remarks to Supreme Soviet of Ukraine."

18. Safire, "After the Fall"; Devroy and Dobbs, "Bush Warns Ukraine."

19. "End of an Era."

20. Nahaylo, "Failed Coup in Moscow."

21. Goldgeier and McFaul, *Power and Purpose*, 34.

22. "At a meeting of top presidential advisors almost two months after the coup and almost a year since his 'Pathways' speech at the Wilson Center, Secretary Baker asserted that 'We should not establish a policy of supporting the breakup of the Soviet Union into twelve republics." Fishel, *The Moscow Factor*, 43.

23. Garthoff, *The Great Transition*, 488.

24. Graham, interview with author.

25. "As the referendum approached, Secretary of Defense Cheney and his aides favored being as forward leaning as possible. Pentagon officials wanted a bold statement from the president immediately following the referendum and argued that Ukrainian commitments to date were sufficient grounds to extend recognition." Goldgeier and McFaul, *Power and Purpose*, 35.

26. Fishel, *The Moscow Factor*, 72–73.

27. Fishel, *The Moscow Factor*, 59; Memorandum of Telephone Conversation, "Telcon with President Boris Yeltsin of Republic of Russia," November 30, 1991, Camp David, George H. W. Bush Presidential Library and Museum, https://bush41library.tamu.edu/files/memcons-telcons/1991-11-30 --Yeltsin.pdf.

CHAPTER 3: DENUCLEARIZATION

1. Fishel, *The Moscow Factor*, 72.

2. Fishel, *The Moscow Factor*, 72–73.

3. Gates, interview with author.

4. National Intelligence Council Memorandum, "Impact of Republic Sovereignty on Soviet Strategic Forces," Central Intelligence Agency, September 1991, declassified in part February 2, 2016, National Security Archive, https://nsarchive.gwu.edu/document/22536-01-first-ever-declassified-listing-strategic; Pifer, *Eagle and Trident*, 21, 43.

5. "It was also in this speech that President Bush made it clear where Europe ended: at the putative Soviet border. While referencing the re-unification of Germany and the fall of communist regimes in Central Europe, he announced that 'Europe has become whole and free.' This framework clearly left nations like Ukraine and others still subject to Moscow's domination on the wrong side of the artificial dividing line." Fishel, *The Moscow Factor*, 41; Garnett, *Keystone in the Arch*, 3.

6. Kotkin, "Russia's Perpetual Geopolitics"; Kryvdyk, interview with author.

7. Turchynov, interview with author.

8. D'Anieri, *Ukraine and Russia*, 76; Kortunov, "Russia in Search of Allies."

9. D'Anieri, *Ukraine and Russia*, 27.

10. Kuzio, *Ukraine*, chap. 2.

11. Kuzio, *Ukraine*, 50.

12. Szporluk, *Russia, Ukraine, and the Breakup*, xxxii–xxxiii.

13. Szporluk, *Russia, Ukraine, and the Breakup*, xxxii.

14. Szporluk, *Russia, Ukraine, and the Breakup*, xxxii.

15. Kuzio, *Ukraine*, 50.

16. Kuzio, *Ukraine*, 431, 452; Pifer, *Eagle and Trident*, 122, 152, 203, 278.

17. Smeshko, interview with author; Horbulin, interview with author.

18. Horbulin, interview with author; Haiduk, interview with author.

19. Horbulin, interview with author.

20. Pifer, *Eagle and Trident*, chap. 2.

21. Pifer, *Eagle and Trident*, chap. 2.

22. Fishel, *The Moscow Factor*, 77–78, 80; Bush, "President's News Conference on Aid to Former Soviet Union"; Memorandum for the Secretary, from Dennis Ross, Policy Planning Staff, "Foreign Policy in the Second Bush Administration: An Overview," April 30, 1992, released in full April 10, 2017.

23. Fishel, *The Moscow Factor*, 80–81; Bush, "Joint Declaration with Kravchuk"; George Bush, "President's News Conference with Kravchuk."

24. Fishel, *The Moscow Factor*, 81; Bush, "President's News Conference with Kravchuk."

25. Gryshchenko, interview with author.

CHAPTER 4: THE END OF HISTORY?

1. Moynihan, "Totalitarianism R.I.P."; Kessler, "Bush's New World Order."

2. Fishel, *The Moscow Factor*, 85; Clinton, "Excerpts of Remarks in Milwaukee."

3. Burns, interview with author.

4. Edelman, interview with author; Fishel, *The Moscow Factor*, 89; Memorandum for Secretary of State-Designate Warren Christopher from Lawrence Eagleburger, "Parting Thoughts: US Foreign Policy in the Years Ahead," January 5, 1993, https://nsarchive.gwu.edu/document/29753-document-1-memorandum-secretary-state-designate-warren-christopher-lawrence-s; D'Anieri, *Ukraine and Russia*, 54.

5. Fishel, *The Moscow Factor*, 89; Statement at Senate Confirmation Hearing, Secretary-Designate Warren Christopher, Senate Foreign Relations Committee, Washington, DC, Office of the Spokesman, US Department of State, January 13, 1993, in "The Clinton Administration Begins," *Foreign Policy Bulletin* 3, no. 4–5 (January 1993), www.cambridge.org/core/journals/foreign-policy-bulletin/article/abs/clinton-administration-begins/9DE8E4D2916C78DDA1A1D66E65E34F90.

6. D'Anieri, *Ukraine and Russia*, 64; Burns, interview with author.

7. Burns, interview with author.

8. Burns, interview with author.

9. Burns, interview with author.

10. Fried, interview with author.

11. Perry, interview with author.

12. Pifer, *Eagle and Trident*, 44.

13. Fishel, *The Moscow Factor*, 103–104; Talbott, *The Russia Hand*, 83.

14. NATO, "Visit to NATO by Kravchuk."

15. Fishel, *The Moscow Factor*, 106–107, 112; Clinton, "President's News Conference with Kravchuk."

16. Nuclear energy provided 50 percent of Ukraine's power. Pifer, *Eagle and Trident*, 57–61.

17. Fishel, *The Moscow Factor*, 106, 112; "A Reality Check."

18. Burns, interview with author.

19. Pifer, *Eagle and Trident*, 65.

20. Burns, interview with author.

21. Pifer, "Getting Rid of Nukes."

CHAPTER 5: A PEACEFUL TRANSFER OF POWER

1. "Borrowing an expression from Italian political vocabulary, one might conclude that the emergence of an independent Ukraine, in the way and form in which it actually occurred, was the result of a 'historic compromise.' One side in that compromise were the party, state, economic, and military elites, including the regional bosses from the east, for whom Russian remained (with some exceptions) the preferred language of daily use after the fall of the Soviet Union. The leaders of the national movement formed the other party. Their background had mainly been in literary and academic fields, and their popular electoral support was concentrated in the western regions and in the capital city." Szporluk, *Russia, Ukraine, and the Breakup*, xxxii.

2. Toth and Ostrow, "Russian Mafia"; Shirley, "Revolution Under the Shadow."

3. Snelbecker, "Political Economy of Privatization"; Gorchinskaya, "Brief History of Corruption."

4. Garnett, *Keystone in the Arch*, 22–26, 32–36; Pifer, *Eagle and Trident*, 7, 35, 112.

5. Pifer, *Eagle and Trident*, 64–66.

6. Kuzio, *Ukraine*, 53.

7. Smeshko, interview with author.

8. D'Anieri, *Ukraine and Russia*, 1–27.

9. Aid was instead outsourced to international organizations like the International Monetary Fund and the World Bank. Kuzio, *Ukraine*, 169.

10. Bakshi, "War in Chechnya."

11. Fishel, *The Moscow Factor*, chap. 3; the Gore-Kuchma Commission was also symbolic because it placed Ukraine on par with Russia, with whom Vice

President Gore conducted the Gore-Chernomyrdin Commission. Gore, interview with author.

12. Dobbs, "Nunn Breaks Ranks"; Arms Control Association, "Opposition to NATO Expansion"; Kennan, "A Fateful Error."

13. Gates, interview with author.

14. Gates, interview with author.

15. Klimkin, interview with author.

CHAPTER 6: THE WAR ON TERROR

1. In a number of ways, the latter part of the Clinton administration marked the then high-water mark of the bilateral relationship, even if Washington's largely positive view of Leonid Kuchma and his presidency was quite unfounded. Pifer, *Eagle and Trident*, 201–208.

2. Gorchinskaya, "Chornovil Dies in Car Crash."

3. Kuchma, interview with author.

4. D'Anieri, *Ukraine and Russia*, 83.

5. Bohlen, "Yeltsin Resigns."

6. Hill and Gaddy, *Mr. Putin*, 22.

7. Hill and Gaddy, *Mr. Putin*, 205.

8. Plokhy, *The Russo-Ukrainian War*, chap. 2.

9. Satter, *The Less You Know*, 12.

10. Hill and Gaddy, *Mr. Putin*, 34.

11. Eckel, "Putin's 'A Solid Man.'"

12. Gentleman, "Secret Tape."

13. Rice, interview with author; Kuchma, interview with author.

14. Fuerth, interview with author.

15. "US support for Ukraine's membership, even as conditioned, was not shared widely at NATO. After joining in 1999, Poland had established itself as Ukraine's foremost advocate, with the United States a close second, but many other allies voiced skepticism." Pifer, *Eagle and Trident*, 222, 223; see also NATO, "Madrid Declaration on Euro-Atlantic Security and Cooperation, Issued by the Heads of State and Government," Madrid, July 8, 1997, www .nato.int/cps/en/natohq/official_texts_25460.htm.

16. Bush made clear his administration's interest in Ukraine in NATO in a speech in Warsaw on June 15. That sentiment did not go down well with Russian president Vladimir Putin, into whose eyes Bush would look the next day in Ljubljana. Pifer, *Eagle and Trident*, 212.

17. Bush, "Press Conference by Bush and Putin."

18. McFaul, "US-Russia Relations."

19. Fishel, *The Moscow Factor*, 127; Graham, interview with author.

20. Goble, "Window on Eurasia."

21. Pifer, *Eagle and Trident*, 209.

22. LaFraniere, "Ukraine Faulted in Probe of Radar Sale."
23. O'Flynn, "Pilot's Last Words."
24. Wesolowsky, "Ukraine: Rice Delivers Strong Message."
25. Pifer, interview with author; Pifer, *Eagle and Trident*, 250.
26. Pifer, *Eagle and Trident*, 216, 234–235.
27. Pifer, *Eagle and Trident*, 250.
28. Pifer, *Eagle and Trident*, 216, 234–235.

CHAPTER 7: A NON-PEACEFUL TRANSFER OF POWER

1. D'Anieri, *Ukraine and Russia*, 27.
2. Hopko, interview with author.
3. D'Anieri, *Ukraine and Russia*, 126–127.
4. Pifer, *Eagle and Trident*, 266.
5. Rice, "US-Russian Relations" interview with Behringer and Miles.
6. Pifer, *Eagle and Trident*, 264.
7. Pifer, *Eagle and Trident*, 266.
8. Kupchinsky, "Mystery Behind Poisoning."
9. Fishel, *The Moscow Factor*, 133.
10. Fishel, *The Moscow Factor*, 131, 142.
11. Ukrainian Central Election Commission.
12. Fishel, *The Moscow Factor*, 132, 257.
13. Pifer, *Eagle and Trident*, 269.
14. Pifer, *Eagle and Trident*, 269.
15. Pifer, *Eagle and Trident*, 269.
16. Pifer, *Eagle and Trident*, 263.
17. Pifer, *Eagle and Trident*, 263; Fishel, *The Moscow Factor*, 137; George W. Bush, "Exchange with Reporters in Crawford, Texas," American Presidency Project, November 26, 2004, www.presidency.ucsb.edu/node/215186.
18. John Tefft later served as ambassador in both Kyiv and Moscow.
19. Fishel, *The Moscow Factor*, 144; Colin L. Powell, interview with Barry Schweid, George Gedda, and Anne Gearan, December 17, 2004, State Department Archives, https://2001-2009.state.gov/secretary/former/powell/remarks/39935.htm.
20. Dick Cheney, *In My Time* (New York: Threshold, 2011), 428.
21. Stent, *Limits of Partnership*, 101.
22. Fishel, *The Moscow Factor*, 153.
23. Haiduk, interview with author.
24. Fishel, *The Moscow Factor*, 154.
25. D'Anieri, *Ukraine and Russia*, 133.

CHAPTER 8: RUSSIA REVANCHIST

1. Haiduk, interview with author.
2. Plokhy, *The Russo-Ukrainian War*, chap. 4; NATO, "Membership Action Plan."
3. Plokhy, *The Russo-Ukrainian War*, 84; Yushchenko, "Opening Statement at NATO-Ukraine Council."
4. Plokhy, *The Russo-Ukrainian War*, 83–84.
5. Yushchenko, "Statement to Press Following NATO-Ukraine Council."
6. Putin, "State of the Nation."
7. Yushchenko, interview with author.
8. Edelman, interview with author.
9. Hoffman, *Conflict in the 21st Century*, 35.
10. Gates, interview with author.
11. Plokhy, *The Russo-Ukrainian War*, chap. 4.
12. Kramer, "Russia Cuts Off Gas."
13. Putin, "Speech and Discussion at Munich."
14. Burns, interview with author.
15. Socor, "Ukraine's Top Leaders Request Membership."
16. Bush, "President's News Conference with Yushchenko."
17. Harding, "Putin Issues Nuclear Threat."
18. Hadley, interview with author.
19. "Yushchenko Dismisses Cabinet."

CHAPTER 9: NATO MEMBERSHIP AND RUSSIA'S WAR ON GEORGIA

1. Rice, interview with author.
2. Rice, interview with author.
3. NATO, "Meetings of Heads of State"; Socor, "NATO Opens Crisis Summit."
4. Robin Oakley, "Bush Stirs Controversy over NATO Membership," *CNN*, April 1, 2008, https://edition.cnn.com/2008/WORLD/europe/04/01/ukraine.analysis/.
5. "President Bush Visits Bucharest"; Socor, "NATO Opens Crisis Summit."
6. Una Hadjari, "How a Name Change Opened the Door to NATO for Macedonia," *New York Times*, February 6, 2019, www.nytimes.com/2019/02/06/world/europe/macedonia-nato.html.
7. NATO, "Bucharest Summit Declaration."
8. Gates, interview with author.
9. Edelman, interview with author.
10. Edelman, interview with author.
11. "Russia Recognizes Abkhazia."
12. Clinton, "Statement on Georgia and Ukraine."

13. Harding, "Putin Issues Nuclear Threat."
14. Marc Champion and Andrew Osborn, "Russia, Georgia Clash over Breakaway Province," *Wall Street Journal*, August 9, 2008; Socor, "Ukraine's Top Leaders Request Membership."
15. Chazan, "Russia Seizes Port"; Shakarian, "2008 Russian Cyber Campaign"; "Media War Flares."
16. Plokhy, *The Russo-Ukrainian War*, chap. 4.
17. "Iraq: Third-Largest Contingent, Georgia"; "Tbilisi Names Street."
18. "US Ship Carrying Aid."
19. Obama, "Statement on Russia's Escalation."
20. McCain, "Statement on Crisis in Georgia."
21. Cooper and Bumiller, "War Puts Focus on McCain."
22. Hagel, interview with author.
23. Shuster, "US-Russia Relations."
24. Graham, interview with author.

CHAPTER 10: THE REVOLUTION OF DIGNITY

1. Plokhy, *The Russo-Ukrainian War*, chap. 4.
2. "Free Trade Agreement."
3. "Trump Pardons Paul Manafort"; Shuster, "How Paul Manafort Helped."
4. Kramer, McIntire, and Meier, "Secret Ledger in Ukraine."
5. "Ukraine's Parliament Votes"; Harding, "Ukraine Extends Lease"; "Yulia Tymoshenko Imprisonment."
6. "Ukraine: Reforms to Pave Way"; "Ukraine-EU Deal Deadlocked."
7. Putin, "New Integration Project for Eurasia."
8. "Romney: Russia Is Number One Foe"; Rayfield, "Obama: The '80s Called."
9. "IRI Ukraine Survey."
10. Kononczuk, "Ukraine Withdraws from Signing."
11. Walker, "Vladimir Putin Offers Incentives."
12. Tomczyk, "Deconstructing the Divide."
13. Grytsenko, "Ukrainian Protesters Flood Kiev."
14. Walker, "Vladimir Putin Offers Incentives"; Schwartz, "Who Killed the Kiev Protesters?"
15. Neuman and Ritchie, "Ukraine President Voted Out"; Amos and Walker, "Fugitive Viktor Yanukovych"; "Putin: Russia Helped Yanukovych Flee."
16. Sutyagin and Clarke, "Ukraine Military Dispositions."

CHAPTER 11: LITTLE GREEN MEN

1. Rawlings, "Putin Calls Uprising 'Unconstitutional.'"
2. "Ukraine Crisis: 'Russians' Occupy Crimea Airports."
3. De Carbonnel, "How the Separatists Delivered."

4. Plokhy, *The Russo-Ukrainian War*, chap. 5.

5. Rogin and Lake, "US Told Ukraine to Stand Down."

6. Turchynov, interview with author.

7. Plokhy, *The Russo-Ukrainian War*, chap. 5.

8. Taylor, "Novorossiya."

9. "MH17 Ukraine Plane Crash."

10. "Kremlin Dismisses Claims."

11. "Protocol on Results (Minsk Agreement)"; "Package of Measures for Implementation of Minsk."

CHAPTER 12: NEO-IDEALISM MEETS PRESIDENT TRUMP

1. National Public Radio, "Vindman Discusses U.S. Options on Russia-Ukraine Tensions."

CONCLUSION: A NEW US FOREIGN POLICY

1. Seldin, "US Sending Ukraine."

2. Snyder, "Ukraine Holds the Future."

BIBLIOGRAPHY

Abbakumova, Natasha, and Kathy Lally. "Russia Boots Out USAID." *Washington Post*, September 18, 2012. www.washingtonpost.com/world/russia-boots -out-usaid/2012/09/18/c2d185a8-01bc-11e2-b260-32f4a8db9b7e_story .html.

Amos, Howard, and Shaun Walker. "Fugitive Viktor Yanukovych Out of Sight but Running Out of Options." *The Guardian*, February 24, 2014. www .theguardian.com/world/2014/feb/24/fugitive-viktor-yanukovych-balaclava -sevastopol-ukraine.

Arms Control Association. "Opposition to NATO Expansion." Arms Control Today, June 26, 1997. www.armscontrol.org/act/1997-06/arms-control -today/opposition-nato-expansion.

Åslund, Anders, and Michael McFaul, eds. *Revolution in Orange: The Origins of Ukraine's Democratic Breakthrough*. Washington, DC: Carnegie Endowment for International Peace, 2006.

Asmus, Ronald. *Opening NATO's Door: How the Alliance Remade Itself for a New Era*. New York: Columbia University Press, 2002.

Bakshi, G. D. "The War in Chechnya: A Military Analysis." *Strategic Analysis* 14, no. 5 (August 2000). https://ciaotest.cc.columbia.edu/olj/sa/sa_aug00 bag01.html.

Bendix, Aria. "Real-Life Characters in HBO's 'Chernobyl' on the Moment They Found Out About the World's Worst Nuclear-Power-Plant Accident." *Business Insider*, September 21, 2019. www.businessinsider.com/real-chernobyl -hbo-characters-moment-the-nuclear-disaster-2019-6?op=1.

Bialer, Seweryn, and Michael Mandelbaum, eds. *Gorbachev's Russia and American Foreign Policy*. Boulder: Westview Press, 1988.

Bohlen, Celestine. "Yeltsin Resigns, Naming Putin as Acting President to Run in March Election." *New York Times*, January 1, 2000. www.nytimes.com /2000/01/01/world/yeltsin-resigns-overview-yeltsin-resigns-naming -putin-acting-president-run-march.html.

Brands, Hal. "American Grand Strategy and the Liberal Order: Continuity, Change, and Options for the Future." RAND Corporation, October 19, 2016. www.rand.org/pubs/perspectives/PE209.html.

Brands, Hal. *The Limits of Offshore Balancing.* Carlisle Barracks, PA: US Army War College Press, 2015. https://press.armywarcollege.edu/monographs /444.

Brands, Hal. *The Promise and Pitfalls of Grand Strategy.* Carlisle Barracks, PA: US Army War College Press, 2015. https://press.armywarcollege.edu /monographs/548.

Brzezinski, Zbigniew. "The Premature Partnership." *Foreign Affairs* 73, no. 2 (March/April 1994).

Bush, George H. W. "Joint Declaration with President Leonid Kravchuk of Ukraine." American Presidency Project, May 6, 1992. www.presidency.ucsb .edu/node/267205.

Bush, George H. W. "The President's News Conference on Aid to the States of the Former Soviet Union." American Presidency Project, April 1, 1992. www .presidency.ucsb.edu/node/267607.

Bush, George H. W. "The President's News Conference with President Leonid Kravchuk of Ukraine." American Presidency Project, May 6, 1992. www .presidency.ucsb.edu/node/267204.

Bush, George H. W. "Remarks to the Supreme Soviet of the Republic of the Ukraine in Kiev, Soviet Union." George H. W. Bush Presidential Library and Museum, August 1, 1991. https://bush41library.tamu.edu/archives/public -papers/3267.

Bush, George W. "President's News Conference with President Viktor Yushchenko of Ukraine in Kiev, Ukraine." Office of the Press Secretary, White House Archives, April 1, 2008. www.govinfo.gov/content/pkg/PPP-2008-book1 /pdf/PPP-2008-book1-doc-pg443.pdf.

Bush, George W. "Press Conference by President Bush and Russian Federation President Putin." White House Archives, June 16, 2001. https://georgewbush -whitehouse.archives.gov/news/releases/2001/06/20010618.html.

Champion, Marc, and Andrew Osborn. "Smoldering Feud, Then War: Tensions at Obscure Border Led to Georgia-Russia Clash." *Wall Street Journal,* August 16, 2008. www.wsj.com/articles/SB121884450978145997.

Chazan, Guy. "Russia Briefly Seizes Georgian Port." *Wall Street Journal,* August 19, 2008. www.wsj.com/articles/SB121913118324652571.

"Chernobyl Accident 1986." World Nuclear Association, April 26, 2024. https: //world-nuclear.org/information-library/safety-and-security/safety-of -plants/chernobyl-accident.

Clinton, Hillary. "Statement by Hillary Clinton on Georgia and Ukraine."

American Presidency Project, April 18, 2008. www.presidency.ucsb.edu /documents/statement-hillary-clinton-georgia-and-ukraine.

Clinton, William J. "Excerpts of Remarks in Milwaukee." American Presidency Project, October 2, 1992. www.presidency.ucsb.edu/node/285621.

Clinton, William J. "The President's News Conference with President Leonid Kravchuk of Ukraine in Kiev," American Presidency Project, January 12, 1994. www.presidency.ucsb.edu/documents/the-presidents-news-conference -with-president-leonid-kravchuk-ukraine-kiev.

Cooper, Michael, and Elisabeth Bumiller. "War Puts Focus on McCain's Hard Line on Russia." New York Times, August 12, 2008. www.nytimes.com /2008/08/12/us/politics/12mccain.html.

D'Anieri, Paul. Ukraine and Russia: From Civilized Divorce to Uncivil War. Cambridge: Cambridge University Press, 2019.

De Carbonnel, Alissa. "How the Separatists Delivered Crimea to Moscow." Reuters, March 12, 2014. www.reuters.com/article/idUSBREA2B13M/.

Devroy, Ann, and Michael Dobbs. "Bush Warns Ukraine on Independence; President Supports Gorbachev's Union Treaty in Kiev Speech." Washington Post, August 2, 1991. https://web.archive.org/web/20140611082257/http: //www.highbeam.com/doc/1P2-1077882.html.

Dobbs, Michael. "Nunn Breaks Ranks on NATO Expansion." Washington Post, June 23, 1995. www.washingtonpost.com/archive/politics/1995/06/23/nunn -breaks-ranks-on-nato-expansion/09e2b0a8-2558-4fcc-9294-e229 b131f7e3/.

Eckel, Mike. "Putin's 'A Solid Man': Declassified Memos Offer Window into Yeltsin-Clinton Relationship." Radio Free Europe/Radio Liberty, August 30, 2018. www.rferl.org/a/putin-s-a-solid-man-declassified-memos-offer-window -into-yeltsin-clinton-relationship/29462317.html.

"End of an Era: The August Coup and the Final Days of the Soviet Union." Association for Diplomatic Studies and Training, August 2014. https://adst .org/2014/08/end-of-an-era-the-august-coup-and-the-final-days-of-the -soviet-union/.

Fishel, Eugene M. The Moscow Factor: US Policy Towards Sovereign Ukraine and the Kremlin. Cambridge, MA: Harvard Ukraine Research Institute, 2022.

"Free Trade Agreement Between Ukraine, Belarus, Kazakhstan, and Russian Federation." World Bank, 2003. https://wits.worldbank.org/GPTAD/PDF /archive/Common_Economic_Zone.pdf.

Garnett, Sherman W. Keystone in the Arch: Ukraine in the Emerging Security Environment of Central and Eastern Europe. Washington, DC: Carnegie Endowment for International Peace, 1997.

Garthoff, Raymond. *The Great Transition: American-Soviet Relations and the End of the Cold War*. Washington, DC: Brookings Institution Press, 1994.

Gentleman, Amelia. "Secret Tape Links Leader to Headless Corpse." *The Guardian*, December 15, 2000. www.theguardian.com/world/2000/dec/15/russia.ameliagentleman1.

Goble, Paul. "Window on Eurasia: The West's Real Double Standards in the Ukrainian Crisis." Window on Eurasia, May 22, 2014. https://windowoneurasia2.blogspot.com/2014/05/window-on-eurasia-wests-real-double.html.

Goldgeier, James M., and Michael McFaul. *Power and Purpose: US Policy Toward Russia After the Cold War*. Washington, DC: Brookings Institution Press, 2003.

Gorchinskaya, Katya. "A Brief History of Corruption in Ukraine: the Kuchma Era." Eurasianet, May 20, 2020. https://eurasianet.org/a-brief-history-of-corruption-in-ukraine-the-kuchma-era.

Gorchinskaya, Katya. "Chornovil Dies in Car Crash." *Kyiv Post*, April 1, 1999. https://archive.kyivpost.com/article/content/ukraine-politics/chornovil-dies-in-car-crash-239.html.

Grytsenko, Oksana. "Ukrainian Protesters Flood Kiev After President Pulls Out of EU Deal." *The Guardian*, November 24, 2013. www.theguardian.com/world/2013/nov/24/ukraine-protesters-yanukovych-aborts-eu-deal-russia.

Harding, Luke. "Medvedev Sworn In as Russian President." *The Guardian*, May 7, 2008. www.theguardian.com/world/2008/may/07/russia.

Harding, Luke. "Putin Issues Nuclear Threat to Ukraine over Plan to Host US Shield." *The Guardian*, February 13, 2008. www.theguardian.com/world/2008/feb/13/russia.putin.

Harding, Luke. "Ukraine Extends Lease for Russia's Black Sea Fleet." *The Guardian*, April 21, 2010. www.theguardian.com/world/2010/apr/21/ukraine-black-sea-fleet-russia.

Hill, Fiona, and Clifford Gaddy. *Mr. Putin: Operative in the Kremlin*. Washington, DC: Brookings Institution Press, 2013.

Hill, Fiona, and Angela Stent. "The World Putin Wants: How Distortions About the Past Feed Delusions About the Future." *Foreign Affairs* 101, no. 5 (September/October 2022). www.foreignaffairs.com/russian-federation/world-putin-wants-fiona-hill-angela-stent.

Hoffman, Frank. *Conflict in the 21st Century: The Rise of Hybrid Wars*. Arlington, VA: Potomac Institute for Policy Studies, 2007. www.comw.org/qdr/fulltext/0712hoffman.pdf.

"Iraq: As Third-Largest Contingent, Georgia Hopes to Show Its Worth." Radio Free Europe/Radio Liberty, September 10, 2007. www.rferl.org/a/1078614 .html.

"IRI Ukraine Survey: Ukrainians Positive About Association Agreement with the EU." International Republican Institute, October 28, 2013. www.iri.org /resources/iri-ukraine-survey-ukrainians-positive-about-association -agreement-with-the-eu/.

Kennan, George. "A Fateful Error." *New York Times*, February 5, 1997. www .nytimes.com/1997/02/05/opinion/a-fateful-error.html.

Kessler, Bart R. "Bush's New World Order: The Meaning Behind the Words." Master's thesis, Air Command and Staff Center, 1997. https://apps.dtic.mil /sti/citations/ADA398504.

Kononczuk, Wojciech. "Ukraine Withdraws from Signing the Association Agreement in Vilnius: The Motives and Implications." Centre for Eastern Studies, November 27, 2013. www.osw.waw.pl/en/publikacje/analyses/2013 -11-27/ukraine-withdraws-signing-association-agreement-vilnius-motives -and.

Kortunov, Sergei. "Russia in Search of Allies." *International Affairs* (Moscow) 42, no. 3 (1996).

Kotkin, Stephen. "Russia's Perpetual Geopolitics: Putin Returns to Historical Patterns." *Foreign Affairs* 95, no. 3 (May/June 2016). www.foreignaffairs .com/articles/ukraine/2016-04-18/russias-perpetual-geopolitics.

Kramer, Andrew E. "Russia Cuts Off Gas to Ukraine in Cost Dispute." *New York Times*, January 1, 2006. www.nytimes.com/2006/01/02/world/europe/russia -cuts-off-gas-to-ukraine-in-cost-dispute.html.

Kramer, Andrew E., Mike McIntire, and Barry Meier. "Secret Ledger in Ukraine Lists Cash for Donald Trump's Campaign Chief." *New York Times*, August 15, 2016. www.nytimes.com/2016/08/15/us/politics/what-is-the-black-ledger .html.

"Kremlin Dismisses Claims Putin Was Involved in MH17 Downing." Reuters, February 9, 2023. www.reuters.com/world/europe/kremlin-dismisses-claims -putin-was-involved-mh17-downing-2023-02-09/.

Kupchinsky, Roman. "Ukraine: Mystery Behind Yushchenko's Poisoning Continues." Radio Free Europe/Radio Liberty, September 18, 2006. www.rferl.org/a /1071434.html.

Kuzio, Taras. *Russian Nationalism and the Russian-Ukrainian War: Autocracy-Orthodoxy-Nationality.* London: Taylor & Francis Group, 2022.

Kuzio, Taras. *Ukraine: Democratization, Corruption, and the New Russian Imperialism.* Santa Barbara, CA: Praeger, 2015.

Kuzio, Taras. *Ukraine Under Kuchma: Political Reform, Economic Transformation and Security Policy in Independent Ukraine.* New York: St. Martin's Press, 1997.

Kuzio, Taras, and Andrew Wilson. *Ukraine: Perestroika to Independence.* New York: St. Martin's Press, 1994.

LaFraniere, Sharon. "Ukraine Faulted in Probe of Radar Sale." *Washington Post,* November 25, 2002. https://www.washingtonpost.com/archive/politics/2002/11/26/ukraine-faulted-in-probe-of-radar-sale/0246c744-c8a6-4783-9378-c4786bac2fd6/.

Martin, Terry. *The Affirmative Action Empire: Nations and Nationalism in the Soviet Union, 1923–1939.* Ithaca, NY: Cornell University Press, 2001.

McCain, John. "Statement by John McCain on the Crisis in Georgia." American Presidency Project, August 11, 2008. www.presidency.ucsb.edu/documents/statement-john-mccain-the-crisis-georgia.

McFaul, Michael. "Putin Hazed Me: How I Was Stalked, Harassed and Surveilled by Kremlin Stooges." *Politico Magazine,* May 19, 2018. www.politico.com/magazine/story/2018/05/19/michael-mcfaul-book-excerpt-218408/.

McFaul, Michael. "US-Russia Relations After September 11, 2001." Carnegie Endowment, October 24, 2001. https://carnegieendowment.org/posts/2001/10/us-russia-relations-after-september-11-2001.

"Media War Flares over S Ossetia." *Al Jazeera,* November 24, 2008. www.aljazeera.com/news/2008/11/24/media-war-flares-over-s-ossetia/.

Memorandum for the Secretary, from Dennis Ross, Policy Planning Staff, "Foreign Policy in the Second Bush Administration: An Overview," April 30, 1992, released in full April 10, 2017. https://ceipfiles.s3.amazonaws.com/pdf/back-channel/1992MemotoBaker.pdf.

"MH17 Ukraine Plane Crash: What We Know." *BBC News,* February 26, 2020. www.bbc.com/news/world-europe-28357880.

Moynihan, Daniel Patrick. "Totalitarianism R.I.P." *Washington Post,* August 22, 1991. www.washingtonpost.com/archive/opinions/1991/08/22/totalitarianism-rip/fcbebb6e-0b71-490d-a75a-1c40d4204b3e/.

Nahaylo, Bohdan. "Failed Coup in Moscow Precipitated Ukraine's Declaration of Independence." *Kyiv Post,* August 19, 2023. www.kyivpost.com/opinion/20707.

National Intelligence Council. "Impact of Republic Sovereignty on Soviet Strategic Forces." National Security Archive, September 1, 1991. https://nsarchive.gwu.edu/document/22536-01-first-ever-declassified-listing-strategic.

National Public Radio. "Vindman Discusses U.S. Options on Russia-Ukraine Tensions." January 10, 2022. https://www.npr.org/2022/01/10/1071896624/vindman-discusses-u-s-options-on-russia-ukraine-tensions.

NATO. "Bucharest Summit Declaration." NATO Newsroom, April 3, 2008. www.nato.int/cps/en/natohq/official_texts_8443.htm.

NATO. "Membership Action Plan (MAP)." NATO, March 28, 2024. www.nato .int/cps/en/natohq/topics_37356.htm.

NATO. "Summit Meetings of Heads of State and Government (Agenda)." NATO Newsroom, April 2, 2008. www.nato.int/cps/en/natohq/events_7344.htm.

NATO. "Visit to NATO by Leonid Kravchuk, President of Ukraine." NATO Newsroom, July 8, 1992. www.nato.int/cps/en/natohq/news_23915.htm.

Neuman, Scott, and L. Carol Ritchie. "Ukrainian President Voted Out; Opposition Leader Freed." *NPR*, February 22, 2014. www.npr.org/sections /thetwo-way/2014/02/22/281083380/unkrainian-protesters-uneasy -president-reportedly-leaves-kiev.

"New Union Treaty: Treaty on the Union of Sovereign States." Seventeen Moments in Soviet History, August 15, 1991. https://soviethistory.msu.edu /1991-2/nine-plus-one-agreement/nine-plus-one-agreement-texts/new -union-treaty/.

Obama, Barack. "Statement from Senator Barack Obama on Russia's Escalation of Violence Against Georgia." American Presidency Project, August 9, 2008. www.presidency.ucsb.edu/documents/statement-from-senator-barack -obama-russias-escalation-violence-against-georgia.

O'Flynn, Kevin. "Pilot's Last Words: 'Where Are We Hit?'" *The Guardian*, October 12, 2001. www.theguardian.com/world/2001/oct/12/russia.

"Package of Measures for the Implementation of the Minsk Agreements." United Nations Peacemaker, February 12, 2015. https://peacemaker.un.org /ukraine-minsk-implementation15.

Pifer, Steven. *The Eagle and the Trident: US-Ukraine Relations in Turbulent Times.* Washington, DC: Brookings Institution Press, 2017.

Pifer, Steven. "Getting Rid of Nukes: The Trilateral Statement at 20 Years." Brookings, January 13, 2014. www.brookings.edu/articles/getting-rid-of -nukes-the-trilateral-statement-at-20-years/.

Plokhy, Serhii. *The Gates of Europe: A History of Ukraine.* New York: Basic Books, 2015.

Plokhy, Serhii. *The Last Empire: The Final Days of the Soviet Union.* New York: Basic Books, 2014.

Plokhy, Serhii. *The Russo-Ukrainian War: The Return of History.* New York: W. W. Norton and Company, 2023.

Plokhy, Serhii. *Ukraine and Russia: Representations of the Past.* Toronto: University of Toronto Press, 2008.

"Poison Pistol, The." *Time*, December 1, 1961. https://web.archive.org/web /20080606005426/http://www.time.com/time/magazine/article /0,9171,938806,00.html.

"President Bush Visits Bucharest, Romania, Discusses NATO." Office of the Press Secretary, White House Archives, April 2, 2008. https://georgewbush -whitehouse.archives.gov/news/releases/2008/04/20080402-2 .html.

"Protocol on the Results of Consultations of the Trilateral Contact Group (Minsk Agreement)." United Nations Peacemaker, September 5, 2014. https: //peacemaker.un.org/UA-ceasefire-2014.

"Putin: Russia Helped Yanukovych to Flee Ukraine." *BBC News*, October 24, 2014. www.bbc.com/news/world-europe-29761799.

Putin, Vladimir. "A New Integration Project for Eurasia: The Future in the Making." Permanent Mission of the Russian Federation to the European Union, October 3, 2011. https://russiaeu.ru/en/news/article-prime-minister -vladimir-putin-new-integration-project-eurasia-future-making-izvestia-3-.

Putin, Vladimir. "Russian President Putin Delivers State of the Nation Address." Federation of American Scientists, April 25, 2005. https://irp.fas.org/news /2005/04/putin042505.html.

Putin, Vladimir. "Speech and the Following Discussion at the Munich Conference on Security Policy." Office of the President of Russia, February 10, 2007. www.en.kremlin.ru/events/president/transcripts/24034.

Rawlings, Nate. "Putin Calls Ukraine Uprising 'Unconstitutional.'" *Time*, March 4, 2014. https://time.com/12161/vladimir-putin-ukraine-russia-crimea/.

Rayfield, Jillian. "Obama: The '80s Called, They Want Their Foreign Policy Back." *Salon*, October 23, 2012. www.salon.com/2012/10/23/obama_the_80s _called_they_want_their_foreign_policy_back/.

"Reality Check, A." *Ukrainian Weekly*, October 17, 1993. www.ukrweekly.com /archive/1993/The_Ukrainian_Weekly_1993-42.pdf.

Rice, Condoleezza. "US-Russian Relations Under Bush and Putin." Interview by Paul Behringer and Simon Miles. SMU Center for Presidential History, April 14, 2022. www.smu.edu/-/media/Site/Dedman/Academics/Institutes Centers/CPH/Bush-Putin-Project/Transcripts/Rice-Condoleezza -FINAL.pdf.

Rogin, Josh, and Eli Lake. "US Told Ukraine to Stand Down as Putin Invaded." Bloomberg, August 21, 2015. www.bloomberg.com/view/articles/2015-08 -21/u-s-told-ukraine-to-stand-down-as-putin-invaded.

"Romney: Russia Is Our Number One Geopolitical Foe." CNN, March 26, 2012. https://cnnpressroom.blogs.cnn.com/2012/03/26/romney-russia-is-our -number-one-geopolitical-foe.

"Russia Recognizes Abkhazia, South Ossetia." Radio Free Europe/Radio Liberty, August 26, 2008. www.rferl.org/a/Russia_Recognizes_Abkhazia_South _Ossetia/1193932.html.

Safire, William. "After the Fall." *New York Times*, August 29, 1991. www.nytimes .com/1991/08/29/opinion/essay-after-the-fall.html.

Sarotte, Mary E. *1989: The Struggle to Create Post–Cold War Europe*. Princeton, NJ: Princeton University Press, 2009.

Sarotte, Mary E. *Not One Inch: America, Russia, and the Making of Post–Cold War Stalemate*. New Haven, CT: Yale University Press, 2021.

Satter, David. *The Less You Know, The Better You Sleep: Russia's Road to Terror and Dictatorship Under Yeltsin and Putin*. New Haven, CT: Yale University Press, 2016. www.fpri.org/books/less-know-better-sleep-russias-road-terror -dictatorship-yeltsin-putin/.

Schwartz, Mattathias. "Who Killed the Kiev Protesters? A 3-D Model Holds the Clues." *New York Times Magazine*, May 30, 2018. www.nytimes.com /2018/05/30/magazine/ukraine-protest-video.html.

Seldin, Jeff. "US Sending Ukraine More Advanced Rocket Systems; Fighter Jets Under Consideration." Voice of America, July 22, 2022. www.voanews .com/a/us-sending-ukraine-more-advanced-rocket-systems-fighter-jets -under-consideration-/6670668.html.

Shakarian, Paulo. "The 2008 Russian Cyber Campaign Against Georgia." *Military Review* 91, no. 6 (November/December 2011). www.armyupress.army.mil /Portals/7/military-review/Archives/English/MilitaryReview_20111231 _art013.pdf.

Shirley, Mike. "Revolution Under the Shadow of the State: Organized Crime in the Soviet Union." *Eurasiatique* 10 (2022). https://eurasiatique.ca/2022/04/04 /revolution-under-the-shadow-of-the-state-organized-crime-in-the-soviet -union/.

Shuster, Simon. "US-Russia Relations: In Need of a New Reset." *Time*, March 16, 2010. https://time.com/archive/6949578/u-s-russia-relations-in-need -of-a-new-reset/.

Shuster, Simon. "How Paul Manafort Helped Elect Russia's Man in Ukraine." *Time*, October 31, 2017. https://time.com/5003623/paul-manafort-mueller -indictment-ukraine-russia/.

Snelbecker, David. "The Political Economy of Privatization in Ukraine." Center for Social and Economic Research, December 1995. https://case-research .eu/sites/default/files/publications/3460183_059_0.pdf.

Snyder, Timothy. "The Making of Modern Ukraine. Class 5: Vikings, Slavers, Lawgivers: The Kyiv State." YaleCourses, YouTube video, September 21, 2022. www.youtube.com/watch?v=36XiKhamtQo.

Snyder, Timothy. "The Making of Modern Ukraine. Class 6: The Grand Duchy of Lithuania." YaleCourses, YouTube video, September 23, 2022. www.youtube .com/watch?v=IlvE6tgPEf8.

Snyder, Timothy. "Ukraine Holds the Future." *Foreign Affairs* 101, no. 5 (September/October 2022). www.foreignaffairs.com/ukraine/ukraine-war -democracy-nihilism-timothy-snyder.

Socor, Vladimir. "NATO Opens a Crisis Summit in Bucharest." Eurasia Daily Monitor, Jamestown Foundation, April 2, 2008. https://jamestown.org /program/nato-opens-a-crisis-summit-in-bucharest/.

Socor, Vladimir. "Ukraine's Top Three Leaders Request NATO Membership Action Plan." Eurasia Daily Monitor, Jamestown Foundation, January 18, 2008. https://jamestown.org/program/ukraines-top-three-leaders-request -nato-membership-action-plan/.

Stent, Angela. *The Limits of Partnership: US-Russian Relations in the Twenty-First Century.* Princeton, NJ: Princeton University Press, 2014.

Sutyagin, Igor, and Michael Clarke. "Ukraine Military Dispositions: The Military Ticks Up While the Clock Ticks Down." Royal United Services Institute, April 2014. https://static.rusi.org/ukranian-military-dispositions-rusibriefing -2014.pdf.

Szporluk, Roman. *Russia, Ukraine, and the Breakup of the Soviet Union.* Stanford, CA: Hoover Institution Press, 2020.

Talbott, Strobe. *The Russia Hand: A Memoir of Presidential Diplomacy.* New York: Random House, 2002.

Tallis, Benjamin. "Neo-idealism: Grand Strategy for the Future of the Transatlantic Community." MacDonald-Laurier Institute, July 18, 2024. https://mac donaldlaurier.ca/neo-idealism-grand-strategy-for-the-future-of-the -transatlantic-community/.

Tallis, Benjamin. "The Rise of the New Idealists." Byline Supplement, July 22, 2023. www.bylinesupplement.com/p/the-rise-of-the-new-idealists.

Tallis, Benjamin. *To Ukraine with Love: Essays on Russia's War and Europe's Future.* Independently published, 2022.

Taylor, Adam. "'Novorossiya,' the Latest Historical Concept to Worry About in Ukraine." *Washington Post,* April 18, 2014. www.washingtonpost.com /news/worldviews/wp/2014/04/18/understanding-novorossiya-the-latest -historical-concept-to-get-worried-about-in-ukraine/.

"Tbilisi City Council Names Street After US President Bush." Civil Georgia, September 15, 2005. https://civil.ge/archives/108851.

Tomczyk, Justin. "Deconstructing the Divide: Armenia and Ukraine in Modern Eurasia." EVN Report, February 17, 2022. https://evnreport.com/politics /deconstructing-the-divide-armenia-and-ukraine-in-modern-eurasia/.

Toth, Robert C., and Ronald J. Ostrow. "'Russian Mafia': KGB Steers Criminals to US Careers." *Los Angeles Times,* February 16, 1988. www.latimes.com /archives/la-xpm-1988-02-16-mn-42975-story.html.

"Trump Pardons Paul Manafort, Roger Stone and Charles Kushner." *BBC News*, December 24, 2020. www.bbc.com/news/world-us-canada-55433522.

"Ukraine Crisis: 'Russians' Occupy Crimea Airports." *BBC News*, February 28, 2014. www.bbc.com/news/world-europe-26379722.

"Ukraine: Reforms to Pave the Way for Association Agreement." European Parliament, February 28, 2013. www.europarl.europa.eu/topics/en/article /20130225STO06079/ukraine-reforms-to-pave-the-way-for-association -agreement.

"Ukraine-EU Trade Deal Deadlocked over Tymoshenko Release." France 24, November 21, 2013. www.france24.com/en/20131121-ukraine-halts-eu -trade-deal-tymoshenko-association-agreement.

"Ukraine's Parliament Votes to Abandon Nato Ambitions." *BBC News*, June 3, 2010. www.bbc.com/news/10229626.

Ukrainian Central Election Commission. "Message from the Central Election Commission on the Results of the Ukrainian Presidential Election." [In Ukrainian.] November 24, 2004. https://web.archive.org/web/20070930223042/http: //www.cvk.gov.ua/postanovy/2004/p1265_2004_d.htm.

"US Ship Carrying Aid Docks at Georgian Port." *New York Times*, August 27, 2008. www.nytimes.com/2008/08/27/world/europe/27iht-georgia.1.1567 9482.html.

Vindman, Alexander. "Stop Tiptoeing Around Russia: It Is Time to End Washington's Decades of Deference to Moscow." *Foreign Affairs*, August 8, 2022. www.foreignaffairs.com/united-states/stop-tiptoeing-around-russia.

Walker, Shaun. "Ukraine Protests: Outrage As Police Attack Kiev Barricades." *The Guardian*, December 11, 2013. www.theguardian.com/world/2013/dec/11 /kiev-protests-police-barricades-chainsaws.

Walker, Shaun. "Vladimir Putin Offers Ukraine Financial Incentives to Stick with Russia." *The Guardian*, December 17, 2013. www.theguardian.com /world/2013/dec/17/ukraine-russia-leaders-talks-kremlin-loan-deal.

Wesolowsky, Tony. "Ukraine: Rice Delivers Stern Message During Kyiv Stopover." Radio Free Europe/Radio Liberty, July 25, 2001. www.rferl.org/a/1097019 .html.

"What Does It Mean to Be Ukrainian? The Life of Taras Shevchenko." Davis Center for Russian and Eurasian Studies, Harvard University, 2024. https: //scalar.fas.harvard.edu/imperiia/what-does-it-mean-to-be-ukrainian-the -life-of-taras-shevchenko.

Wilson, Damon. "President George H. W. Bush Had 'the Vision Thing' in Spades." Atlantic Council, December 3, 2018. www.atlanticcouncil.org/blogs /new-atlanticist/president-george-h-w-bush-had-the-vision-thing-in -spades/.

"Yulia Tymoshenko Imprisonment 'Politically Motivated.'" *The Guardian*, April 30, 2013. www.theguardian.com/world/2013/apr/30/yulia-tymoshenko-jailing-politically-motivated.

"Yushchenko Dismisses Ukraine Cabinet." *The Guardian*, September 8, 2005. www.theguardian.com/world/2005/sep/08/ukraine.

Yushchenko, Viktor. "Opening Statement by Viktor Yushchenko, President of Ukraine at the Meeting of the NATO-Ukraine Council at the Level of Heads of State and Government." NATO Newsroom, February 22, 2005. www.nato.int/cps/en/natohq/opinions_21972.htm.

Yushchenko, Viktor. "Statement to the Press by Viktor Yushchenko, President of Ukraine at the Press Conference Following the Meeting of the NATO-Ukraine Council at the Level of Heads of State and Government." NATO Newsroom, February 22, 2005. www.nato.int/cps/en/natohq/opinions_21969.htm.

INDEX

Dr. Alexander Vindman, Lieutenant Colonel US Army (Retired), was the director for European affairs on the White House's National Security Council, former Pentagon political-military affairs officer for Russia, and attaché at the American embassies in Moscow and Kyiv. He holds a doctorate in international affairs from the School of Advanced International Studies at Johns Hopkins where he is a senior fellow. He is the author of the *New York Times*–bestselling memoir *Here, Right Matters* and leads the Institute for Informed American Leadership at the Vet Voice Foundation and the Here Right Matters Foundation, which focuses on helping Ukraine win the war against Russia. He lives in Fort Lauderdale, Florida.

PublicAffairs is a publishing house founded in 1997. It is a tribute to the standards, values, and flair of three persons who have served as mentors to countless reporters, writers, editors, and book people of all kinds, including me.

I. F. STONE, proprietor of *I. F. Stone's Weekly*, combined a commitment to the First Amendment with entrepreneurial zeal and reporting skill and became one of the great independent journalists in American history. At the age of eighty, Izzy published *The Trial of Socrates*, which was a national bestseller. He wrote the book after he taught himself ancient Greek.

BENJAMIN C. BRADLEE was for nearly thirty years the charismatic editorial leader of *The Washington Post*. It was Ben who gave the *Post* the range and courage to pursue such historic issues as Watergate. He supported his reporters with a tenacity that made them fearless and it is no accident that so many became authors of influential, best-selling books.

ROBERT L. BERNSTEIN, the chief executive of Random House for more than a quarter century, guided one of the nation's premier publishing houses. Bob was personally responsible for many books of political dissent and argument that challenged tyranny around the globe. He is also the founder and longtime chair of Human Rights Watch, one of the most respected human rights organizations in the world.

· · ·

For fifty years, the banner of Public Affairs Press was carried by its owner Morris B. Schnapper, who published Gandhi, Nasser, Toynbee, Truman, and about 1,500 other authors. In 1983, Schnapper was described by *The Washington Post* as "a redoubtable gadfly." His legacy will endure in the books to come.

Peter Osnos, *Founder*